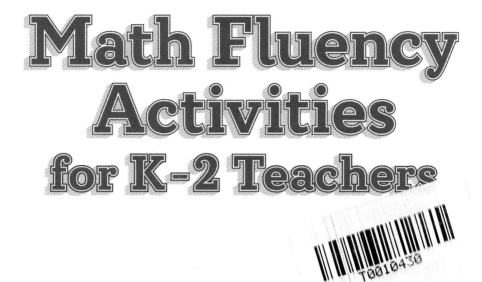

Math Fluency Activities
for K-2 Teachers

Math Fluency Activities for K-2 Teachers

Fun Classroom Games That Teach Basic Math Facts, Promote Number Sense, and Create Engaging and Meaningful Practice

NANCY HUGHES

Published by:
Ulysses Press
PO Box 3440
Berkeley, CA 94703
www.ulyssespress.com

ISBN: 978-1-64604-357-6
Library of Congress Control Number: 2022932297

Printed in the United States by Versa Press
10 9 8 7 6 5 4 3 2 1

Acquisitions editor: Casie Vogel
Managing editor: Claire Chun
Editor: Anne Healey
Proofreader: Barbara Schultz
Front cover and interior design: Jake Flaherty
Production: Yesenia Garcia, what!design @ whatweb.com
Cover art: octopus © BNP Design Studio/shutterstock.com; chalkboard © GraphicsRF/shutterstock.com
Interior art: shutterstock.com

Contents

Introduction

Math fluency is developed over time. All students should receive a solid mathematical foundation. It is important to actively engage students in their learning. Early deficits have enduring and devastating effects on later learning. Working on math activities daily, over time, is a powerful way to enable students to become fluent mathematical thinkers, efficient and accurate with computation, and ready to problem solve.

Teaching, reviewing, and reinforcing reasoning strategies gives students the tools they need for lifelong learning. Each student will comprehend math differently, so teaching multiple strategies in a variety of ways is necessary for all students to make sense of math.

What Is Math Fluency?

According to the National Council of Teachers of Mathematics, "procedural fluency is a critical component of mathematical proficiency. Procedural fluency is the ability to apply procedures accurately, efficiently, and flexibly; to transfer procedures to different problems and contexts; to build or modify procedures from other procedures; and to recognize when one strategy or procedure is more appropriate to apply than another."[1] In other words, fluency is reaching beyond procedures and computation. It is much more than speed and accuracy. It is understanding math and being able to apply math to a variety of mathematical situations. It is important to be efficient and accurate by using a variety of strategies (computational fluency) and to apply computational fluency to procedural fluency (flexibly, accurately, and efficiently). This creates a bridge for students to access more complex concepts and procedures.

---

1   https://www.nctm.org/Standards-and-Positions/Position-Statements/Procedural-Fluency-in-Mathematics.

Here are the kindergarten through grade 2 Common Core fluency standards, which require teaching with a depth of understanding.

GRADE	REQUIRED FLUENCY
K	**K.OA.A.5** Add/subtract within 5.
1	**1.OA.C.6** Add/subtract within 10.
2	**2.OA.B.2** Add/subtract within 20; by the end of year, know from memory all sums of two one-digit numbers. **2.NBT.B.5** Add/subtract within 100.

Engaging and Meaningful Fluency Activities

Focusing on the math fluency standards, I've provided activities and ideas that easily and efficiently teach math fluency; teachers, parents, interventionists, and students will be provided with a variety of suggestions to support success for all students through their mathematical journey. Mastering basic math facts requires a shift from memorizing to understanding. The end goal of learning math facts is to recall math from memory (quickly, efficiently, and accurately). Developing fluency requires ongoing practice (such as number talks) and moving students from concrete examples to representational and finally to abstract thought (activities and ideas like those in this book).

In these early grades, the focus should be on number sense. Using a timed test does not gauge understanding. Teaching for mastery requires time and frequent practice: practice that is engaging and meaningful. The ideas and activities shared in this book are ideal for guided math, center time, instructional focus time, reteaching, at-home practice, intervention, or general education class time.

CHAPTER 1

Kindergarten

GRADE	REQUIRED FLUENCY
K	**K.OA.A.5** Add/subtract within 5.

This concept is one of the more important mathematical concepts students must master in order to progress to the next level of mathematical development. In kindergarten, students learn mathematics through concrete and verbal representations. It is important for students to learn to compose and decompose numbers within 10. The following activities are aligned with student mastery of adding and subtracting within 5.

Using Number Bonds to Add Numbers

MATERIALS NEEDED: Color counters

★ Copy the pages with the number bond cards and give them to each student or group of students, or project the cards for whole class discussion.

★ Use five color counters or have five virtual color counters on the screen for students to drag and drop within the number bond.

★ Have students, working in groups or individually, drag and drop the color counters onto the circles on the card either virtually or physically. With younger students it is ideal for them to accomplish this with their own number bond and color counters.

★ Students then move the counters to the lower circles on the number bond, discovering all the different combinations of the number.

★ Discuss the number sentences that the students construct.

★ Finally, share and discuss the results with your students.

Number Bonds

★ Place 6 color counters on each small circle within the upper large circle.

★ Using different combinations, drag the counters to the lower large circles to make as many different number sentences as you can.

★ Record your sentences in the space provided.

★ Share and discuss your findings.

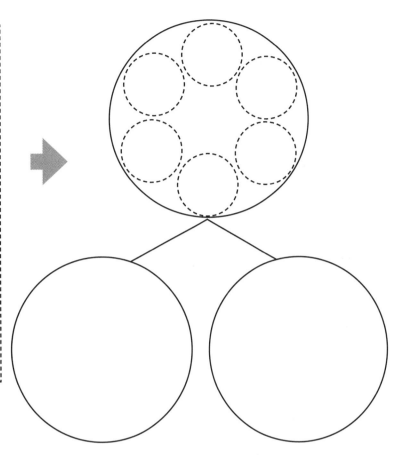

How many different number sentences can you make?

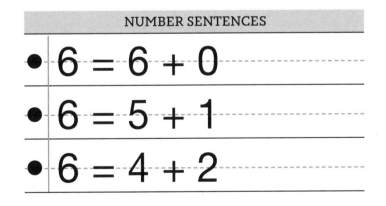

NUMBER SENTENCES

$6 = 6 + 0$

$6 = 5 + 1$

$6 = 4 + 2$

Number Bonds

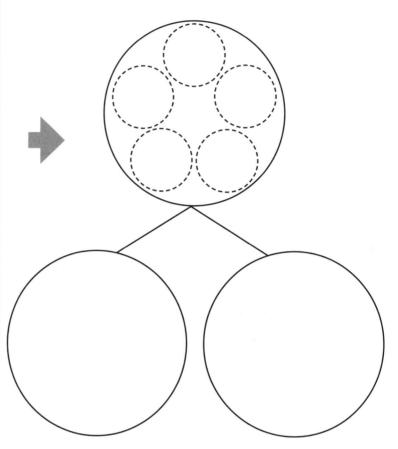

★ Place 5 color counters on each small circle within the upper large circle.

★ Using different combinations, drag the counters to the lower large circles to make as many different number sentences as you can.

★ Record your sentences in the space provided.

★ Share and discuss your findings.

How many different number sentences can you make?

NUMBER SENTENCES
• 5 =
• 5 =
• 5 =

Number Bonds

★ Place 4 color counters on each small circle within the upper large circle.

★ Using different combinations, drag the counters to the lower large circles to make as many different number sentences as you can.

★ Record your sentences in the space provided.

★ Share and discuss your findings.

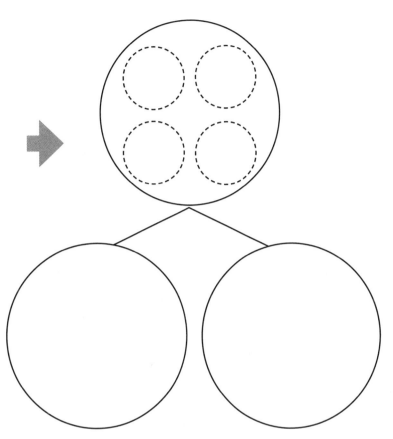

How many different number sentences can you make?

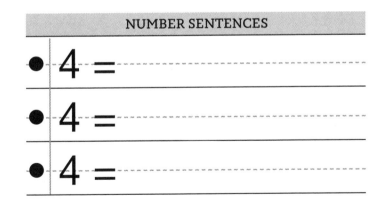

NUMBER SENTENCES
• $4 =$
• $4 =$
• $4 =$

Number Bonds

★ Place 3 color counters on each small circle within the upper large circle.

★ Using different combinations, drag the counters to the lower large circles to make as many different number sentences as you can.

★ Record your sentences in the space provided.

★ Share and discuss your findings.

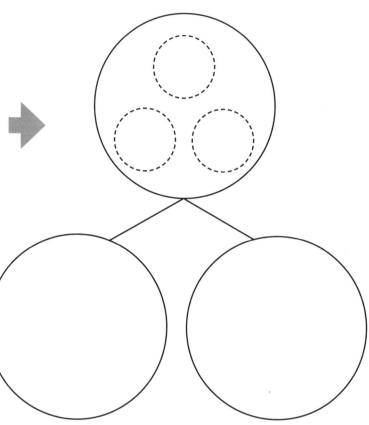

How many different number sentences can you make?

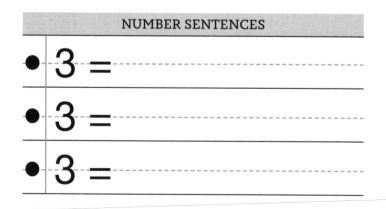

NUMBER SENTENCES
● 3 =
● 3 =
● 3 =

Math Fluency Activities for K–2 Teachers

Number Bonds

- ★ Place 2 color counters on each small circle within the upper large circle.

- ★ Using different combinations, drag the counters to the lower large circles to make as many different number sentences as you can.

- ★ Record your sentences in the space provided.

- ★ Share and discuss your findings.

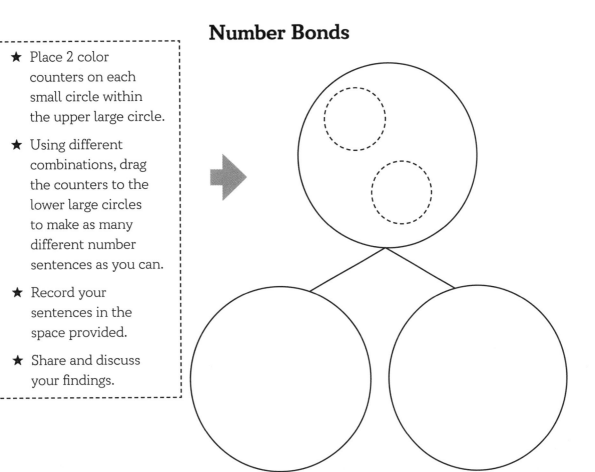

How many different number sentences can you make?

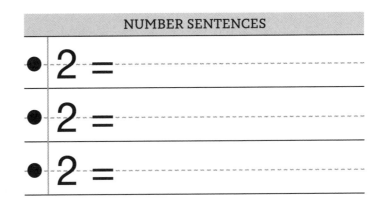

NUMBER SENTENCES
● 2 =
● 2 =
● 2 =

Adding and Subtracting on a Ten-Frame

★ Copy the task cards and number sentence cards for students, or project the cards for whole class discussion.

★ Place students in groups and have them match the ten-frame with the number sentence.

★ Make sure to have students share and discuss their results.

In the example below, there are 3 dragons and 2 additional different dragons. It is matched with the card that shows that 3 plus 2 is the same as 5. In other words, there are 5 total dragons in the ten-frame. We know this because 3 plus 2 additional dragons will make a total of 5.

EXAMPLE

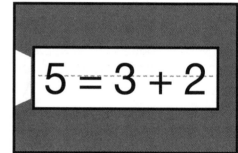

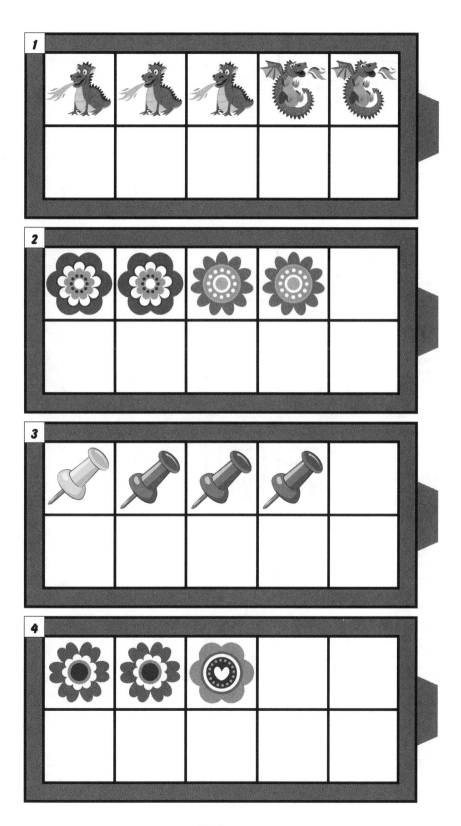

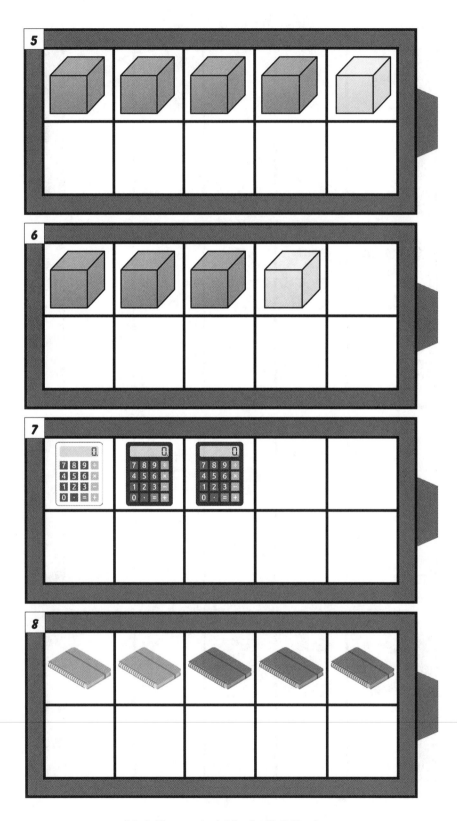

Math Fluency Activities for K–2 Teachers

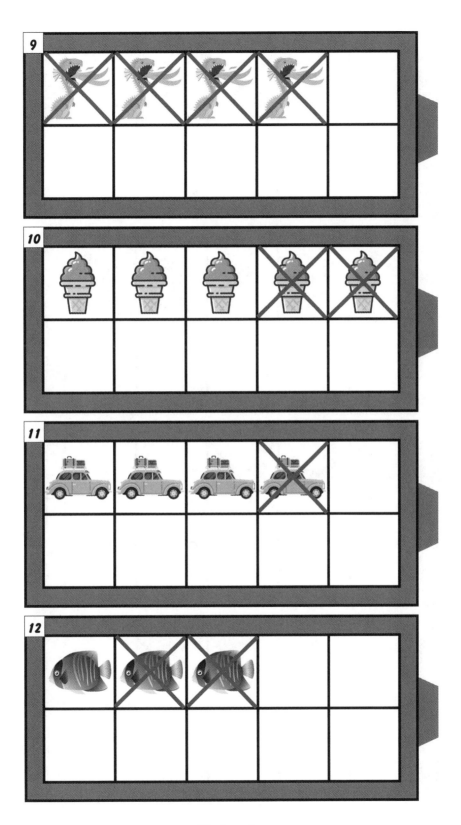

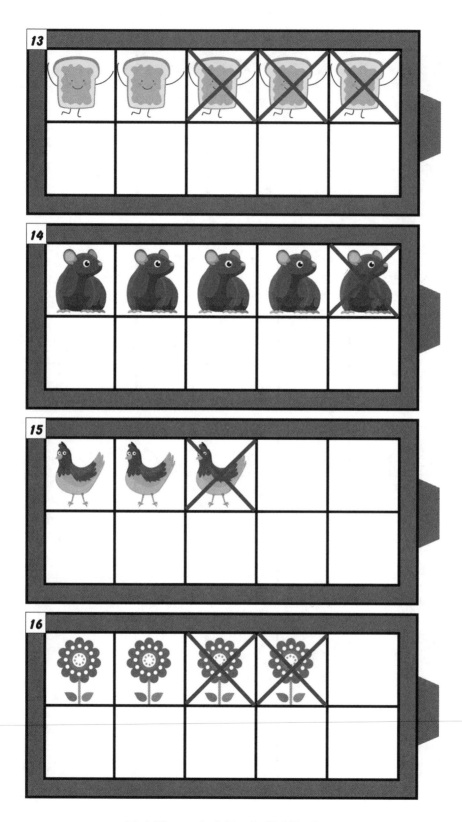

Math Fluency Activities for K–2 Teachers

$4 = 2 + 2$

$4 = 1 + 3$

$5 = 3 + 2$

$3 = 2 + 1$

$5 = 1 + 4$

$3 = 1 + 2$

$4 = 3 + 1$

$5 = 2 + 3$

$3 = 5 - 2$

$3 = 4 - 1$

$0 = 4 - 4$

$1 = 3 - 2$

$2 = 5 - 3$

$2 = 3 - 1$

$4 = 5 - 1$

$2 = 4 - 2$

Math Fluency Activities for K-2 Teachers

ANSWER KEY:
Adding and Subtracting on a Ten-Frame

PROBLEM	NUMBER SENTENCE	PROBLEM	NUMBER SENTENCE
1.	5 = 3 + 2	9.	0 = 4 − 4
2.	4 = 2 + 2	10.	3 = 5 − 2
3.	4 = 1 + 3	11.	3 = 4 − 1
4.	3 = 2 + 1	12.	1 = 3 − 2
5.	5 = 4+ 1	13.	2 = 5 − 3
6.	4 = 3 + 1	14.	4 = 5 − 1
7.	3 = 1 + 2	15.	2 = 3 − 1
8.	5 = 2 + 3	16.	2 = 4 − 2

Number Sentences and the Number Line

★ Copy the number sentences and number line for student use or project the number lines for whole class discussion.

★ Place students in groups to find the number sentence shown on the number line. Record student answers.

★ Have students share and discuss their results.

Use the example below to discuss and share results for this number sentence and number line. From this example, we know that one jump from 0 to 1 on the number line with an additional jump of 2 more places brings the frog to 3 on the number line. Therefore, we can conclude that 1 plus 2 more is the same as 3.

EXAMPLE

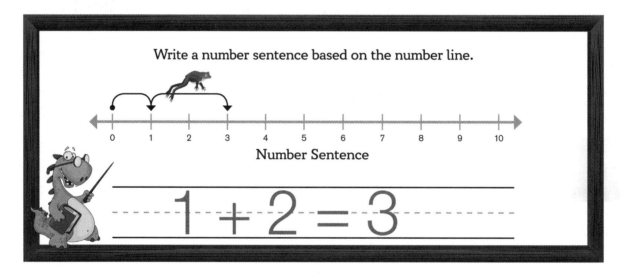

1

Write a number sentence based on the number line.

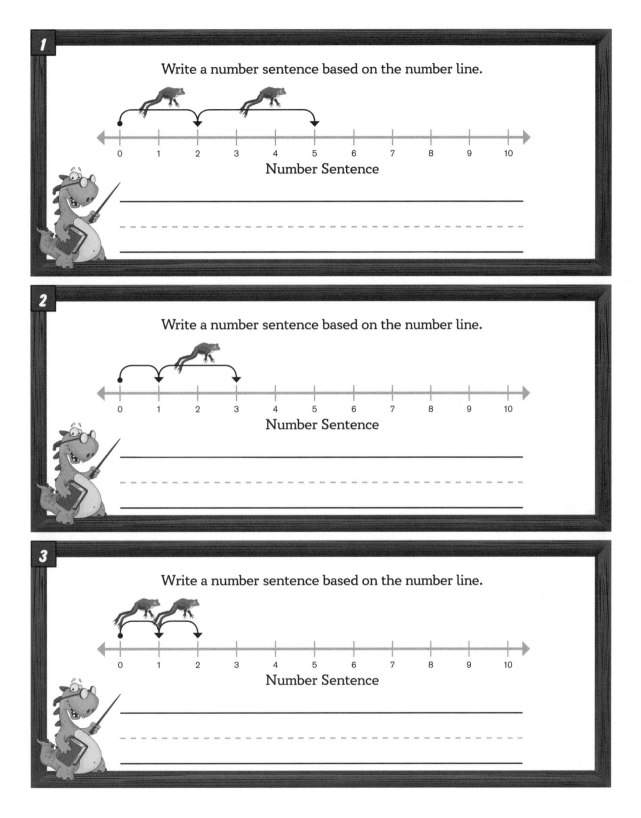

Number Sentence

_____

- -

_____

2

Write a number sentence based on the number line.

Number Sentence

_____

- -

_____

3

Write a number sentence based on the number line.

Number Sentence

_____

- -

_____

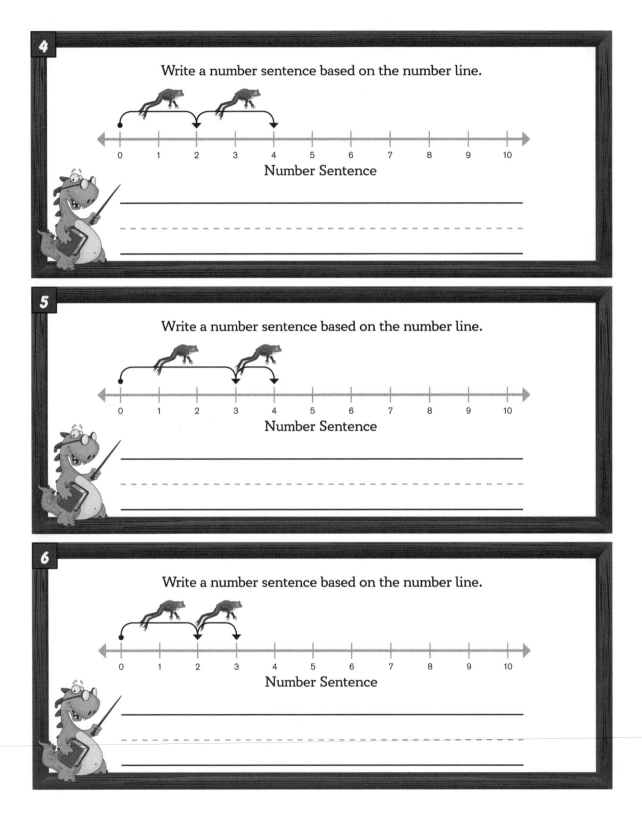

4

Write a number sentence based on the number line.

0   1   2   3   4   5   6   7   8   9   10

Number Sentence

_____

- -

_____

5

Write a number sentence based on the number line.

0   1   2   3   4   5   6   7   8   9   10

Number Sentence

_____

- -

_____

6

Write a number sentence based on the number line.

0   1   2   3   4   5   6   7   8   9   10

Number Sentence

_____

- -

_____

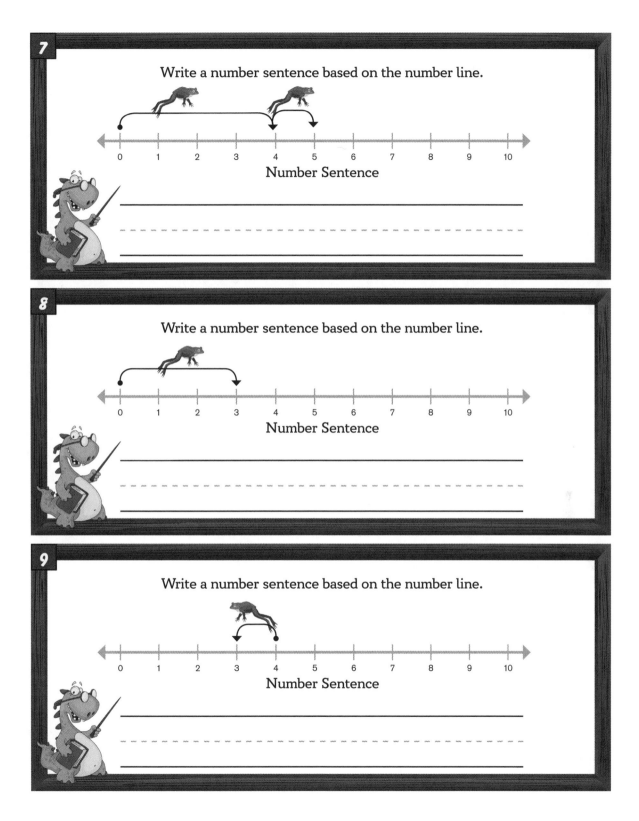

7

Write a number sentence based on the number line.

0 1 2 3 4 5 6 7 8 9 10

Number Sentence

_____

- - - - - - - - - - - - - - - - - -

_____

8

Write a number sentence based on the number line.

0 1 2 3 4 5 6 7 8 9 10

Number Sentence

_____

- - - - - - - - - - - - - - - - - -

_____

9

Write a number sentence based on the number line.

0 1 2 3 4 5 6 7 8 9 10

Number Sentence

_____

- - - - - - - - - - - - - - - - - -

_____

10

Write a number sentence based on the number line.

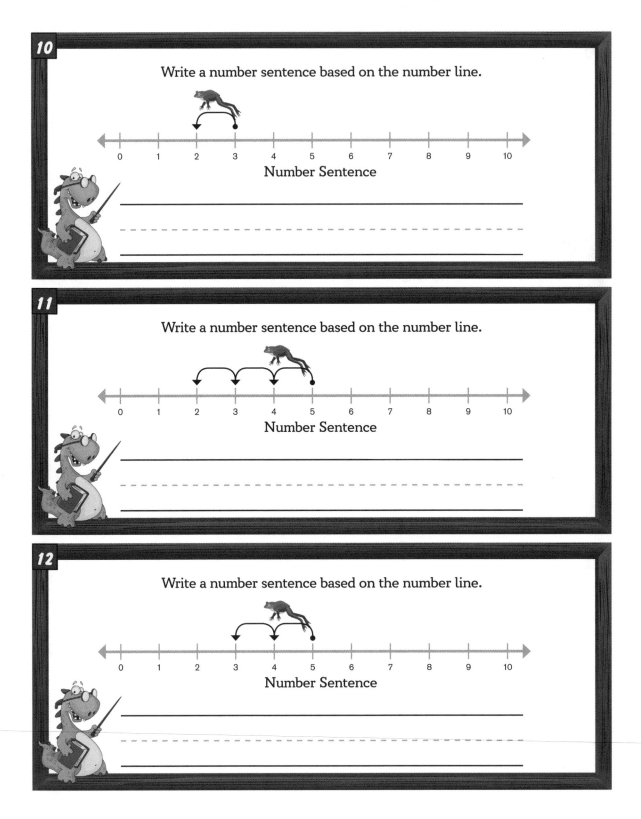

Number Sentence

_____

- -

_____

11

Write a number sentence based on the number line.

Number Sentence

_____

- -

_____

12

Write a number sentence based on the number line.

Number Sentence

_____

- -

_____

Math Fluency Activities for K–2 Teachers

13

Write a number sentence based on the number line.

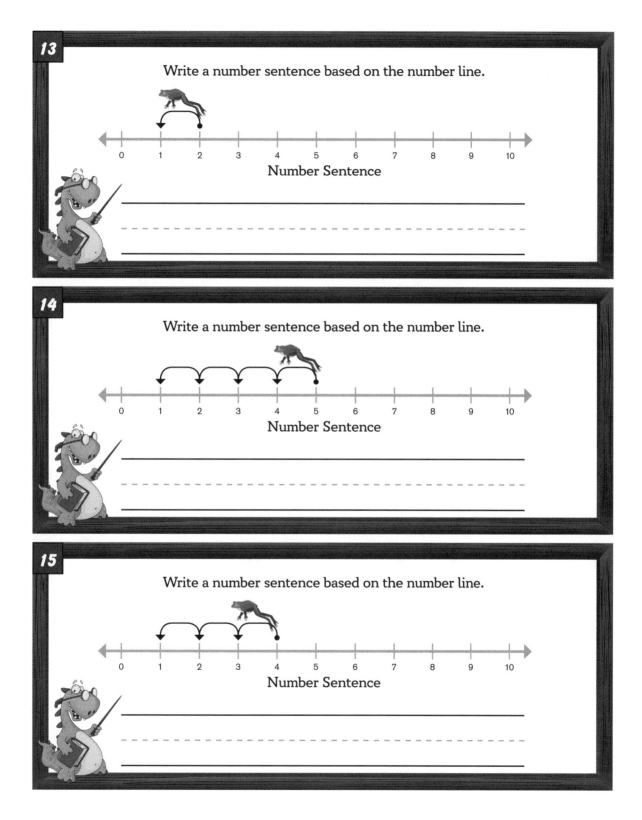

Number Sentence

_____

- -

_____

14

Write a number sentence based on the number line.

Number Sentence

_____

- -

_____

15

Write a number sentence based on the number line.

Number Sentence

_____

- -

_____

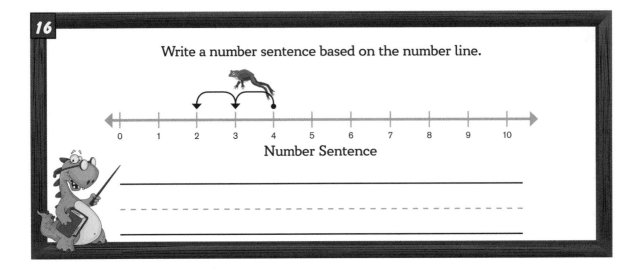

Write a number sentence based on the number line.

0 1 2 3 4 5 6 7 8 9 10

Number Sentence

_____

- - - - - - - - - - - - - - - - -

_____

ANSWER KEY:
Number Sentences and the Number Line

PROBLEM	NUMBER SENTENCE
1.	$2 + 3 = 5$
2.	$1 + 2 = 3$
3.	$1 + 1 = 2$
4.	$2 + 2 = 4$
5.	$3 + 1 = 4$
6.	$2 + 1 = 3$
7.	$4 + 1 = 5$
8.	$3 + 0 = 3$

PROBLEM	NUMBER SENTENCE
9.	$4 - 1 = 3$
10.	$3 - 1 = 2$
11.	$5 - 3 = 2$
12.	$5 - 2 = 3$
13.	$2 - 1 = 1$
14.	$5 - 4 = 1$
15.	$4 - 3 = 1$
16.	$4 - 2 = 2$

Real-World Application

★ Either copy the task cards for student use or project the cards for class discussion. Place students in groups to solve the problems on the cards.

★ Draw in your solutions using the ten-frame or use color counters to illustrate each of the real-world problems.

★ Make sure to draw in the jumps on the number line as well. Record the number sentence that goes with each problem.

★ Finally, have students share and discuss their results for each problem.

Use the example below as a talking point with students. Discuss and solve the problem.

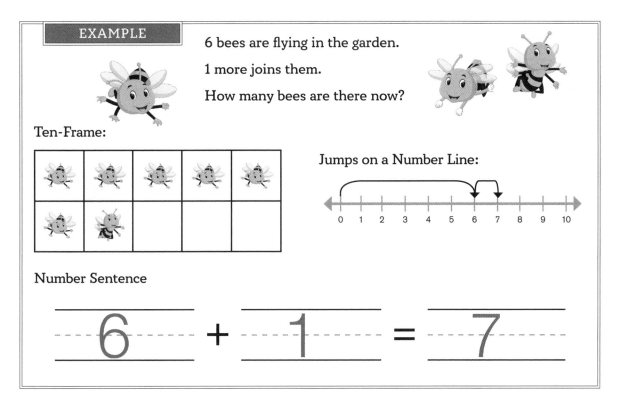

EXAMPLE

6 bees are flying in the garden.

1 more joins them.

How many bees are there now?

Ten-Frame:

Jumps on a Number Line:

Number Sentence

$$6 + 1 = 7$$

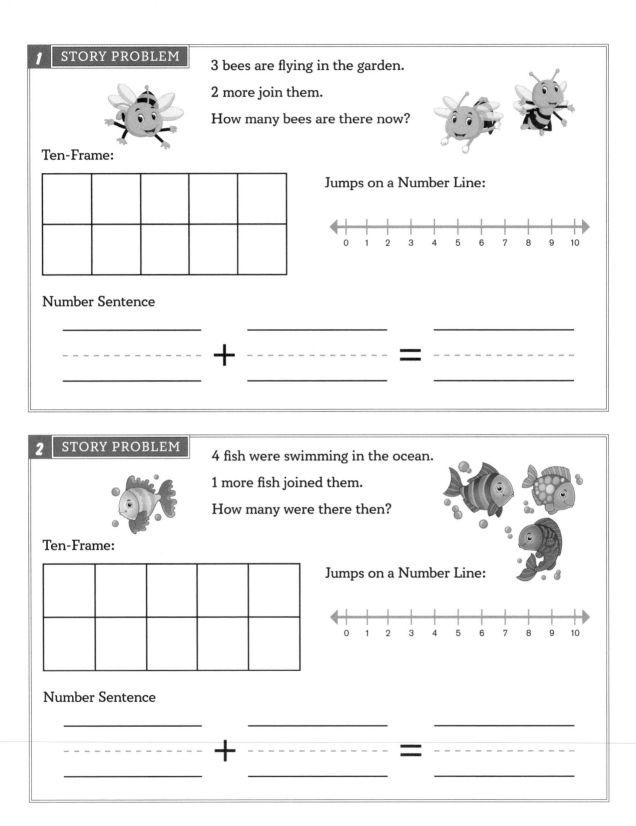

1 STORY PROBLEM

3 bees are flying in the garden.

2 more join them.

How many bees are there now?

Ten-Frame:

Jumps on a Number Line:

0 1 2 3 4 5 6 7 8 9 10

Number Sentence

_____ + _____ = _____

2 STORY PROBLEM

4 fish were swimming in the ocean.

1 more fish joined them.

How many were there then?

Ten-Frame:

Jumps on a Number Line:

0 1 2 3 4 5 6 7 8 9 10

Number Sentence

_____ + _____ = _____

3 | **STORY PROBLEM**

3 girls are swinging.

1 boy joins them.

How many children are there in all?

Ten-Frame:

Jumps on a Number Line:

0 1 2 3 4 5 6 7 8 9 10

Number Sentence

_____ + _____ = _____

4 | **STORY PROBLEM**

2 children are flying kites.

2 children join them.

How many children are swinging?

Ten-Frame:

Jumps on a Number Line:

0 1 2 3 4 5 6 7 8 9 10

Number Sentence

_____ + _____ = _____

5 | **STORY PROBLEM**

Jan has 1 pencil.

She is given 3 more.

How many pencils are there in all?

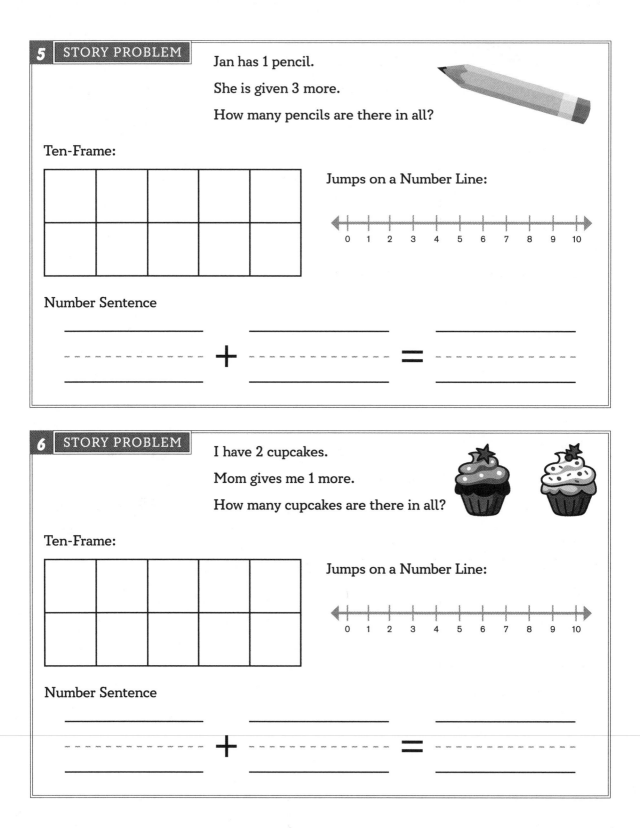

Ten-Frame:

Jumps on a Number Line:

0 1 2 3 4 5 6 7 8 9 10

Number Sentence

_____ **+** _____ **=** _____

---

6 | **STORY PROBLEM**

I have 2 cupcakes.

Mom gives me 1 more.

How many cupcakes are there in all?

Ten-Frame:

Jumps on a Number Line:

0 1 2 3 4 5 6 7 8 9 10

Number Sentence

_____ **+** _____ **=** _____

7 STORY PROBLEM

Nemo has 2 friends.

3 more become his friends.

How many friends does he have?

Ten-Frame:

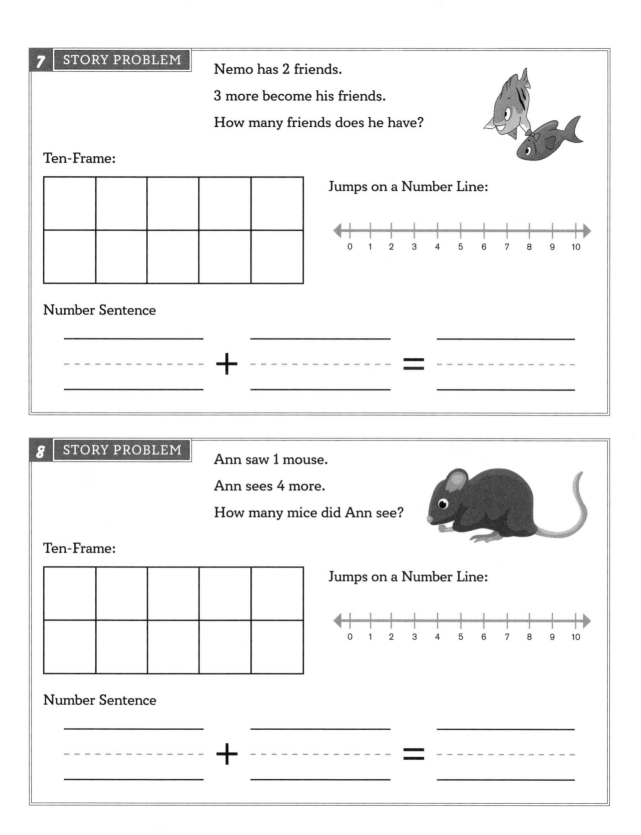

Jumps on a Number Line:

0 1 2 3 4 5 6 7 8 9 10

Number Sentence

_____ + _____ = _____

8 STORY PROBLEM

Ann saw 1 mouse.

Ann sees 4 more.

How many mice did Ann see?

Ten-Frame:

Jumps on a Number Line:

0 1 2 3 4 5 6 7 8 9 10

Number Sentence

_____ + _____ = _____

9 | STORY PROBLEM

1 turtle crossed the road.

2 more joined them.

How many turtles are there in all?

Ten-Frame:

Jumps on a Number Line:

0 1 2 3 4 5 6 7 8 9 10

Number Sentence

_____ **+** _____ **=** _____

10 | STORY PROBLEM

Ken has 0 sandwiches.

Ken's dad gives him 1 sandwich.

How many sandwiches are there in all?

Ten-Frame:

Jumps on a Number Line:

0 1 2 3 4 5 6 7 8 9 10

Number Sentence

_____ **+** _____ **=** _____

11 | STORY PROBLEM

David sees 5 caterpillars.

Then 2 walk away.

How many are left?

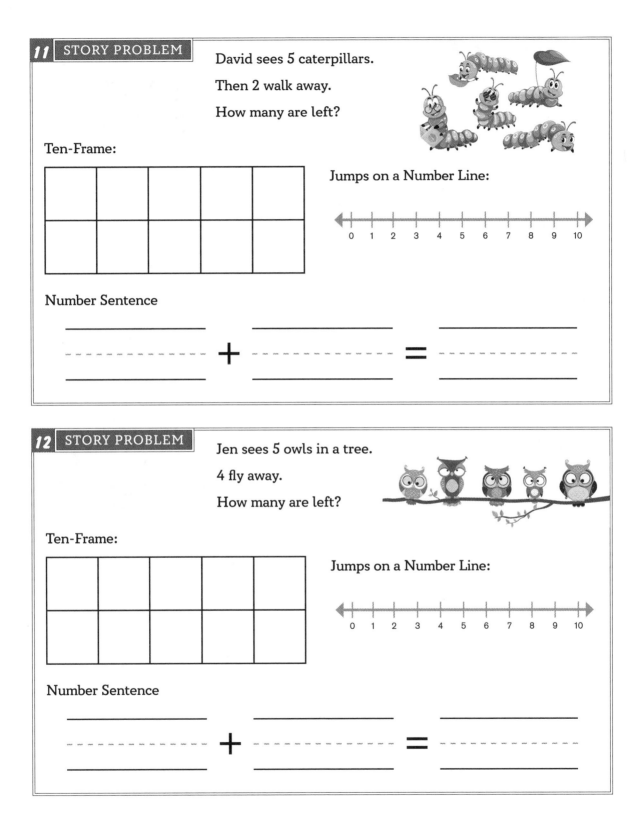

Ten-Frame:

Jumps on a Number Line:

```
0  1  2  3  4  5  6  7  8  9  10
```

Number Sentence

_____ + _____ = _____

12 | STORY PROBLEM

Jen sees 5 owls in a tree.

4 fly away.

How many are left?

Ten-Frame:

Jumps on a Number Line:

```
0  1  2  3  4  5  6  7  8  9  10
```

Number Sentence

_____ + _____ = _____

13 | STORY PROBLEM

4 passengers are riding a train.

2 get off.

How many are left on the train?

Ten-Frame:

Jumps on a Number Line:

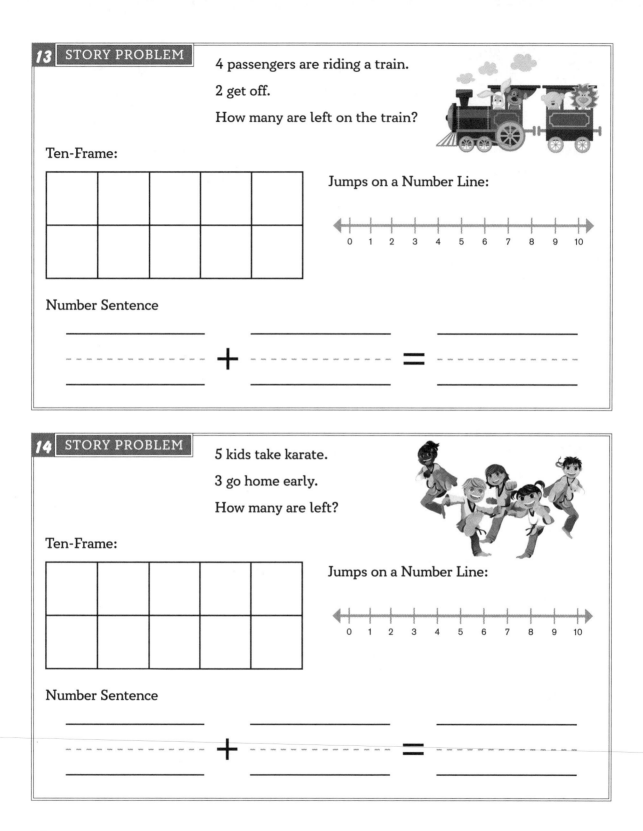

Number Sentence

_____   +   _____   =   _____

---

14 | STORY PROBLEM

5 kids take karate.

3 go home early.

How many are left?

Ten-Frame:

Jumps on a Number Line:

Number Sentence

_____   +   _____   =   _____

15 STORY PROBLEM

4 dragons are playing.

4 dragons go home.

How many are left playing?

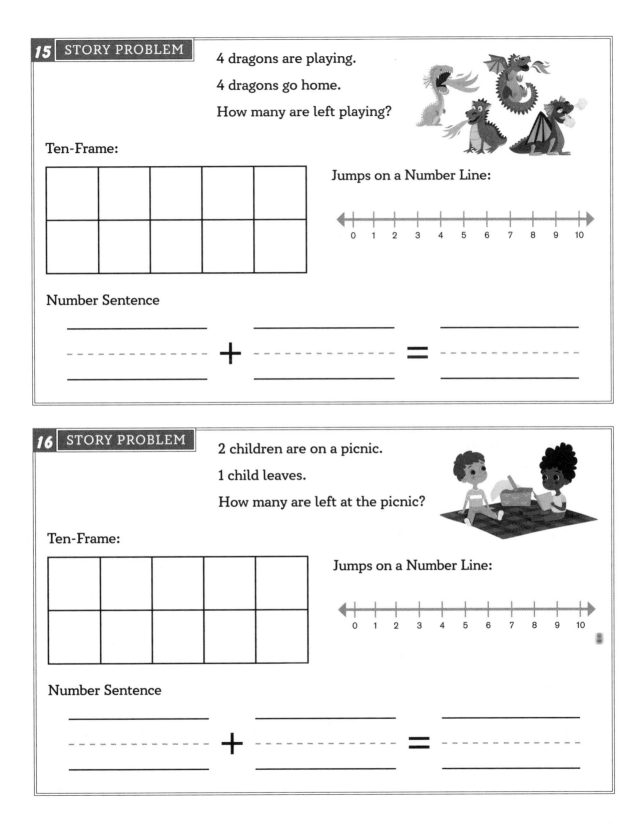

Ten-Frame:

Jumps on a Number Line:

0 1 2 3 4 5 6 7 8 9 10

Number Sentence

_____ + _____ = _____

16 STORY PROBLEM

2 children are on a picnic.

1 child leaves.

How many are left at the picnic?

Ten-Frame:

Jumps on a Number Line:

0 1 2 3 4 5 6 7 8 9 10

Number Sentence

_____ + _____ = _____

17 STORY PROBLEM

Ben has 4 apples.

He gives 3 away.

How many are left?

Ten-Frame:

Jumps on a Number Line:

0 1 2 3 4 5 6 7 8 9 10

Number Sentence

_____ **+** _____ **=** _____

18 STORY PROBLEM

Rich has 4 pencils.

He gives 1 away.

How many does he have left?

Ten-Frame:

Jumps on a Number Line:

0 1 2 3 4 5 6 7 8 9 10

Number Sentence

_____ **+** _____ **=** _____

19 STORY PROBLEM

There are 3 squirrels.

1 runs away.

How many are left?

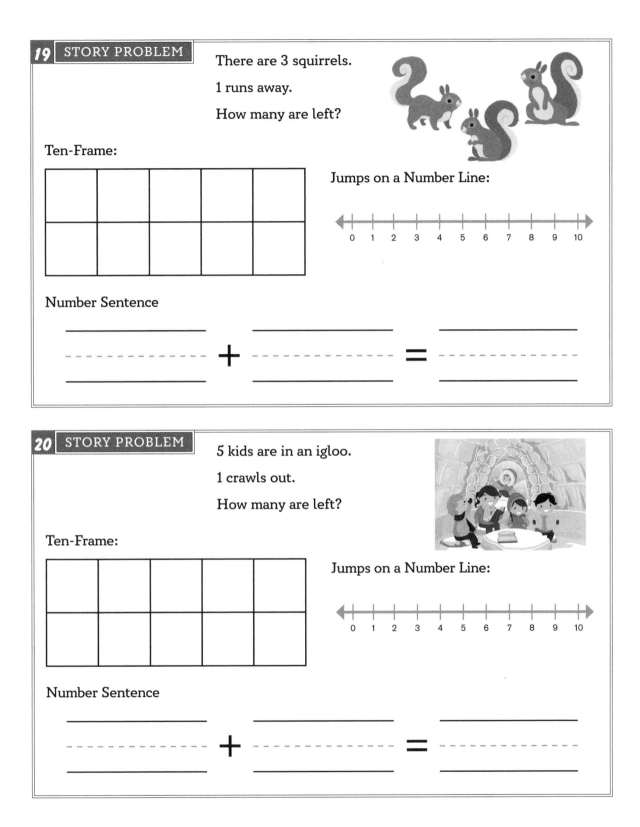

Ten-Frame:

Jumps on a Number Line:

0 1 2 3 4 5 6 7 8 9 10

Number Sentence

‾‾‾‾‾‾‾‾‾   **+**   ‾‾‾‾‾‾‾‾‾   **=**   ‾‾‾‾‾‾‾‾‾

---

20 STORY PROBLEM

5 kids are in an igloo.

1 crawls out.

How many are left?

Ten-Frame:

Jumps on a Number Line:

0 1 2 3 4 5 6 7 8 9 10

Number Sentence

‾‾‾‾‾‾‾‾‾   **+**   ‾‾‾‾‾‾‾‾‾   **=**   ‾‾‾‾‾‾‾‾‾

ANSWER KEY:
Real-World Application

PROBLEM	NUMBER SENTENCE
1.	3 + 2 = 5
2.	4 + 1 = 5
3.	3 + 1 = 4
4.	2 + 2 = 4
5.	1 + 3 = 4
6.	2 + 1 = 3
7.	2 + 3 = 5
8.	1 + 4 = 5
9.	1 + 2 = 3
10.	0 + 1 = 1

PROBLEM	NUMBER SENTENCE
11.	5 − 2 = 3
12.	5 − 4 = 1
13.	4 − 2 = 2
14.	5 − 3 = 2
15.	4 − 4 = 0
16.	2 − 1 = 1
17.	4 − 3 = 1
18.	4 − 1 = 3
19.	3 − 1 = 2
20.	5 − 1 = 4

Math Fluency Activities for K–2 Teachers

Building Automaticity with Addition and Subtraction

All students should receive a solid mathematical foundation. It is important to actively engage students in their learning. Early deficits have enduring and devastating effects on later learning. In the past, math teaching utilized "drill and kill" repetitive practices, whereas teaching for fluency requires conceptual understanding. Conceptual understanding starts with visual images such as concrete examples and then shifts the learner to more of a representational model in order to achieve abstract thought. Automaticity should not be considered a substitute or replacement for teaching and learning math conceptually. Automaticity requires understanding. The goal of instruction is to teach strategies—strategies based on understanding the relationship between numbers, so that math is automatic and can be recalled from memory. Effective, engaging, and focused practice is important. During practice, focus on mastery rather than speed. One such activity is using number bonds. A number bond is a mental picture of the relationships between a number and the parts that make the whole. Number bonds lead to part-part-whole relationships. A whole thing is made of parts. If you know the parts, you can put them together to find the whole. If you know the whole and one part, you can subtract to find the unknown part. Practice using cards such as the ones here. This will lead to fluency with numbers.

Number Bonds

★ Copy or project the cards for students.

★ Have students find the whole or missing part.

★ Make sure to have students discuss and share their strategies for finding the whole or part.

In the example shown here, we show a missing whole with two parts, 2 and 3. In order to find the missing whole, we must add the parts.

Hence, we know that 2 and 3 more make 5, our whole.

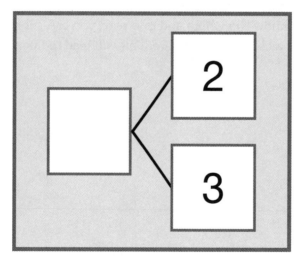

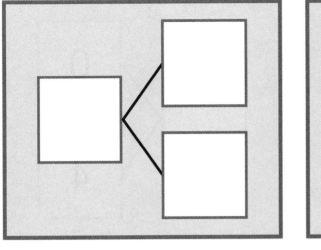

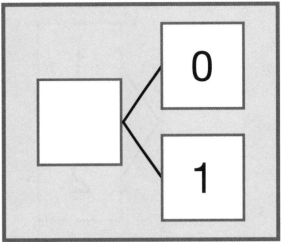

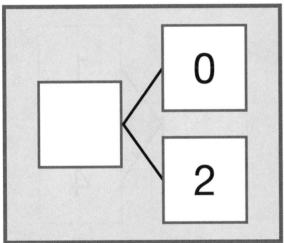

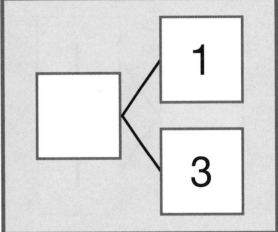

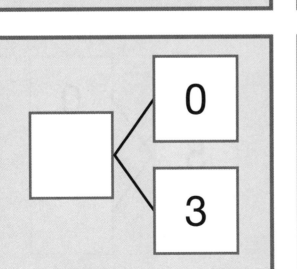

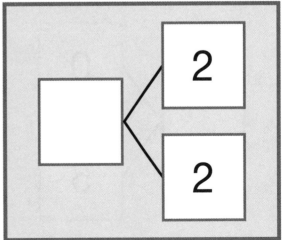

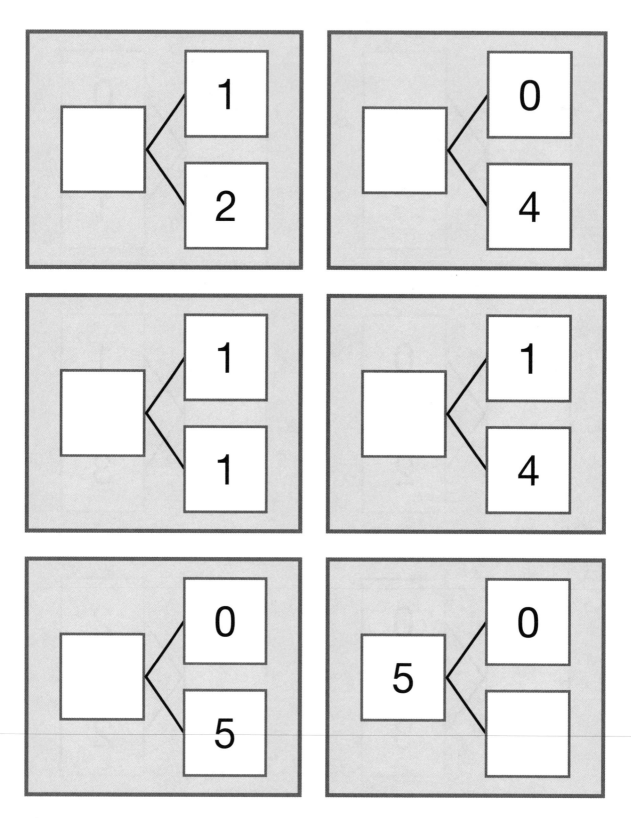

Math Fluency Activities for K–2 Teachers

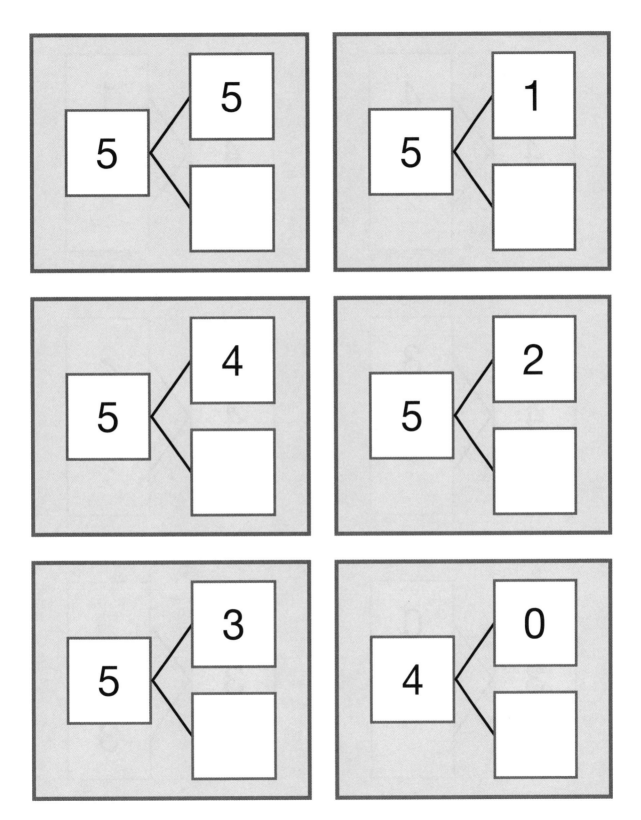

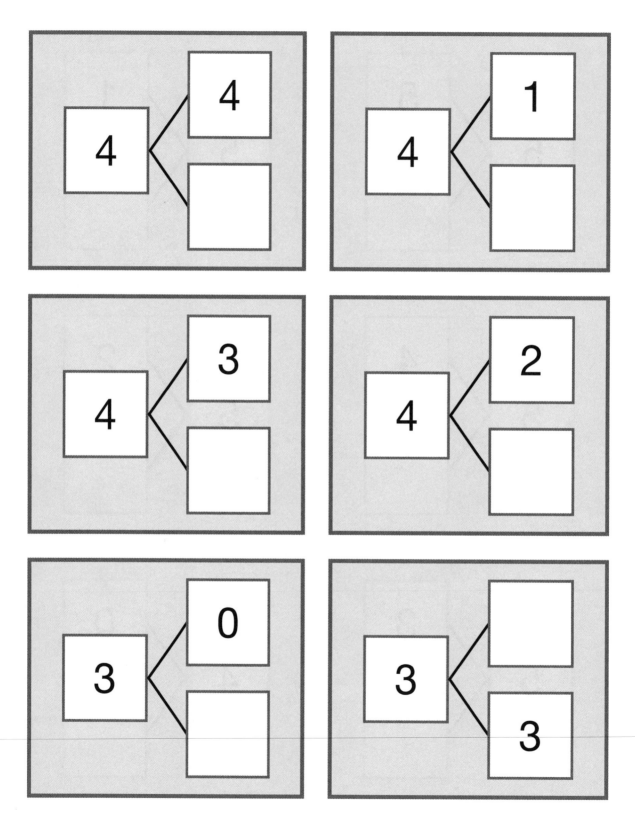

Math Fluency Activities for K–2 Teachers

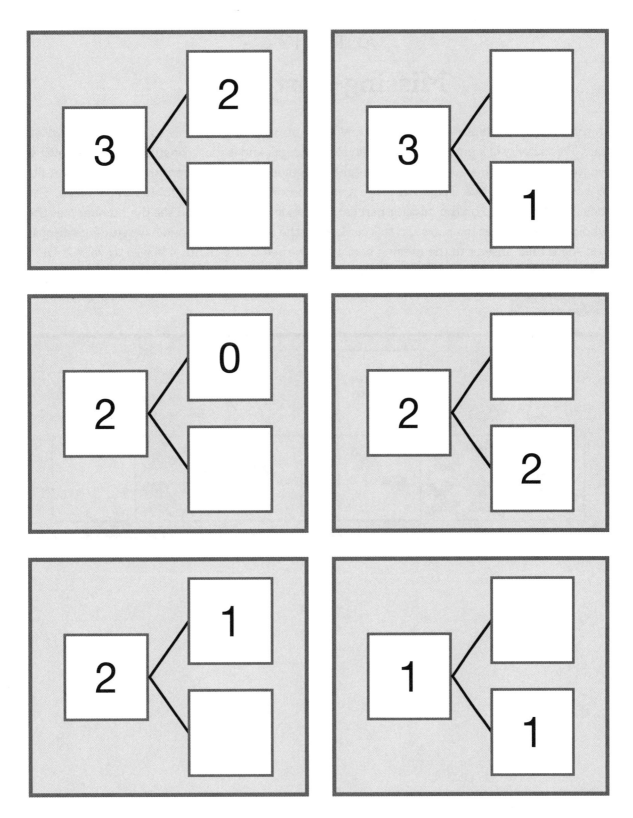

Missing-Part Cards

In this activity, students will use their knowledge of parts of the whole to identify the hidden part. This activity is a precursor to subtraction concepts and is ideal for students in any setting, whether it is whole class instruction, center time, guided math, intervention, or wherever it fits as a wonderful practice. These cards are a variation on an activity by John Van de Walle. The idea is to flip the flap on the missing-part card. For example, below you see the number 6 as the whole with 4 and 2 as the parts. On this card, place the flap over the 2 and have students discuss and share their answer to the missing part. Here we see that 6 minus 4 leaves us with 2. Or, 6 = 4 + 2.

EXAMPLE

Flip the flap on the
missing-part card → five and zero is
the same as five

5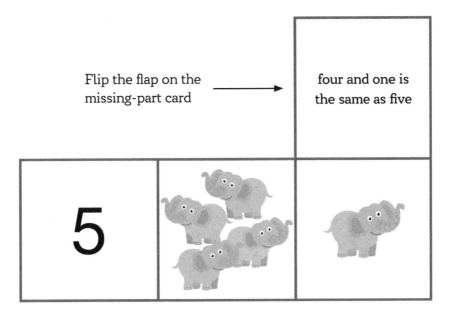

Flip the flap on the
missing-part card → four and one is
the same as five

5

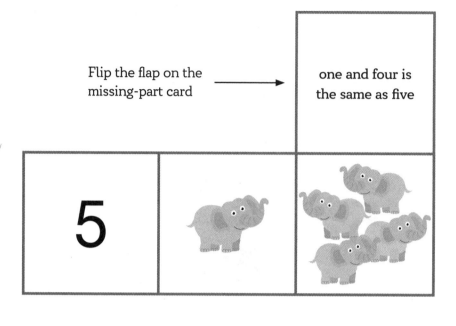

Flip the flap on the missing-part card → one and four is the same as five

5

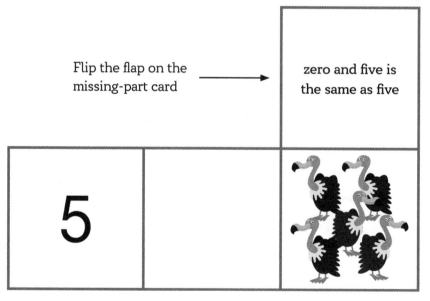

Flip the flap on the missing-part card → zero and five is the same as five

5

Flip the flap on the missing-part card → two and three is the same as five

5

Flip the flap on the missing-part card → three and two is the same as five

5

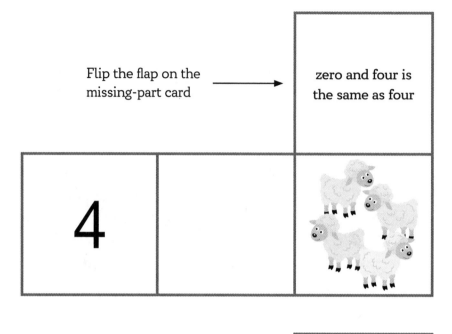

Flip the flap on the missing-part card → zero and four is the same as four

4

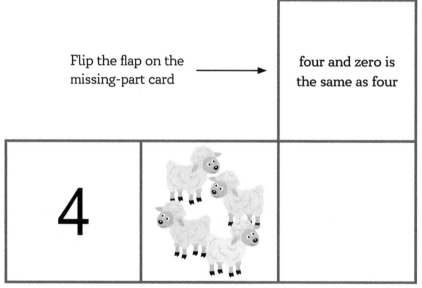

Flip the flap on the missing-part card → four and zero is the same as four

4

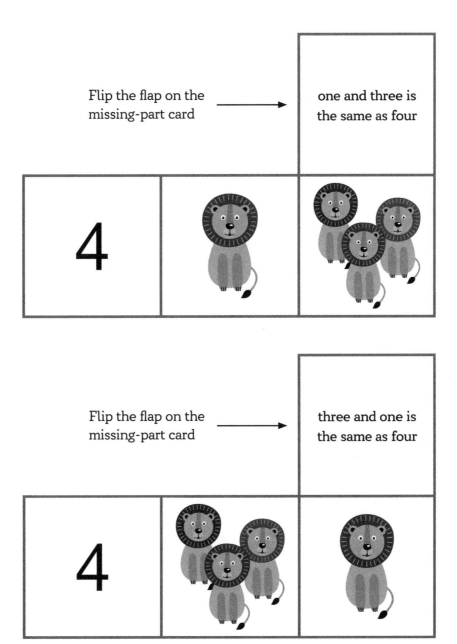

Flip the flap on the
missing-part card → one and three is
the same as four

4

Flip the flap on the
missing-part card → three and one is
the same as four

4

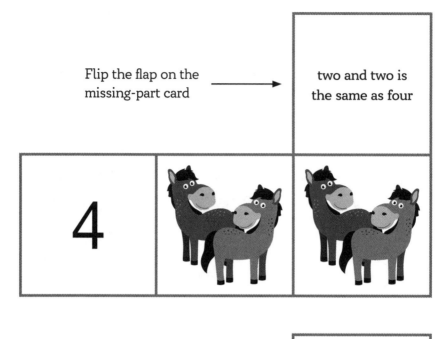

Flip the flap on the missing-part card → two and two is the same as four

4

Flip the flap on the missing-part card → zero and three is the same as three

3

Flip the flap on the missing-part card $\longrightarrow$ one and two is the same as three

| 3 | | |

Flip the flap on the missing-part card $\longrightarrow$ three and zero is the same as three

| 3 | | |

Flip the flap on the missing-part card ⟶ two and one is the same as three

Post Office

★ This activity is designed to reinforce addition and subtraction and to check for understanding.

★ Copy and cut out the six Post Office box fronts provided on the next three pages. These will be glued onto six facial tissue boxes (the kind that looks most like a cube). Make six mailboxes. Cut out the oval for the opening of the box.

★ Glue the boxes together to make an apartment-style mailbox. Copy and cut out the letters on the following pages.

★ Students will work in groups to find the answer to each of the number sentences. Once an answer is agreed upon, deliver the letter to the corresponding box matching the answer choice.

★ Have students discuss and share their solutions.

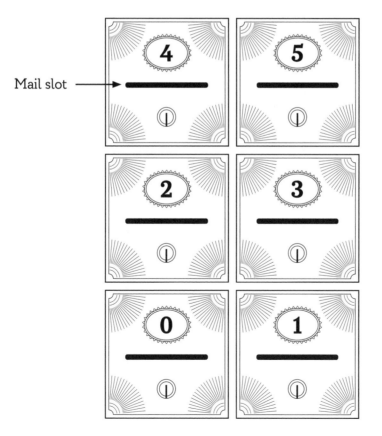

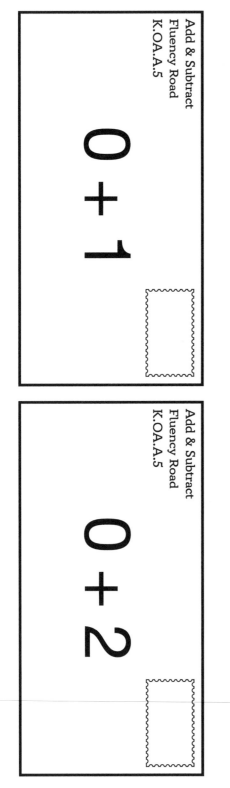

Add & Subtract
Fluency Road
K.OA.A.5

0 + 1

Add & Subtract
Fluency Road
K.OA.A.5

0 + 2

0 + 3

0 + 4

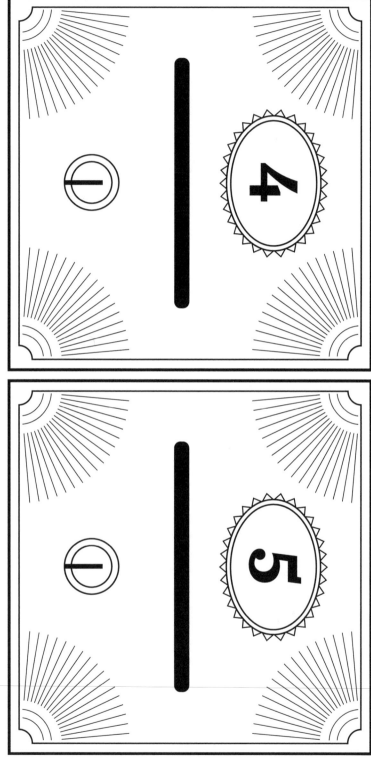

Add & Subtract
Fluency Road
K.OA.A.5

$0 + 5$

Add & Subtract
Fluency Road
K.OA.A.5

$1 + 0$

Math Fluency Activities for K–2 Teachers

Add & Subtract
Fluency Road
K.OA.A.5

1 + 1

Add & Subtract
Fluency Road
K.OA.A.5

1 + 3

Add & Subtract
Fluency Road
K.OA.A.5

2 + 5

Add & Subtract
Fluency Road
K.OA.A.5

1 + 2

Add & Subtract
Fluency Road
K.OA.A.5

1 + 4

Add & Subtract
Fluency Road
K.OA.A.5

2 + 1

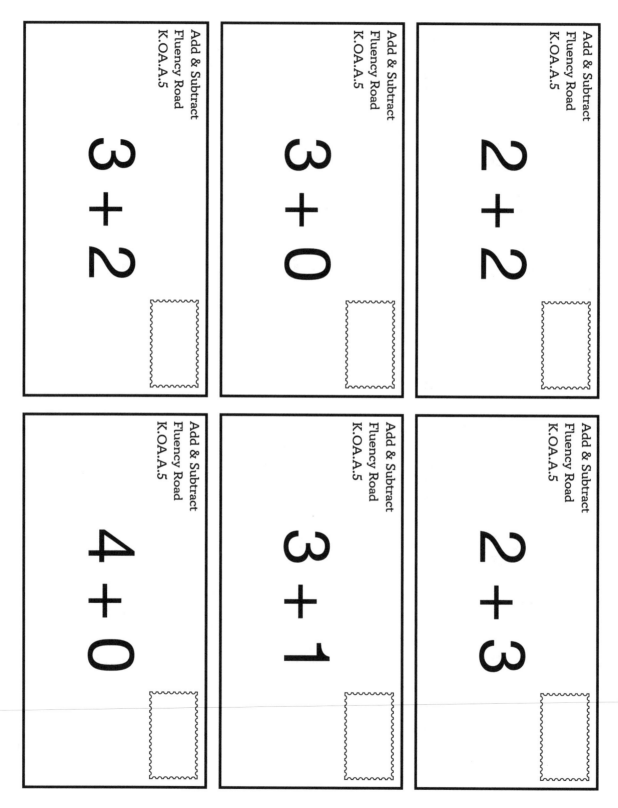

Add & Subtract
Fluency Road
K.OA.A.5

2 + 2

Add & Subtract
Fluency Road
K.OA.A.5

3 + 0

Add & Subtract
Fluency Road
K.OA.A.5

3 + 2

Add & Subtract
Fluency Road
K.OA.A.5

2 + 3

Add & Subtract
Fluency Road
K.OA.A.5

3 + 1

Add & Subtract
Fluency Road
K.OA.A.5

4 + 0

Add & Subtract
Fluency Road
K.OA.A.5

4 + 1

Add & Subtract
Fluency Road
K.OA.A.5

5 − 0

Add & Subtract
Fluency Road
K.OA.A.5

5 − 2

Add & Subtract
Fluency Road
K.OA.A.5

5 + 0

Add & Subtract
Fluency Road
K.OA.A.5

5 − 1

Add & Subtract
Fluency Road
K.OA.A.5

5 − 3

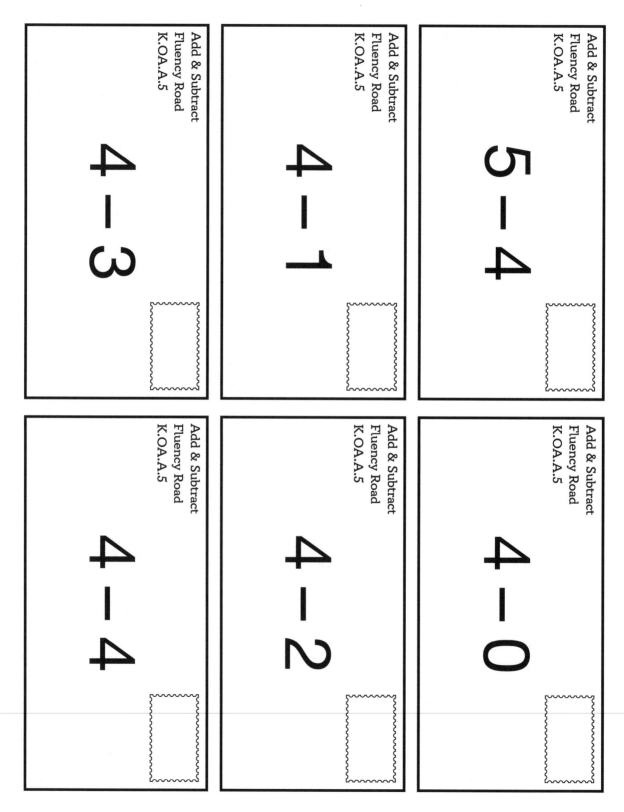

Add & Subtract
Fluency Road
K.OA.A.5

5 − 4

Add & Subtract
Fluency Road
K.OA.A.5

4 − 1

Add & Subtract
Fluency Road
K.OA.A.5

4 − 3

Add & Subtract
Fluency Road
K.OA.A.5

4 − 0

Add & Subtract
Fluency Road
K.OA.A.5

4 − 2

Add & Subtract
Fluency Road
K.OA.A.5

4 − 4

Math Fluency Activities for K–2 Teachers

3 – 0

3 – 1

3 – 3

2 – 0

3 – 2

2 – 1

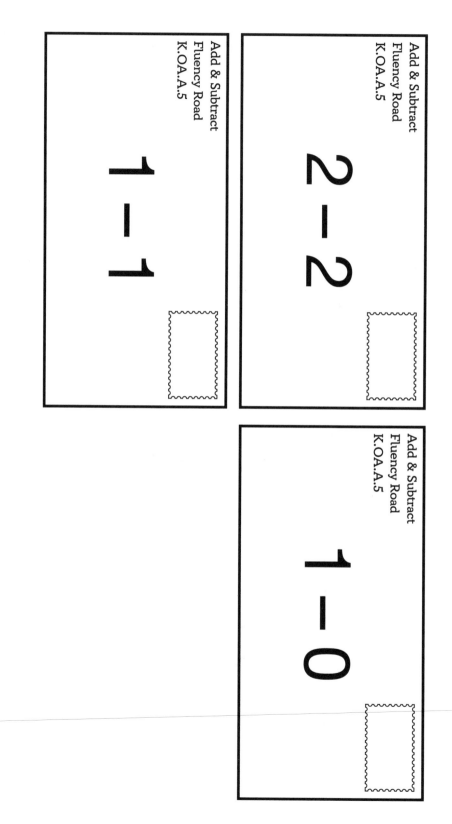

Add & Subtract
Fluency Road
K.OA.A.5

2 − 2

Add & Subtract
Fluency Road
K.OA.A.5

1 − 1

Add & Subtract
Fluency Road
K.OA.A.5

1 − 0

Facts Strategy Check

Name: _____   Date: _____

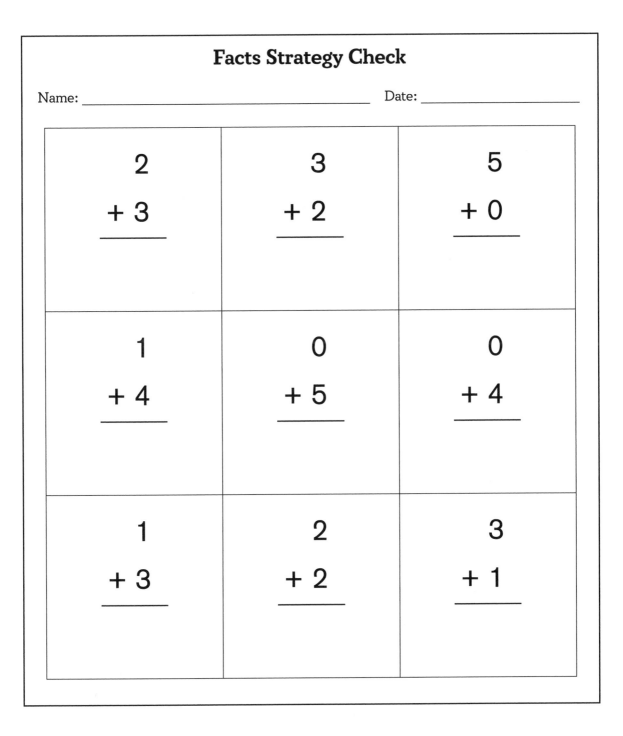

2 + 3 ___	3 + 2 ___	5 + 0 ___
1 + 4 ___	0 + 5 ___	0 + 4 ___
1 + 3 ___	2 + 2 ___	3 + 1 ___

Facts Strategy Check

Name: _____ Date: _____

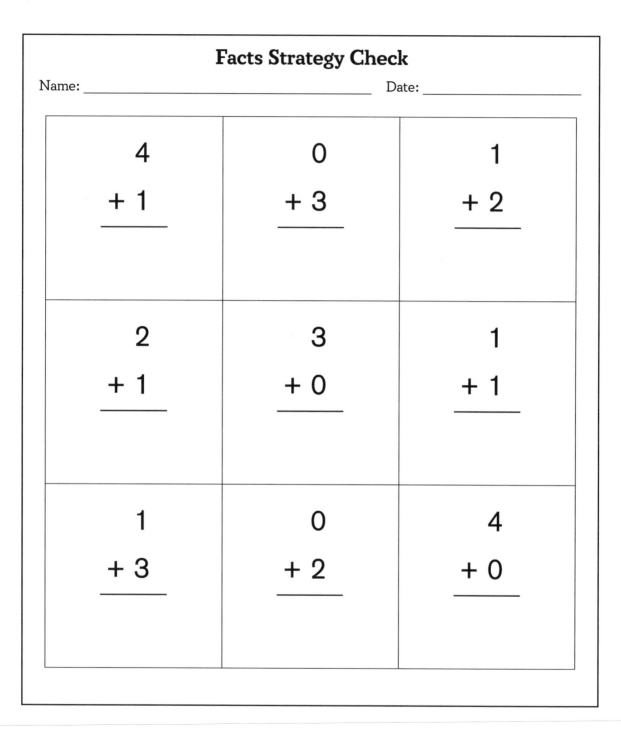

4 + 1	0 + 3	1 + 2
2 + 1	3 + 0	1 + 1
1 + 3	0 + 2	4 + 0

Math Fluency Activities for K–2 Teachers

Facts I Know!

Name: _____

+	0	1	2	3	4	5
0						
1						
2						
3						
4						
5						

★ Do not time.

★ Do not have students compete against other students.

★ Have students set personal goals.

★ Look for growth.

★ Highlight facts they know.

Facts I Know!

Name: _____

+	0	1	2	3	4	5
0						
1						
2						
3						
4						
5						

CHAPTER 2

Grade 1

GRADE	REQUIRED FLUENCY
1	**1.OA.C.6** Add/subtract within 10. Use strategies such as counting on; making 10 (e.g., 8 + 6 = 8 + 2 + 4 = 10 + 4 = 14); decomposing a number leading to a 10 (e.g., 13 − 4 = 13 − 3 − 1 = 10 − 1 = 9); using the relationship between addition and subtraction (e.g., knowing that 8 + 4 = 12, one knows 12 − 8 = 4); and creating equivalent but easier or known sums (e.g., adding 6 + 7 by creating the known equivalent 6 + 6 + 1 = 12 + 1 = 13).

In grade 1, students build on their knowledge of operations and algebraic thinking from kindergarten standard K.OA.A.5 to include numbers within 10. Activities in this section will assume student mastery of numbers within 5. If students are struggling with these activities, step back to kindergarten standards and progress from concrete to representational examples. This standard is critical for mathematical development with addition and subtraction since, with mastery, students will have the skills to be fluent with basic facts.

Basic facts are facts with addends of 0 to 10 and facts with factors of 0 to 10. To be fluent means to be able to recall basic facts accurately, quickly, and effortlessly. When automaticity is mastered, facts can be retrieved from long-term memory without thinking about it. As stated earlier, drilling does not produce mastery. Mastery comes from understanding math skills and concepts, not from memorizing facts and procedures. The end goal is to retrieve from memory through understanding. Being fluent requires ongoing practice and moving students from concrete to representational to abstract strategies. Keep in mind that all students move through these phases at individual rates. In grades kindergarten, first, and second, the focus should be on number sense. Just as we checked for mastery in kindergarten, make sure to inventory what facts they know and do not know before sending them on to the next grade's standards. If a student is struggling, make sure to provide the necessary intervention to help them be successful. Focus on reasoning strategies, build in success, and provide engaging activities like the ones in this section. The following activities, ideas, and games will provide support in mastering addition and subtraction in an engaging, meaningful way that will support mastering from understanding. These activities use the first grade fluency standard shown above as their focus.

The following strategies are essential for conceptual understanding and procedural fluency: counting on, decomposing a number leading to 10, relationships between addition and subtraction, and finally, equivalent or easier sums.

Concrete Activities

Representational Activities

Abstract Activities

Counting On Using Connecting Cubes

MATERIALS NEEDED: Connecting cubes (any kind)

Students will use cubes and these task cards to find the solution to the number sentence. Once all cards have been solved, make sure students discuss and share their solutions. These activities can be done as a whole class, in small groups, or individually.

Copy the cards or display for the class and use a virtual connecting cube manipulative. Drag and drop the cubes to make the number sentence.

I see 6 cubes with 2 more added to them. How many cubes do I have now? I know that 6 + 2 = 8

What is 6 + 2 = ?

What is 7 – 4 = ?

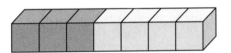

I see 7 total cubes. If I remove 4 cubes, how many cubes are left? I know that 7 – 4 = 3

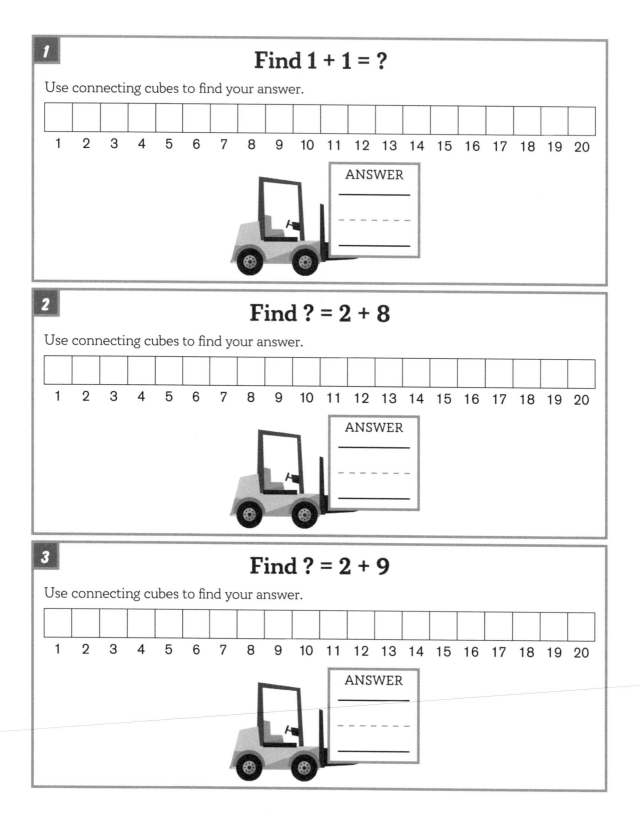

1

Find 1 + 1 = ?

Use connecting cubes to find your answer.

| | | | | | | | | | | | | | | | | | | | |
|1|2|3|4|5|6|7|8|9|10|11|12|13|14|15|16|17|18|19|20|

ANSWER

2

Find ? = 2 + 8

Use connecting cubes to find your answer.

| | | | | | | | | | | | | | | | | | | | |
|1|2|3|4|5|6|7|8|9|10|11|12|13|14|15|16|17|18|19|20|

ANSWER

3

Find ? = 2 + 9

Use connecting cubes to find your answer.

| | | | | | | | | | | | | | | | | | | | |
|1|2|3|4|5|6|7|8|9|10|11|12|13|14|15|16|17|18|19|20|

ANSWER

4

Find ? = 1 + 8

Use connecting cubes to find your answer.

1	2	3	4	5	6	7	8	9	10	11	12	13	14	15	16	17	18	19	20

ANSWER

5

Find ? = 1 + 6

Use connecting cubes to find your answer.

1	2	3	4	5	6	7	8	9	10	11	12	13	14	15	16	17	18	19	20

ANSWER

6

Find ? = 1 + 3

Use connecting cubes to find your answer.

1	2	3	4	5	6	7	8	9	10	11	12	13	14	15	16	17	18	19	20

ANSWER

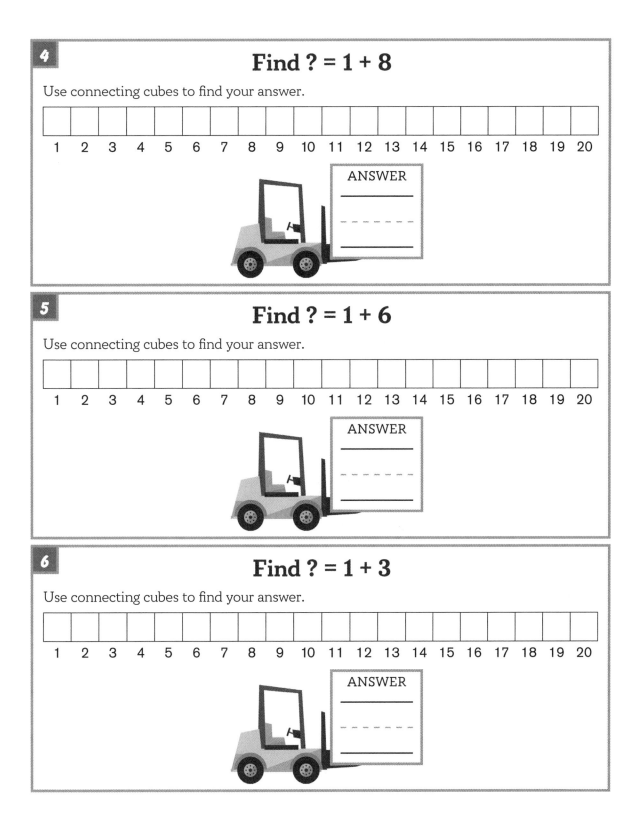

7

Find ? = 2 + 4

Use connecting cubes to find your answer.

1	2	3	4	5	6	7	8	9	10	11	12	13	14	15	16	17	18	19	20

ANSWER

_____

– – – – –

_____

8

Find ? = 2 + 3

Use connecting cubes to find your answer.

1	2	3	4	5	6	7	8	9	10	11	12	13	14	15	16	17	18	19	20

ANSWER

_____

– – – – –

_____

9

Find ? = 1 + 7

Use connecting cubes to find your answer.

1	2	3	4	5	6	7	8	9	10	11	12	13	14	15	16	17	18	19	20

ANSWER

_____

– – – – –

_____

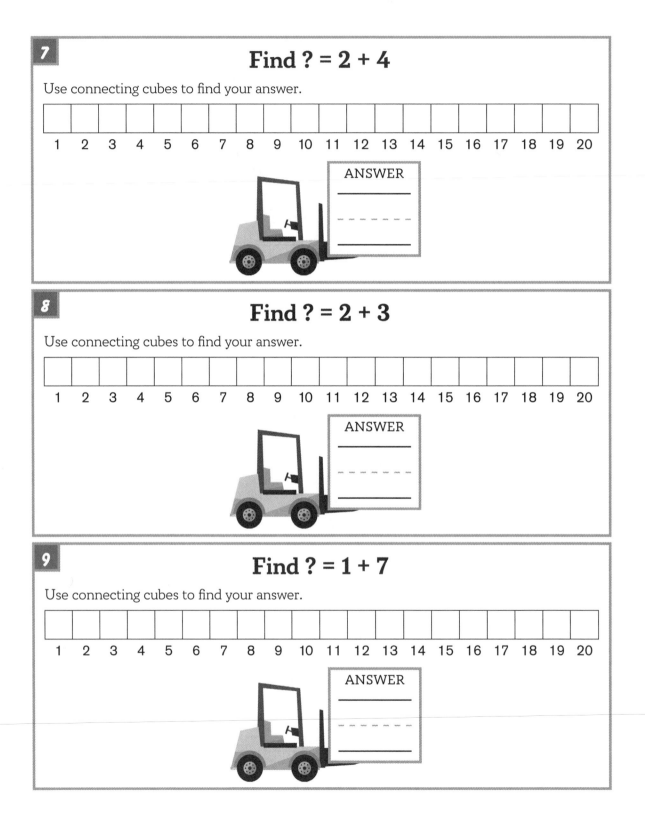

10

Find ? = 1 + 5

Use connecting cubes to find your answer.

1	2	3	4	5	6	7	8	9	10	11	12	13	14	15	16	17	18	19	20

ANSWER
_____
- - - - -
_____

11

Find ? = 5 + 4

Use connecting cubes to find your answer.

1	2	3	4	5	6	7	8	9	10	11	12	13	14	15	16	17	18	19	20

ANSWER
_____
- - - - -
_____

12

Find ? = 6 + 2

Use connecting cubes to find your answer.

1	2	3	4	5	6	7	8	9	10	11	12	13	14	15	16	17	18	19	20

ANSWER
_____
- - - - -
_____

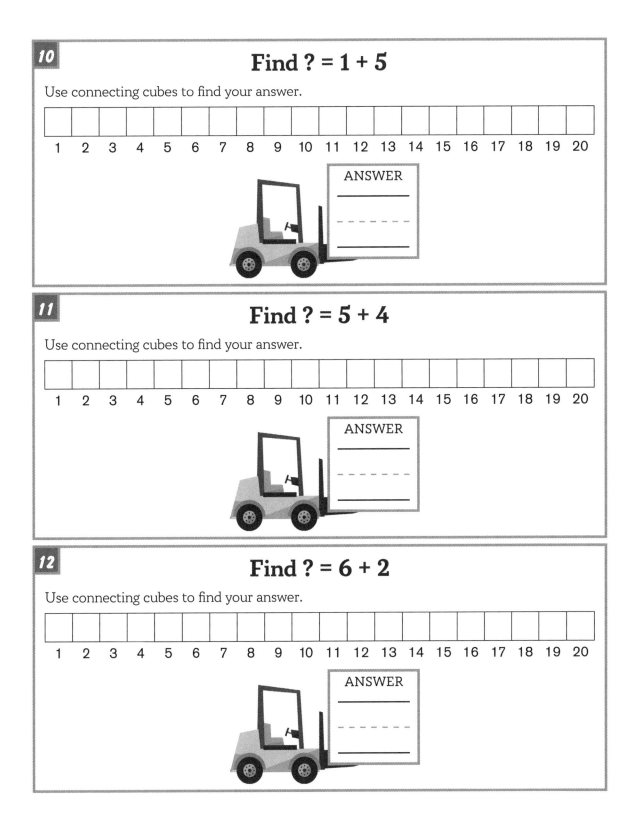

13

Find ? = 1 + 2

Use connecting cubes to find your answer.

1	2	3	4	5	6	7	8	9	10	11	12	13	14	15	16	17	18	19	20

ANSWER

14

Find ? = 2 + 6

Use connecting cubes to find your answer.

1	2	3	4	5	6	7	8	9	10	11	12	13	14	15	16	17	18	19	20

ANSWER

15

Find ? = 4 + 4

Use connecting cubes to find your answer.

1	2	3	4	5	6	7	8	9	10	11	12	13	14	15	16	17	18	19	20

ANSWER

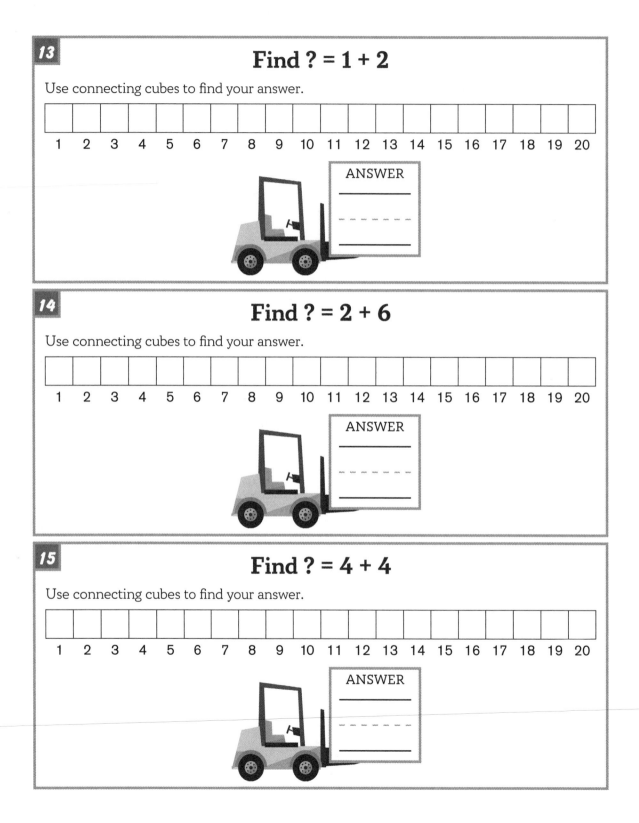

16   Find ? = 3 + 7

Use connecting cubes to find your answer.

1	2	3	4	5	6	7	8	9	10	11	12	13	14	15	16	17	18	19	20

ANSWER

17   Find ? = 5 + 3

Use connecting cubes to find your answer.

1	2	3	4	5	6	7	8	9	10	11	12	13	14	15	16	17	18	19	20

ANSWER

18   Find ? = 4 + 5

Use connecting cubes to find your answer.

1	2	3	4	5	6	7	8	9	10	11	12	13	14	15	16	17	18	19	20

ANSWER

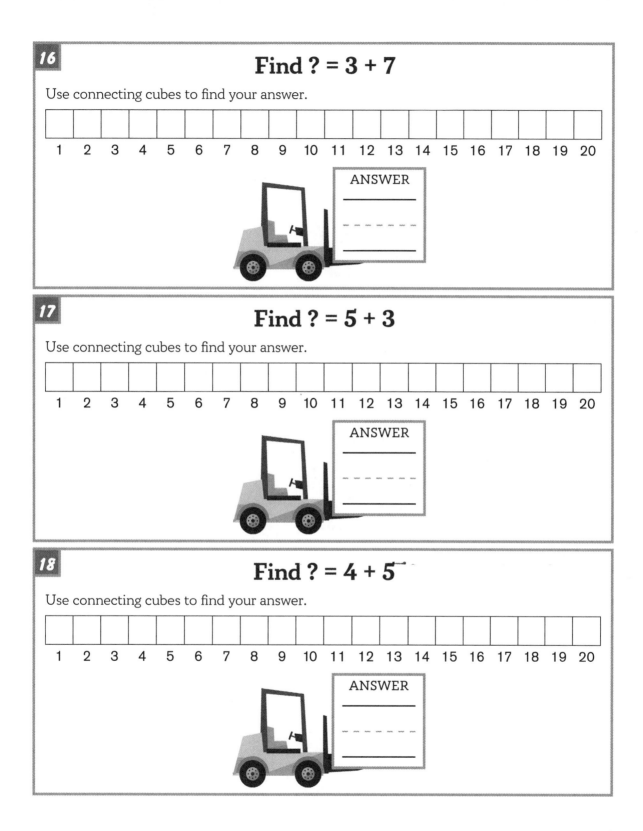

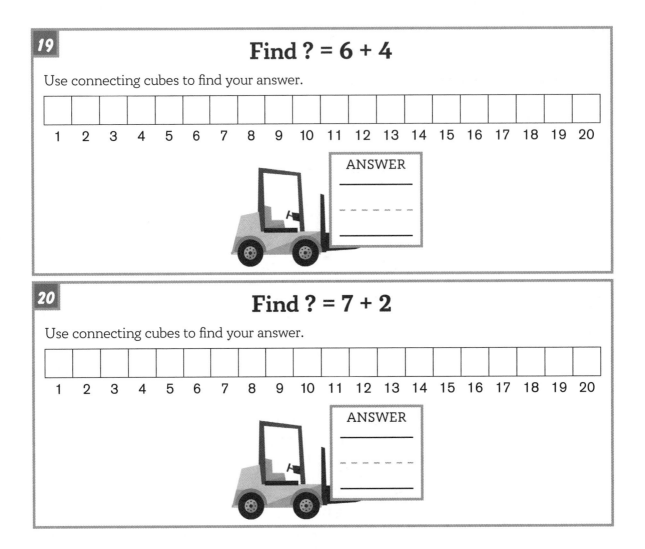

19 **Find ? = 6 + 4**

Use connecting cubes to find your answer.

1	2	3	4	5	6	7	8	9	10	11	12	13	14	15	16	17	18	19	20

ANSWER

20 **Find ? = 7 + 2**

Use connecting cubes to find your answer.

1	2	3	4	5	6	7	8	9	10	11	12	13	14	15	16	17	18	19	20

ANSWER

ANSWER KEY:
Counting On Using Connecting Cubes

QUESTION	ANSWER		QUESTION	ANSWER
1.	2		11.	9
2.	10		12.	8
3.	11		13.	3
4.	9		14.	8
5.	7		15.	8
6.	4		16.	10
7.	6		17.	8
8.	5		18.	9
9.	8		19.	10
10.	6		20.	9

Adding on a Ten-Frame

> **OBJECTIVE:** Students use ten-frames on the task cards to find the solutions to the number sentences. Once all task cards have been solved, share solutions. This activity can be done as a whole class, in a small group setting, such as a guided math group, or individually.

MATERIALS NEEDED: Task cards and two-color counters

DIRECTIONS: Copy the task cards or project for all students to see. Students should place the first addend (red counter) on the upper part of the ten-frame and then place the second addend (yellow counter) on the lower part of the ten-frame. In the example below, there are 4 red counters and 5 yellow counters. By moving one of the yellow counters to the upper part of the ten-frame we make a 5. Now addition is easy. 5 plus an additional 4 will give us 9. Or, students can also see that 10 less 1 gives us 9. So, 4 + 5 = 9 and 10 − 1 = 9.

EXAMPLE

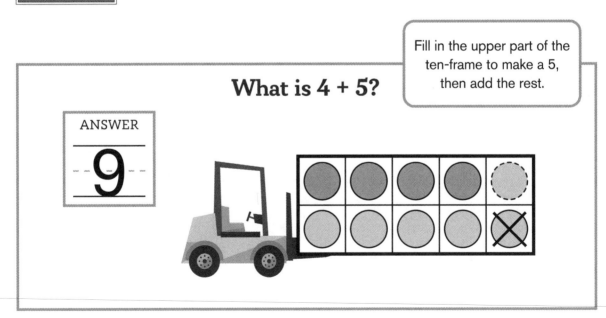

Fill in the upper part of the ten-frame to make a 5, then add the rest.

What is 4 + 5?

ANSWER

9

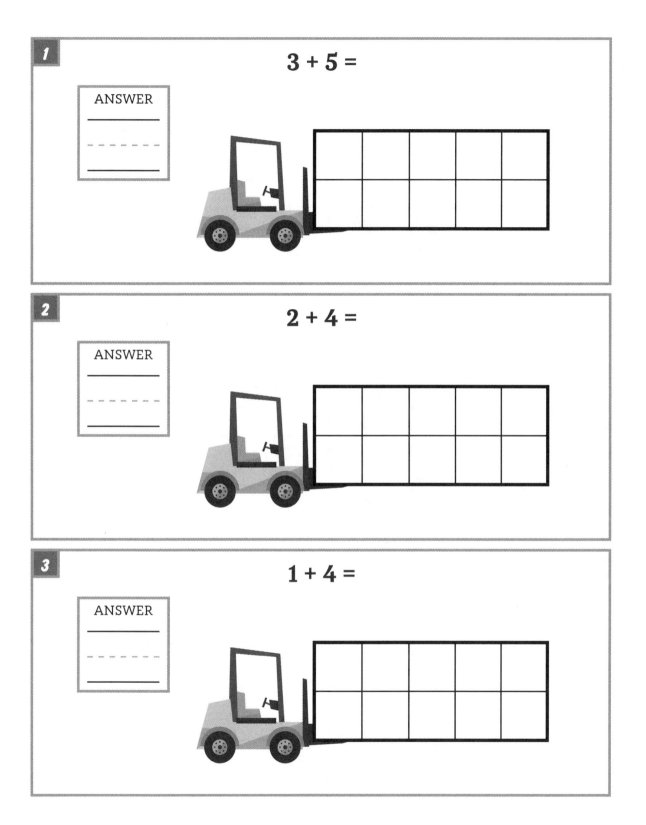

1

3 + 5 =

ANSWER

2

2 + 4 =

ANSWER

3

1 + 4 =

ANSWER

4

$$2 + 3 =$$

ANSWER

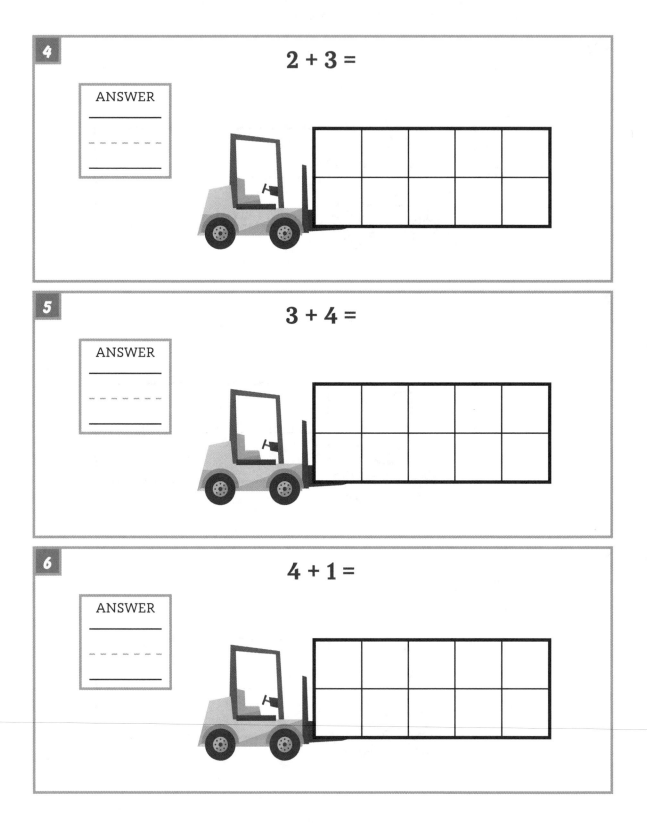

5

$$3 + 4 =$$

ANSWER

6

$$4 + 1 =$$

ANSWER

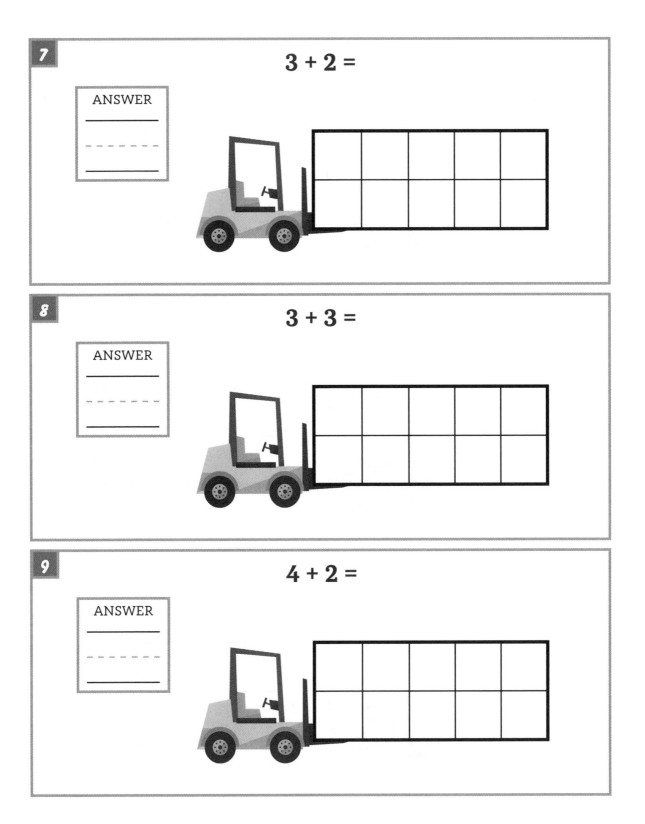

7

3 + 2 =

ANSWER

8

3 + 3 =

ANSWER

9

4 + 2 =

ANSWER

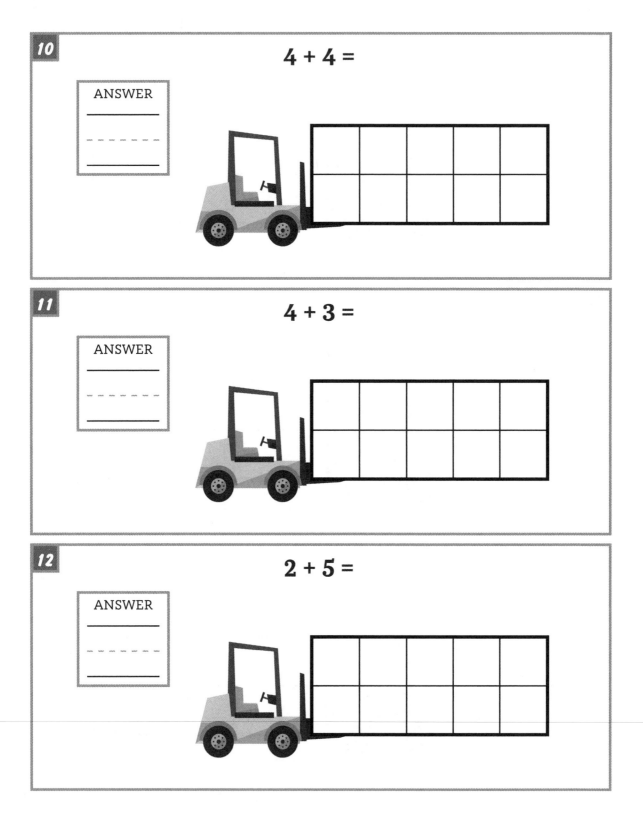

10

4 + 4 =

ANSWER

11

4 + 3 =

ANSWER

12

2 + 5 =

ANSWER

13

5 + 3 =

ANSWER
_____
- - - - - - - -
_____

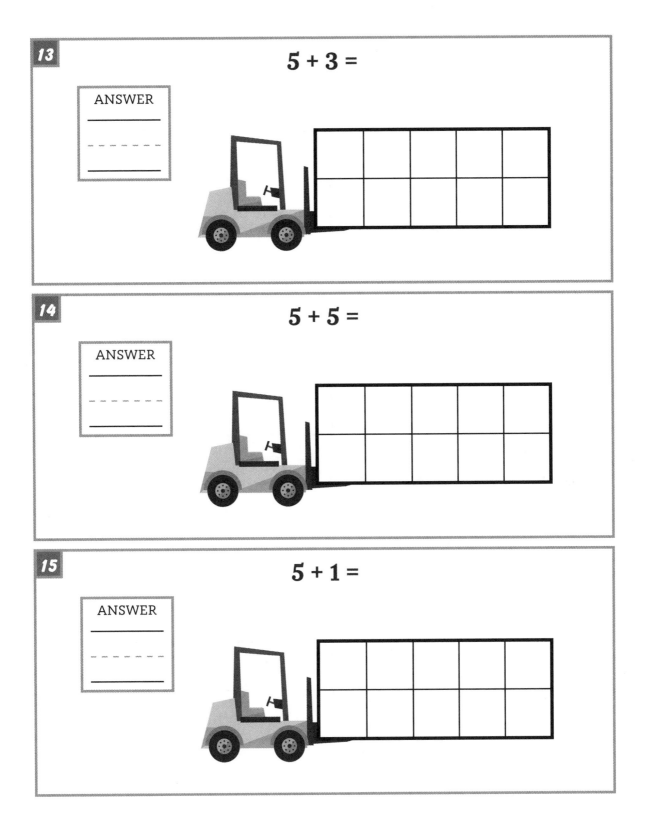

14

5 + 5 =

ANSWER
_____
- - - - - - - -
_____

15

5 + 1 =

ANSWER
_____
- - - - - - - -
_____

16

$5 + 4 =$

ANSWER

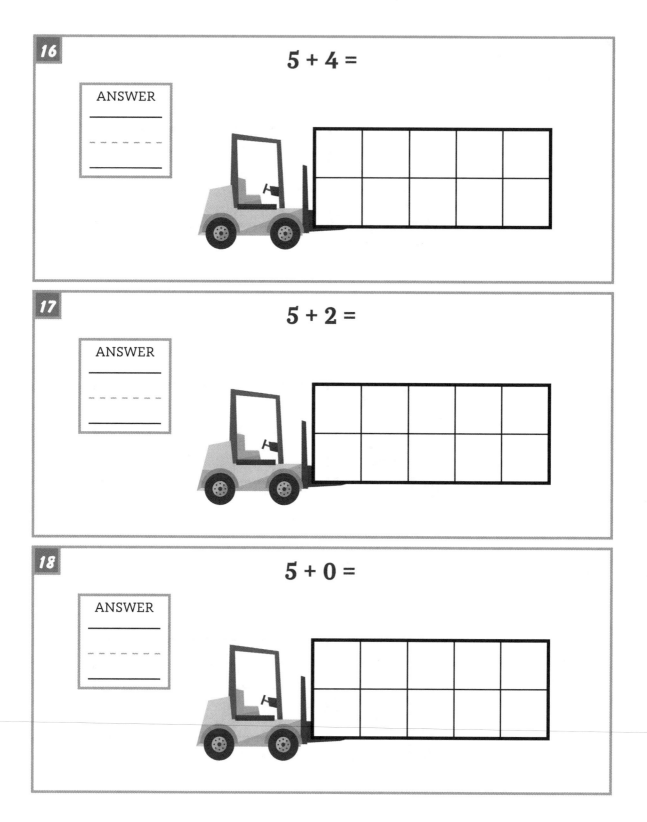

17

$5 + 2 =$

ANSWER

18

$5 + 0 =$

ANSWER

19

7 + 1 =

ANSWER

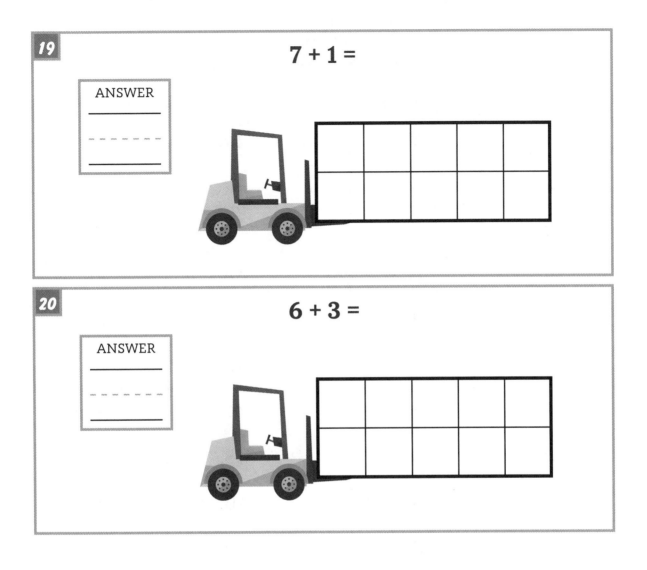

20

6 + 3 =

ANSWER

ANSWER KEY:
Adding on a Ten-Frame

QUESTION	ANSWER
1.	8
2.	6
3.	5
4.	5
5.	7
6.	5
7.	5
8.	6
9.	6
10.	8

QUESTION	ANSWER
11.	7
12.	7
13.	8
14.	10
15.	6
16.	9
17.	7
18.	5
19.	8
20.	9

Subtracting on a Ten-Frame

OBJECTIVE: Students use ten-frames on the task cards to find the solutions to the number sentences. Once all task cards have been solved, discuss and share solutions. This activity can be done as a whole class, in a small group setting, such as a guided math group, or individually.

MATERIALS NEEDED: Task cards and two-color counters

DIRECTIONS: Copy the task cards or project for all class viewing. Students place the minuend on the ten-frames. Decompose the subtrahend to count down to 10, then remove the rest. In this example, there are 9 red color counters on the ten-frame. Removing 6 will leave us with 3. We see that 9 – 6 = 3.

EXAMPLE

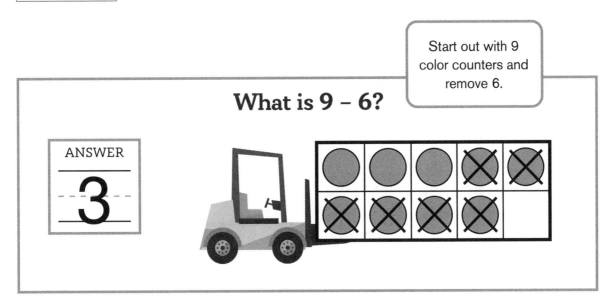

Start out with 9 color counters and remove 6.

What is 9 – 6?

ANSWER

3

1

What is 3 – 2?

ANSWER

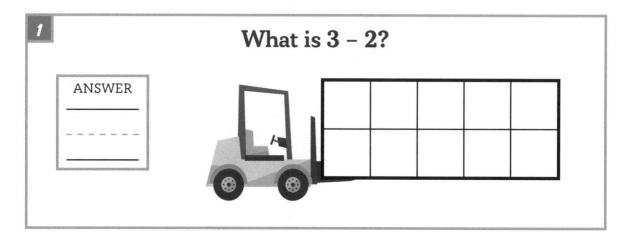

2

What is 4 – 3?

ANSWER

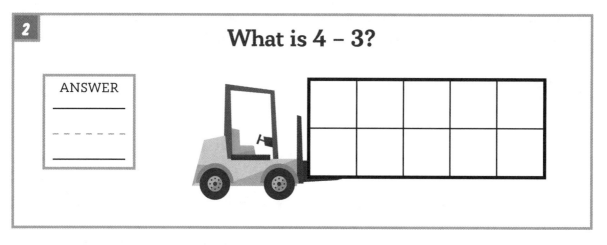

3

What is 5 – 2?

ANSWER

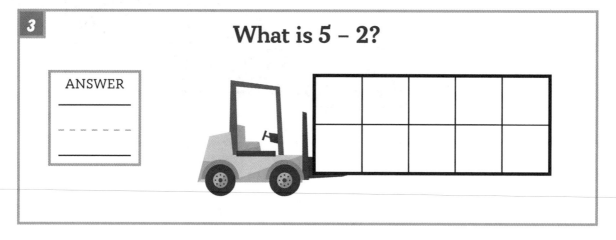

4

What is 2 – 2?

ANSWER
_____
- - - - - - -
_____

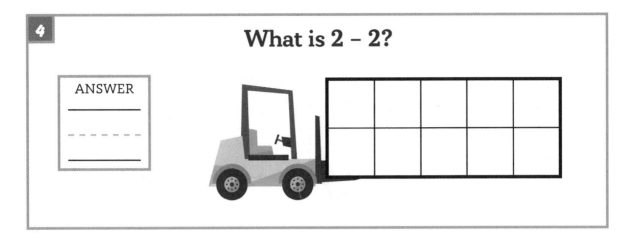

5

What is 6 – 4?

ANSWER
_____
- - - - - - -
_____

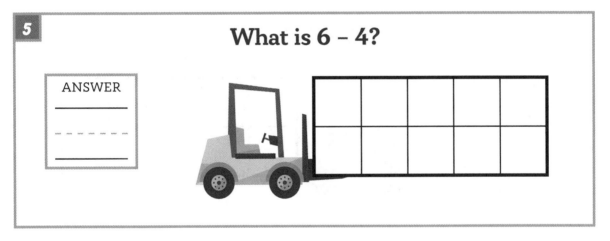

6

What is 4 – 1?

ANSWER
_____
- - - - - - -
_____

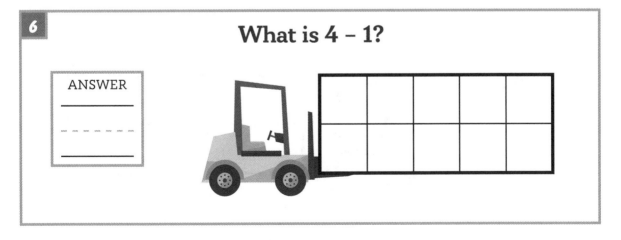

7 What is 8 − 5?

ANSWER

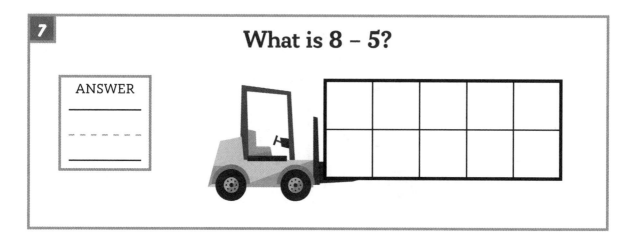

8 What is 7 − 3?

ANSWER

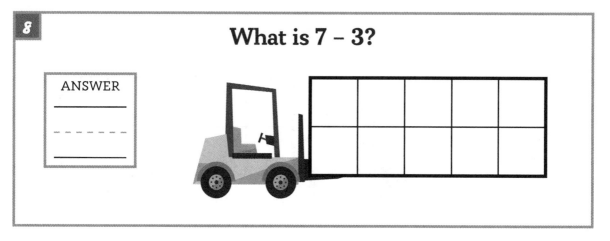

9 What is 9 − 5?

ANSWER

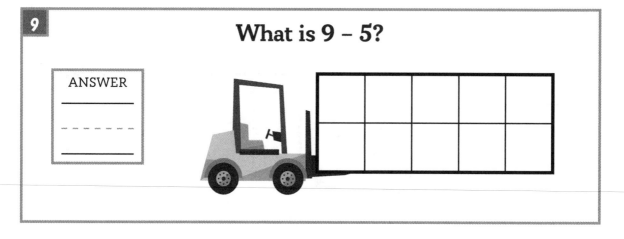

10 **What is 6 – 1?**

ANSWER
_____
- - - - - - - - -
_____

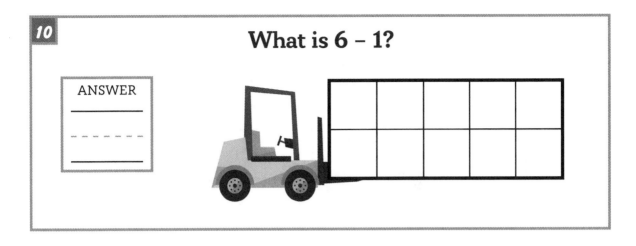

11 **What is 9 – 7?**

ANSWER
_____
- - - - - - - - -
_____

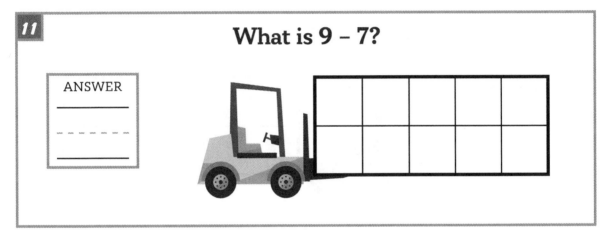

12 **What is 8 – 6?**

ANSWER
_____
- - - - - - - - -
_____

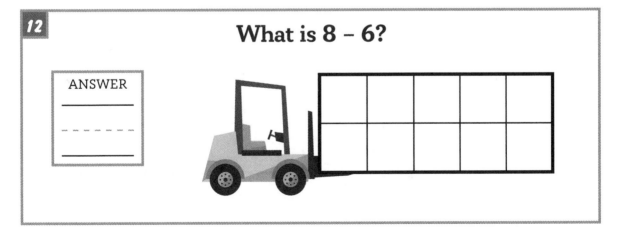

13 What is 7 – 6?

ANSWER

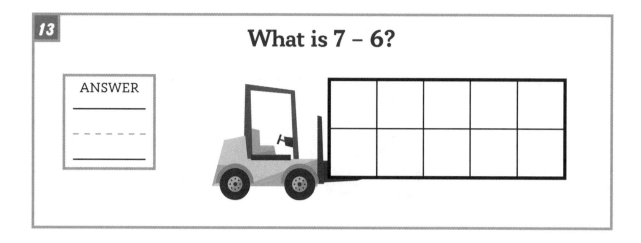

14 What is 6 – 3?

ANSWER

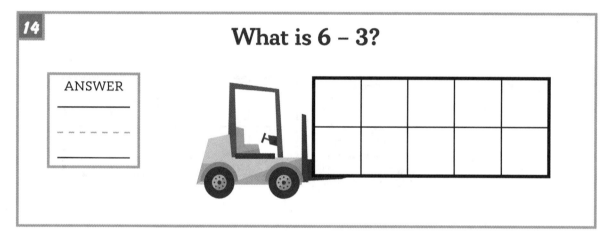

15 What is 9 – 2?

ANSWER

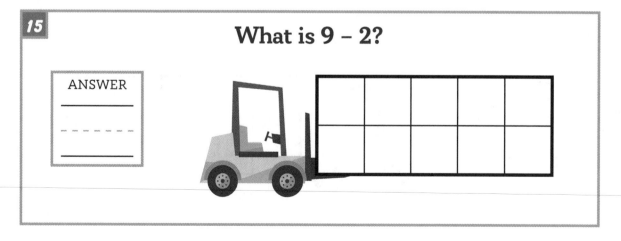

Math Fluency Activities for K–2 Teachers

16 What is 9 – 4?

ANSWER
_____
- - - - - - - -
_____

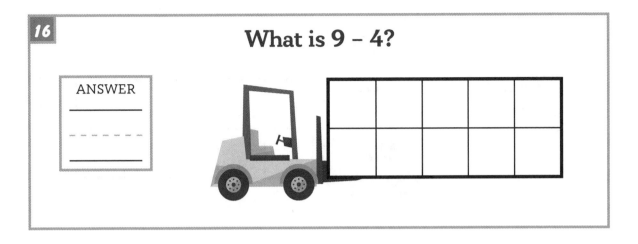

17 What is 8 – 2?

ANSWER
_____
- - - - - - - -
_____

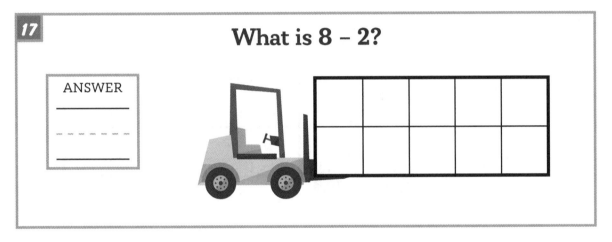

18 What is 7 – 4?

ANSWER
_____
- - - - - - - -
_____

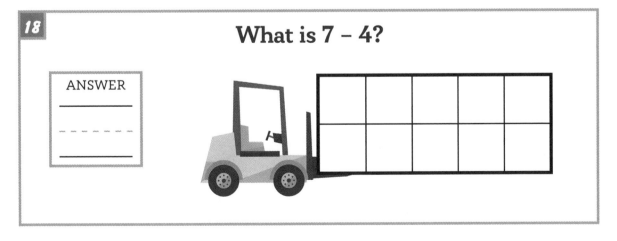

19

What is 9 – 3?

ANSWER
_____
- - - - - - -
_____

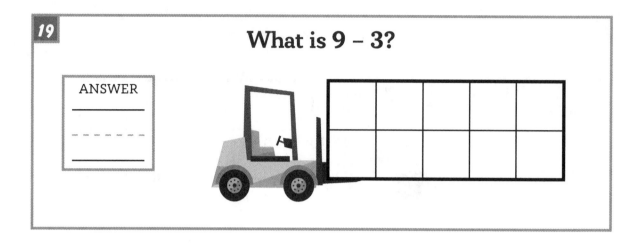

20

What is 8 – 4?

ANSWER
_____
- - - - - - -
_____

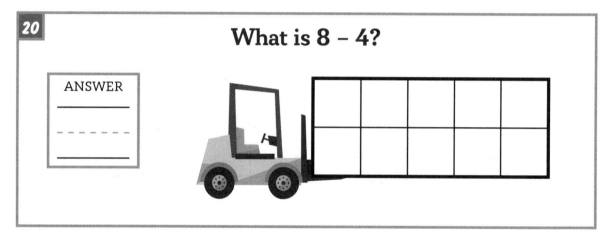

Math Fluency Activities for K–2 Teachers

ANSWER KEY:
Subtracting on a Ten-Frame

QUESTION	ANSWER
1.	1
2.	1
3.	3
4.	0
5.	2
6.	3
7.	3
8.	4
9.	4
10.	5

QUESTION	ANSWER
11.	2
12.	2
13.	1
14.	3
15.	7
16.	5
17.	6
18.	3
19.	6
20.	4

Using Doubles for Addition and Subtraction

MATERIALS NEEDED: Connector cubes along with these task cards

DIRECTIONS: Copy or display the task cards for students to use. Students will practice finding the sum or difference by using the strategy of "doubles." Have students discuss and share their strategies. Examples are given to start students on the right track. In the first example, we see a stack of 5 cubes and a stack of 3 cubes. If we remove 2 cubes from the stack of 5, we have a set of doubles, 3 plus 3, with 2 remaining. Using our knowledge of doubles, in this instance 3 + 3 = 6, we simply add 2 more to the doubles of 6 to make a total of 8. Therefore, we now know that 5 + 3 = 8 using the doubles plus 2 strategy. In the second example, we show 5 cubes in the first group and 3 in the second group. Removing the 2 cubes again from the set of 5, we have 2 groups of 3 with 2 left over. We now have a zero pair because we know that 3 − 3 = 0, which leaves us with the final 2 cubes. Hence, we know that 5 − 3 = 2.

EXAMPLE

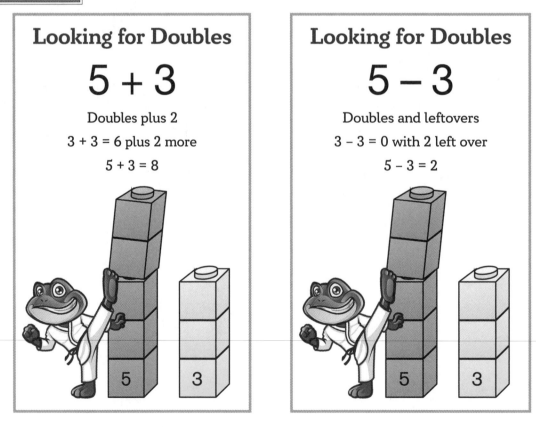

Looking for Doubles

$$5 + 3$$

Doubles plus 2

3 + 3 = 6 plus 2 more

5 + 3 = 8

Looking for Doubles

$$5 - 3$$

Doubles and leftovers

3 − 3 = 0 with 2 left over

5 − 3 = 2

Looking for Doubles

9 + 9

Looking for Doubles

9 – 9

Looking for Doubles

9 + 8

9   8

Looking for Doubles

9 − 8

9   8

Looking for Doubles

9 + 7

Looking for Doubles

9 − 7

Looking for Doubles

9 + 6

Looking for Doubles

9 − 6

Looking for Doubles

9 + 5

Looking for Doubles

9 − 5

Looking for Doubles

8 + 8

Looking for Doubles

8 − 8

Looking for Doubles

8 + 7

Looking for Doubles

8 − 7

Looking for Doubles

$8 + 6$

Looking for Doubles

$8 - 6$

Looking for Doubles

8 + 5

Looking for Doubles

8 − 5

Looking for Doubles

7 + 7

Looking for Doubles

7 − 7

Math Fluency Activities for K–2 Teachers

Looking for Doubles

7 + 6

Looking for Doubles

7 − 6

Looking for Doubles

7 + 5

Looking for Doubles

7 – 5

Looking for Doubles

7 + 4

Looking for Doubles

7 − 4

Looking for Doubles

6 + 6

Looking for Doubles

6 − 6

Math Fluency Activities for K–2 Teachers

Looking for Doubles

6 + 5

Looking for Doubles

6 − 5

Looking for Doubles

6 + 4

Looking for Doubles

6 − 4

Math Fluency Activities for K–2 Teachers

Looking for Doubles

5 + 5

Looking for Doubles

5 − 5

Looking for Doubles

5 + 4

Looking for Doubles

5 − 4

Looking for Doubles

5 + 3

Looking for Doubles

5 − 3

Looking for Doubles

4 + 4

Looking for Doubles

4 − 4

Looking for Doubles

4 + 3

Looking for Doubles

4 − 3

Looking for Doubles

3 + 3

Looking for Doubles

3 − 3

Looking for Doubles

3 + 2

Looking for Doubles

3 − 2

ANSWER KEY:
Using Doubles for Addition and Subtraction

QUESTION	ANSWER
9 + 9	18
9 − 9	0
9 + 8	$(8 + 8) + 1 = 17$
9 − 8	$(8 − 8) + 1 = 1$
9 + 7	$(7 + 7) + 2 = 16$
9 − 7	$(7 − 7) + 2 = 2$
9 + 6	$(6 + 6) + 3 = 15$
9 − 6	$(6 − 6) + 3 = 3$
9 + 5	$(5 + 5) + 4 = 14$
9 − 5	$(5 − 5) + 4 = 4$
8 + 8	16
8 − 8	0

QUESTION	ANSWER
8 + 7	$(7 + 7) + 1 = 15$
8 − 7	$(7 − 7) + 1 = 1$
8 + 6	$(6 + 6) + 2 = 14$
8 − 6	$(6 − 6) + 2 = 2$
8 + 5	$(5 + 5) + 3 = 13$
8 − 5	$(5 − 5) + 3 = 3$
7 + 7	14
7 − 7	0
7 + 6	$(6 + 6) + 1 = 13$
7 − 6	$(6 − 6) + 1 = 1$
7 + 5	$(5 + 5) + 2 = 12$
7 − 5	$(5 − 5) + 2 = 2$

ANSWER KEY:
Using Doubles for Addition and Subtraction

QUESTION	ANSWER
7 + 4	$(4+4)+3=11$
7 − 4	$(4-4)+3=3$
6 + 6	12
6 − 6	0
6 + 5	$(5+5)+1=11$
6 − 5	$(5-5)+1=1$
6 + 4	$(4+4)+2=10$
6 − 4	$(4-4)+2=2$
5 + 5	10
5 - 5	0
5 + 4	$(4+4)+1=9$
5 - 4	$(4-4)+1=1$

QUESTION	ANSWER
5 + 3	$(3+3)+2=8$
5 − 3	$(3-3)+2=2$
4 + 4	8
4 − 4	0
4 + 3	$(3+3)+1=7$
4 − 3	$(3-3)+1=1$
3 + 3	6
3 − 3	0
3 + 2	$(2+2)+1=5$
3 − 2	$(2-2)+1=1$
3 + 2	$(2+2)+1=5$
3 − 2	$(2-2)+1=1$

Adding on a Number Line (Counting On Strategy)

OBJECTIVE: Students use a number line to find the solutions to the number sentences. Once all task cards have been solved, discuss and share solutions.

MATERIALS NEEDED: Task cards

DIRECTIONS: Copy the task cards or project for students to see. Show several examples before using the task cards. In the example below, we are asked to add 7 and 5. To visualize this, we start with the first addend 7 on the number line and jump 5 places to find our total. Now we can easily see that 7 + 5 = 12.

EXAMPLE

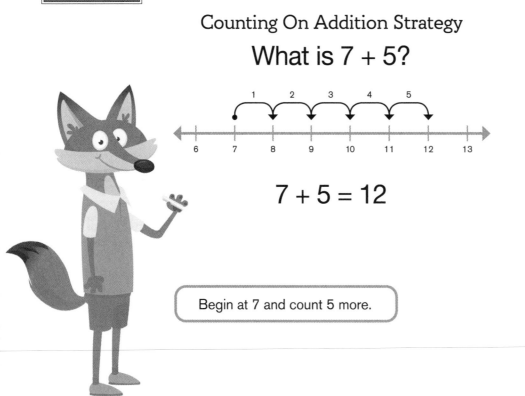

Counting On Addition Strategy
What is 7 + 5?

$$7 + 5 = 12$$

Begin at 7 and count 5 more.

1

Counting On Addition Strategy

What is 2 + 9?

0 1 2 3 4 5 6 7 8 9 10 11 12 13 14 15 16 17 18 19 20

2 + 9 =

2

Counting On Addition Strategy

What is 5 + 6?

0 1 2 3 4 5 6 7 8 9 10 11 12 13 14 15 16 17 18 19 20

5 + 6 =

3

Counting On Addition Strategy

What is 10 + 3?

0 1 2 3 4 5 6 7 8 9 10 11 12 13 14 15 16 17 18 19 20

10 + 3 =

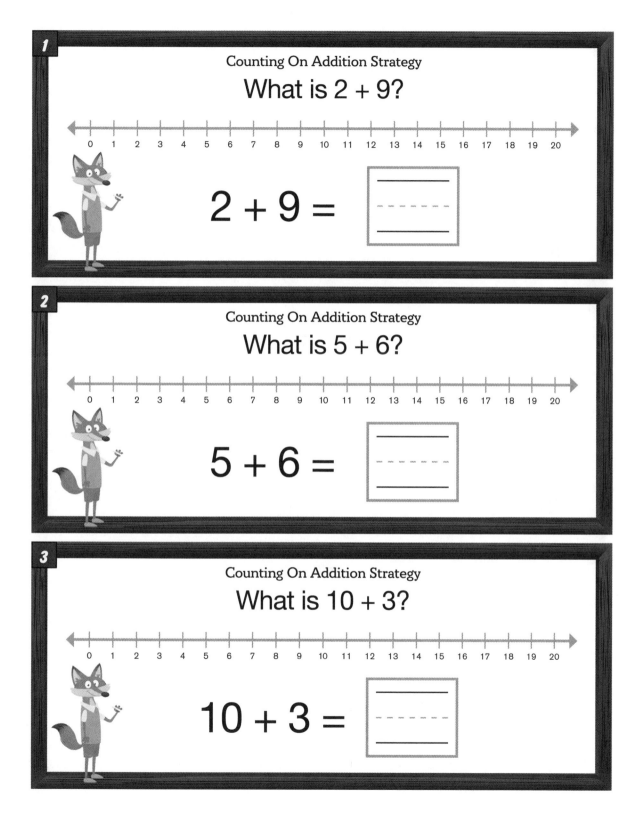

4

Counting On Addition Strategy

What is 9 + 1?

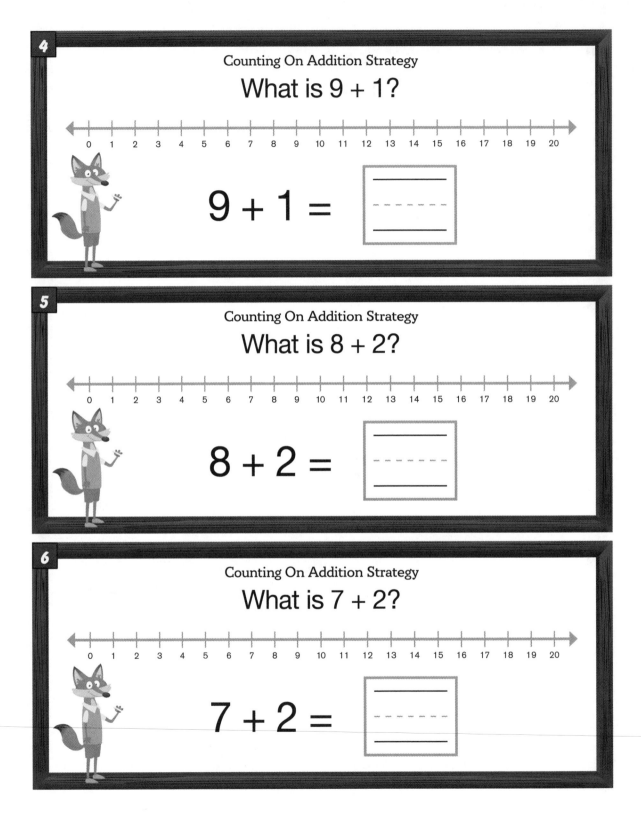

0 1 2 3 4 5 6 7 8 9 10 11 12 13 14 15 16 17 18 19 20

9 + 1 =

5

Counting On Addition Strategy

What is 8 + 2?

0 1 2 3 4 5 6 7 8 9 10 11 12 13 14 15 16 17 18 19 20

8 + 2 =

6

Counting On Addition Strategy

What is 7 + 2?

0 1 2 3 4 5 6 7 8 9 10 11 12 13 14 15 16 17 18 19 20

7 + 2 =

7

Counting On Addition Strategy

What is 3 + 8?

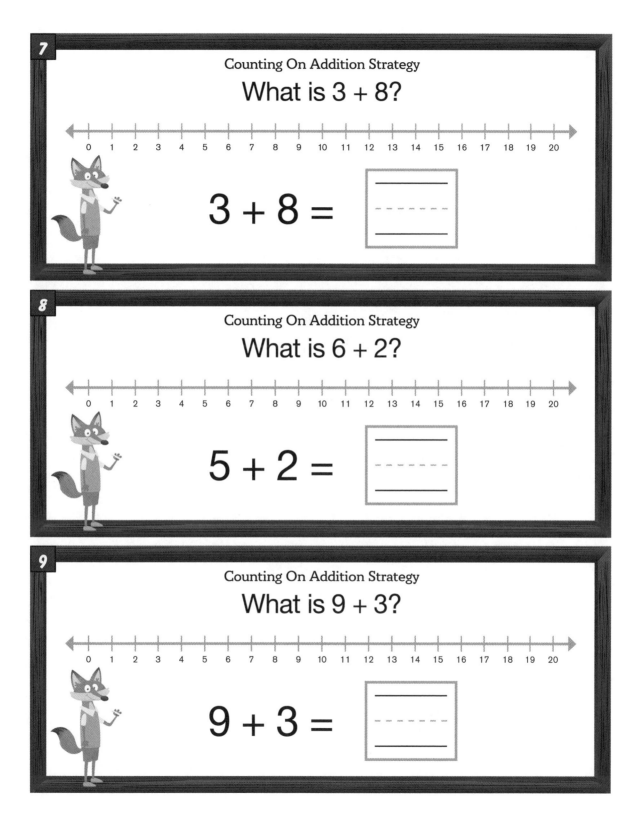

0 1 2 3 4 5 6 7 8 9 10 11 12 13 14 15 16 17 18 19 20

3 + 8 =

8

Counting On Addition Strategy

What is 6 + 2?

0 1 2 3 4 5 6 7 8 9 10 11 12 13 14 15 16 17 18 19 20

5 + 2 =

9

Counting On Addition Strategy

What is 9 + 3?

0 1 2 3 4 5 6 7 8 9 10 11 12 13 14 15 16 17 18 19 20

9 + 3 =

10

Counting On Addition Strategy
What is 6 + 7?

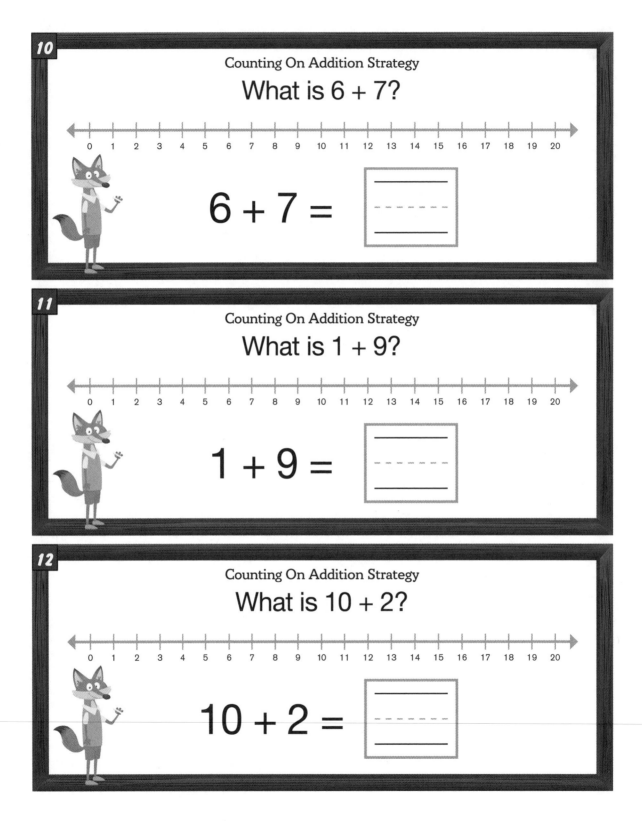

0 1 2 3 4 5 6 7 8 9 10 11 12 13 14 15 16 17 18 19 20

6 + 7 =

11

Counting On Addition Strategy
What is 1 + 9?

0 1 2 3 4 5 6 7 8 9 10 11 12 13 14 15 16 17 18 19 20

1 + 9 =

12

Counting On Addition Strategy
What is 10 + 2?

0 1 2 3 4 5 6 7 8 9 10 11 12 13 14 15 16 17 18 19 20

10 + 2 =

13

Counting On Addition Strategy

What is 7 + 4?

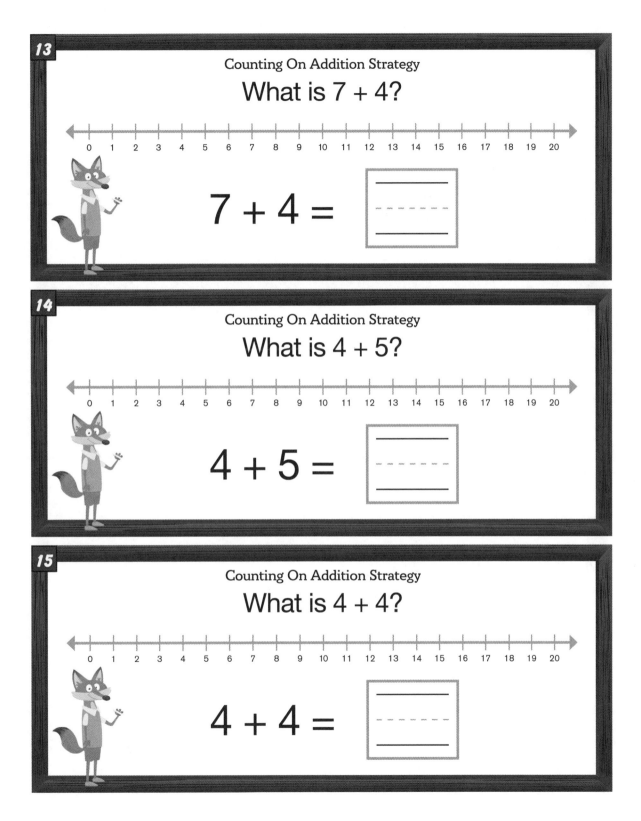

0 1 2 3 4 5 6 7 8 9 10 11 12 13 14 15 16 17 18 19 20

$7 + 4 =$

14

Counting On Addition Strategy

What is 4 + 5?

0 1 2 3 4 5 6 7 8 9 10 11 12 13 14 15 16 17 18 19 20

$4 + 5 =$

15

Counting On Addition Strategy

What is 4 + 4?

0 1 2 3 4 5 6 7 8 9 10 11 12 13 14 15 16 17 18 19 20

$4 + 4 =$

16

Counting On Addition Strategy

What is 7 + 8?

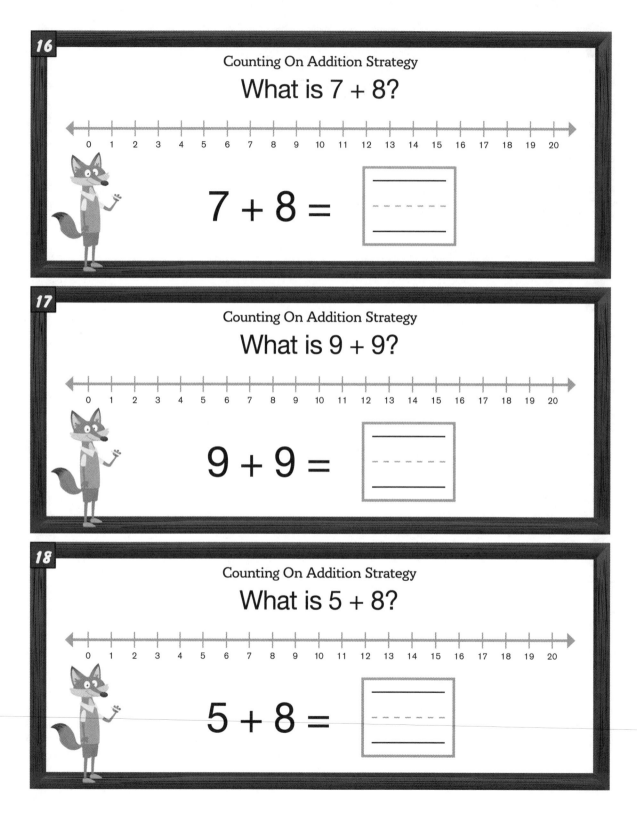

0 1 2 3 4 5 6 7 8 9 10 11 12 13 14 15 16 17 18 19 20

$$7 + 8 =$$

17

Counting On Addition Strategy

What is 9 + 9?

0 1 2 3 4 5 6 7 8 9 10 11 12 13 14 15 16 17 18 19 20

$$9 + 9 =$$

18

Counting On Addition Strategy

What is 5 + 8?

0 1 2 3 4 5 6 7 8 9 10 11 12 13 14 15 16 17 18 19 20

$$5 + 8 =$$

Math Fluency Activities for K–2 Teachers

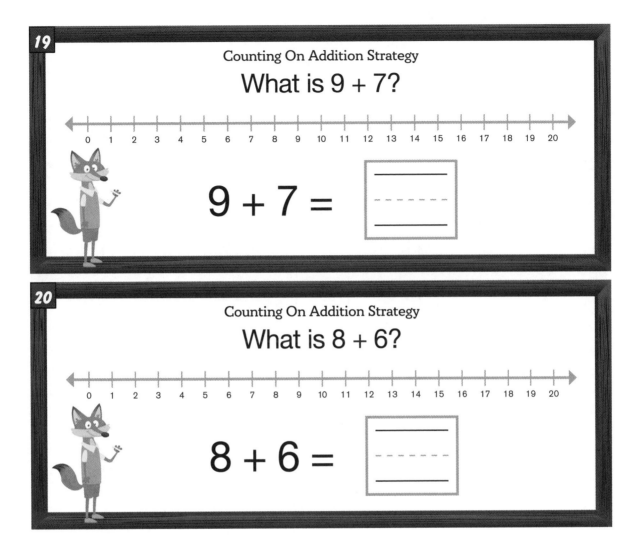

19
Counting On Addition Strategy
What is 9 + 7?

0 1 2 3 4 5 6 7 8 9 10 11 12 13 14 15 16 17 18 19 20

9 + 7 =

20
Counting On Addition Strategy
What is 8 + 6?

0 1 2 3 4 5 6 7 8 9 10 11 12 13 14 15 16 17 18 19 20

8 + 6 =

ANSWER KEY:
Adding on a Number Line (Counting On Strategy)

QUESTION	ANSWER	QUESTION	ANSWER
1.	11	11.	10
2.	11	12.	12
3.	13	13.	11
4.	10	14.	9
5.	10	15.	8
6.	9	16.	15
7.	11	17.	18
8.	8	18.	13
9.	12	19.	16
10.	13	20.	14

Subtracting on a Number Line (Counting Back Strategy)

OBJECTIVE: Students use a number line to find the solutions to the number sentences. Once all task cards have been solved, discuss and share solutions.

MATERIALS NEEDED: Task cards

DIRECTIONS: Copy the task cards or project for classroom use. Show several examples before using the task cards. In the example below we are asked to solve 9 – 5. We begin on the number line with the minuend 9 and jump back 5 places, the subtrahend, to arrive at 4. So, 9 – 5 = 4.

EXAMPLE

Counting Back Subtraction Strategy
What is 9 – 5?

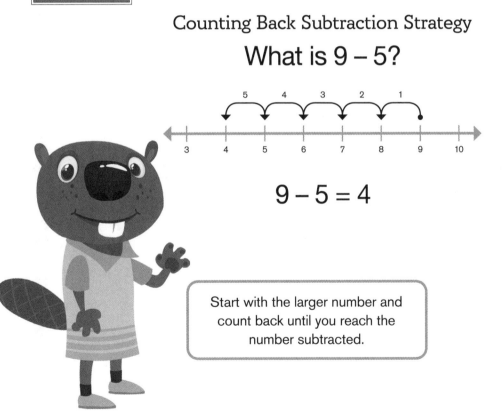

$$9 - 5 = 4$$

Start with the larger number and count back until you reach the number subtracted.

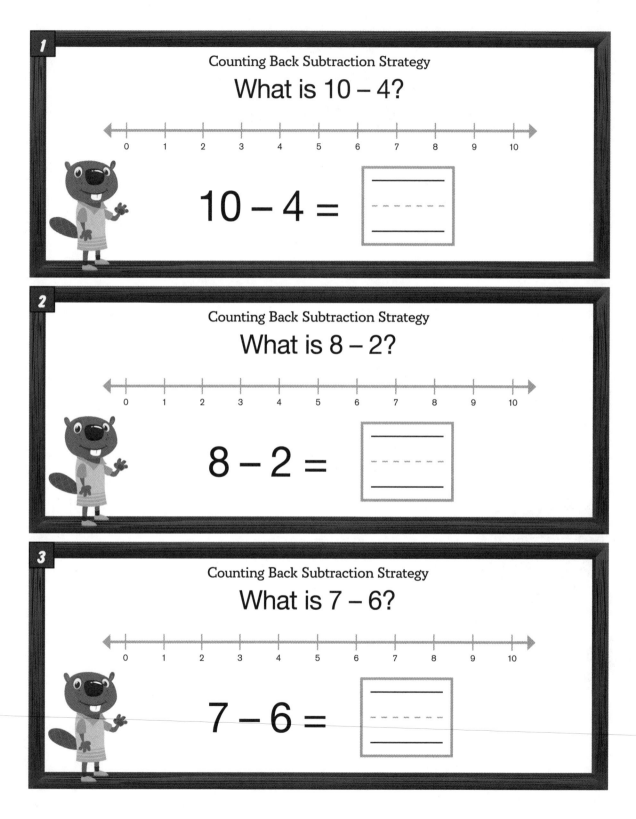

1

Counting Back Subtraction Strategy

What is 10 – 4?

0   1   2   3   4   5   6   7   8   9   10

$$10 - 4 =$$

2

Counting Back Subtraction Strategy

What is 8 – 2?

0   1   2   3   4   5   6   7   8   9   10

$$8 - 2 =$$

3

Counting Back Subtraction Strategy

What is 7 – 6?

0   1   2   3   4   5   6   7   8   9   10

$$7 - 6 =$$

Math Fluency Activities for K–2 Teachers

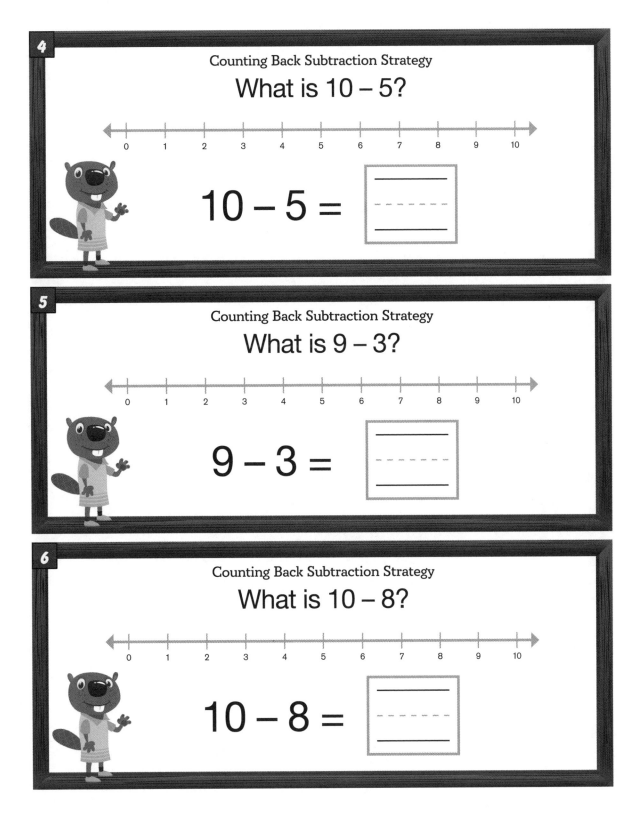

4

Counting Back Subtraction Strategy

What is 10 – 5?

0 1 2 3 4 5 6 7 8 9 10

10 – 5 =

5

Counting Back Subtraction Strategy

What is 9 – 3?

0 1 2 3 4 5 6 7 8 9 10

9 – 3 =

6

Counting Back Subtraction Strategy

What is 10 – 8?

0 1 2 3 4 5 6 7 8 9 10

10 – 8 =

7

Counting Back Subtraction Strategy

What is 8 − 4?

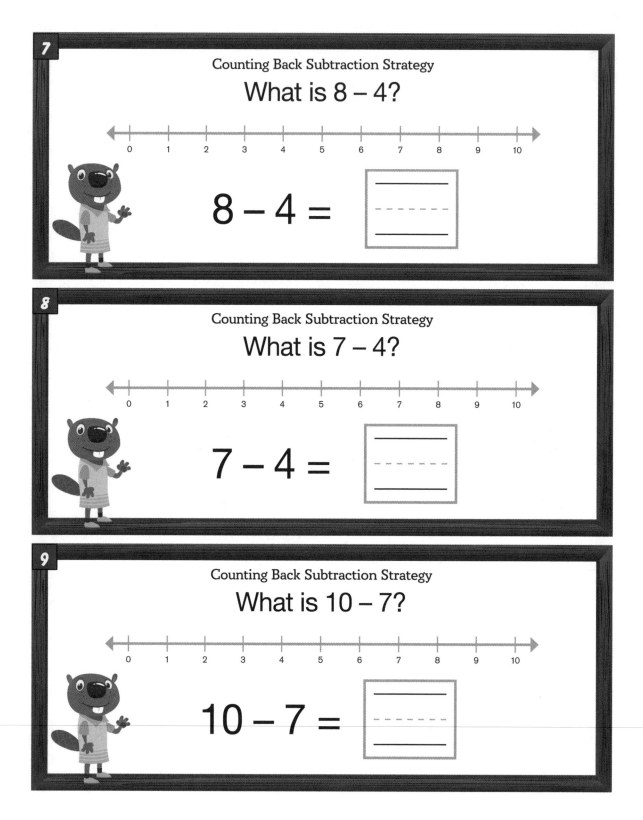

8 − 4 =

8

Counting Back Subtraction Strategy

What is 7 − 4?

7 − 4 =

9

Counting Back Subtraction Strategy

What is 10 − 7?

10 − 7 =

Math Fluency Activities for K–2 Teachers

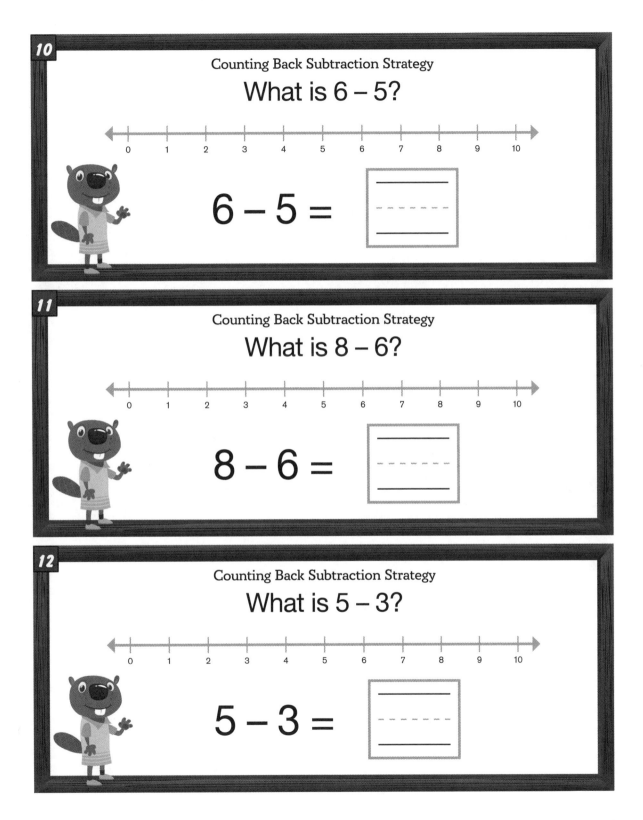

10

Counting Back Subtraction Strategy

What is 6 – 5?

0 1 2 3 4 5 6 7 8 9 10

6 – 5 =

11

Counting Back Subtraction Strategy

What is 8 – 6?

0 1 2 3 4 5 6 7 8 9 10

8 – 6 =

12

Counting Back Subtraction Strategy

What is 5 – 3?

0 1 2 3 4 5 6 7 8 9 10

5 – 3 =

13

Counting Back Subtraction Strategy

What is 7 – 3?

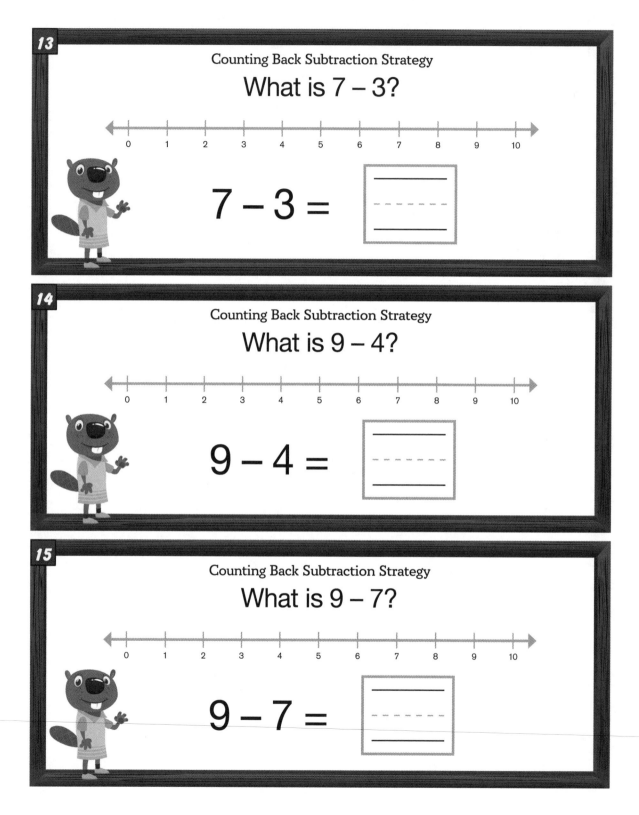

0 1 2 3 4 5 6 7 8 9 10

7 – 3 =

14

Counting Back Subtraction Strategy

What is 9 – 4?

0 1 2 3 4 5 6 7 8 9 10

9 – 4 =

15

Counting Back Subtraction Strategy

What is 9 – 7?

0 1 2 3 4 5 6 7 8 9 10

9 – 7 =

Math Fluency Activities for K–2 Teachers

16

Counting Back Subtraction Strategy

What is 5 – 5?

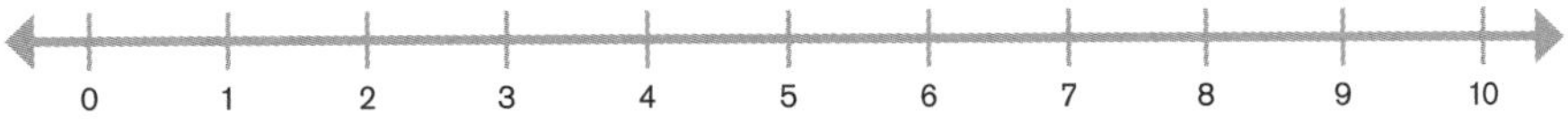

$$5 - 5 = $$

17

Counting Back Subtraction Strategy

What is 6 – 4?

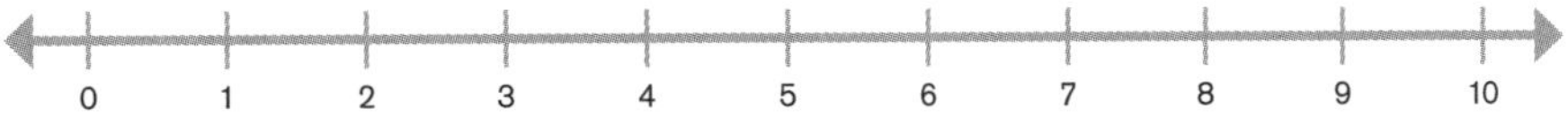

$$6 - 4 = $$

18

Counting Back Subtraction Strategy

What is 7 – 2?

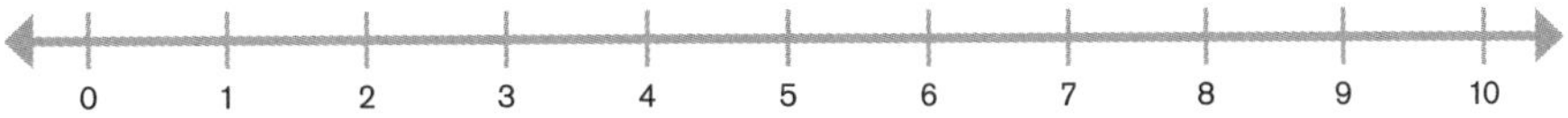

$$7 - 2 = $$

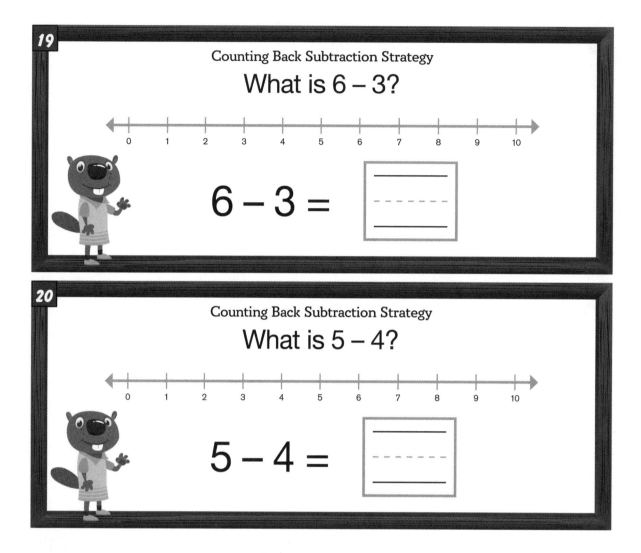

19

Counting Back Subtraction Strategy

What is 6 – 3?

0 1 2 3 4 5 6 7 8 9 10

6 – 3 =

20

Counting Back Subtraction Strategy

What is 5 – 4?

0 1 2 3 4 5 6 7 8 9 10

5 – 4 =

Math Fluency Activities for K–2 Teachers

Subtracting on a Number Line (Counting Back Strategy)

QUESTION	ANSWER	QUESTION	ANSWER
1.	6	11.	2
2.	6	12.	2
3.	1	13.	4
4.	5	14.	5
5.	6	15.	2
6.	2	16.	0
7.	4	17.	2
8.	3	18.	5
9.	3	19.	3
10.	1	20.	1

Subtracting on a Number line (Counting Up Strategy)

OBJECTIVE: Students use a number line to find the solutions to the number sentences. Once all task cards have been solved, discuss and share solutions.

MATERIALS NEEDED: Task cards

DIRECTIONS: Copy the task cards or project for classroom use. Show several examples before using the task cards. In the example below, we start with the subtrahend on the number line (3). Now we look for the distance between the minuend and subtrahend by jumping up on the number line to the minuend, 8. It is 5 jumps or units from 3 to 8. Therefore, the difference or distance between the two numbers is 5.

EXAMPLE

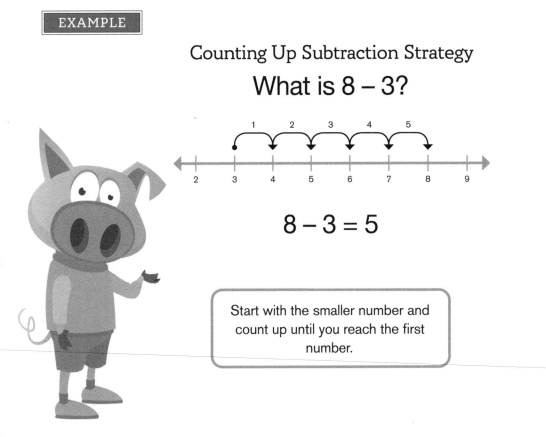

Counting Up Subtraction Strategy
What is 8 – 3?

$$8 - 3 = 5$$

Start with the smaller number and count up until you reach the first number.

1

Counting Up Subtraction Strategy
What is 9 – 5?

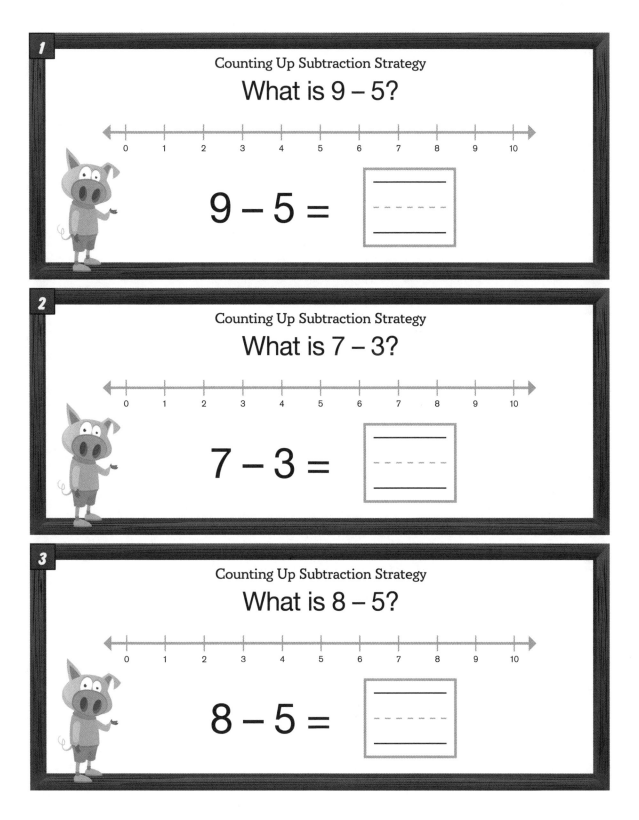

$$9 - 5 =$$

2

Counting Up Subtraction Strategy
What is 7 – 3?

$$7 - 3 =$$

3

Counting Up Subtraction Strategy
What is 8 – 5?

$$8 - 5 =$$

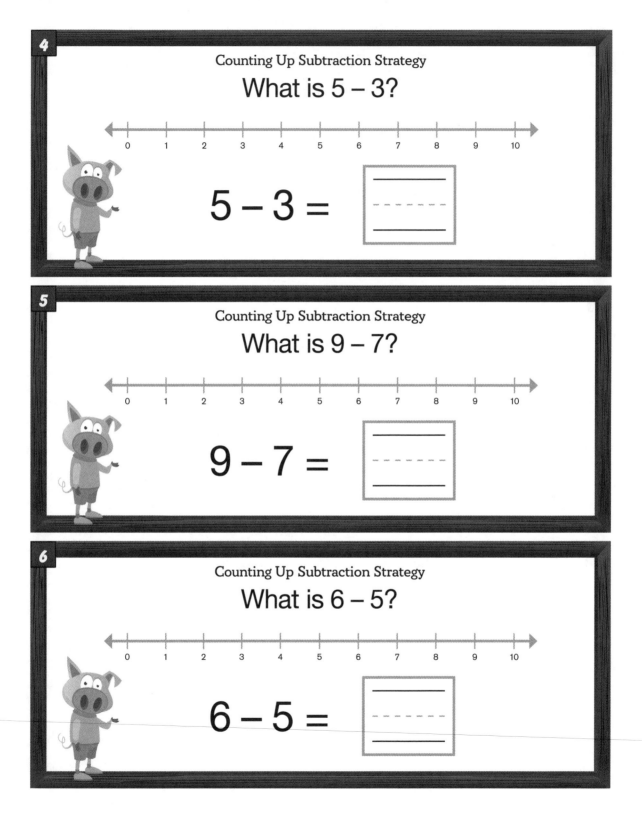

4

Counting Up Subtraction Strategy

What is 5 − 3?

0 1 2 3 4 5 6 7 8 9 10

5 − 3 =

5

Counting Up Subtraction Strategy

What is 9 − 7?

0 1 2 3 4 5 6 7 8 9 10

9 − 7 =

6

Counting Up Subtraction Strategy

What is 6 − 5?

0 1 2 3 4 5 6 7 8 9 10

6 − 5 =

Math Fluency Activities for K–2 Teachers

7

What is 7 – 2?

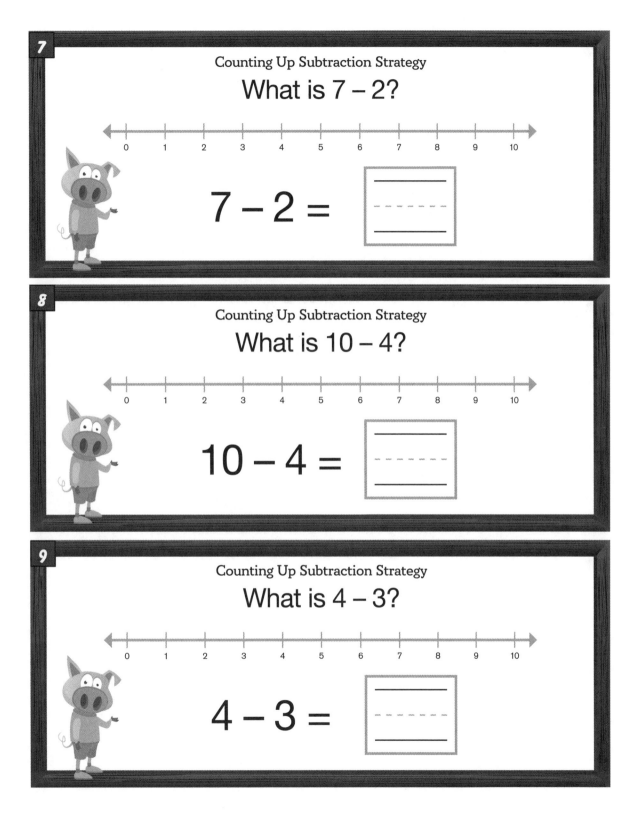

0 1 2 3 4 5 6 7 8 9 10

7 – 2 =

8

Counting Up Subtraction Strategy

What is 10 – 4?

0 1 2 3 4 5 6 7 8 9 10

10 – 4 =

9

Counting Up Subtraction Strategy

What is 4 – 3?

0 1 2 3 4 5 6 7 8 9 10

4 – 3 =

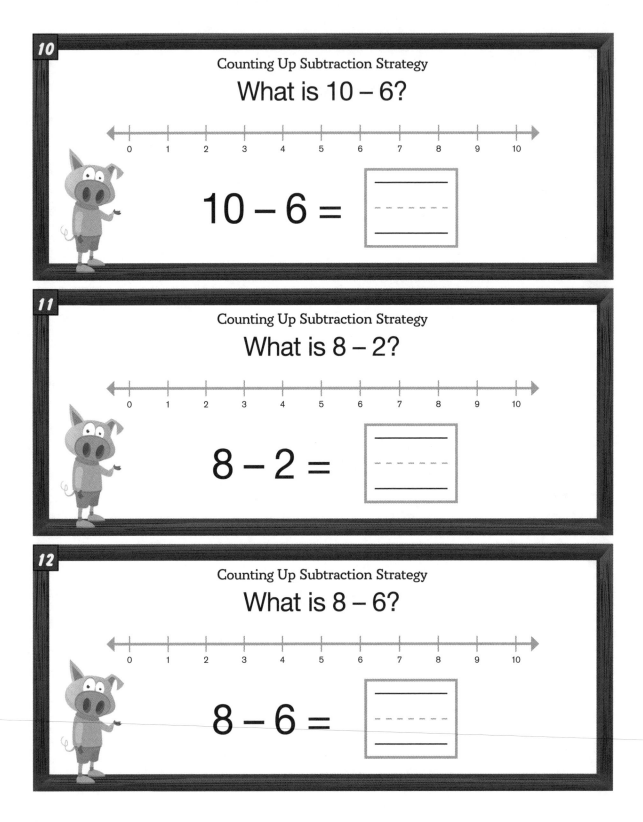

10

Counting Up Subtraction Strategy
What is 10 – 6?

0 1 2 3 4 5 6 7 8 9 10

$$10 - 6 =$$

11

Counting Up Subtraction Strategy
What is 8 – 2?

0 1 2 3 4 5 6 7 8 9 10

$$8 - 2 =$$

12

Counting Up Subtraction Strategy
What is 8 – 6?

0 1 2 3 4 5 6 7 8 9 10

$$8 - 6 =$$

　Math Fluency Activities for K–2 Teachers

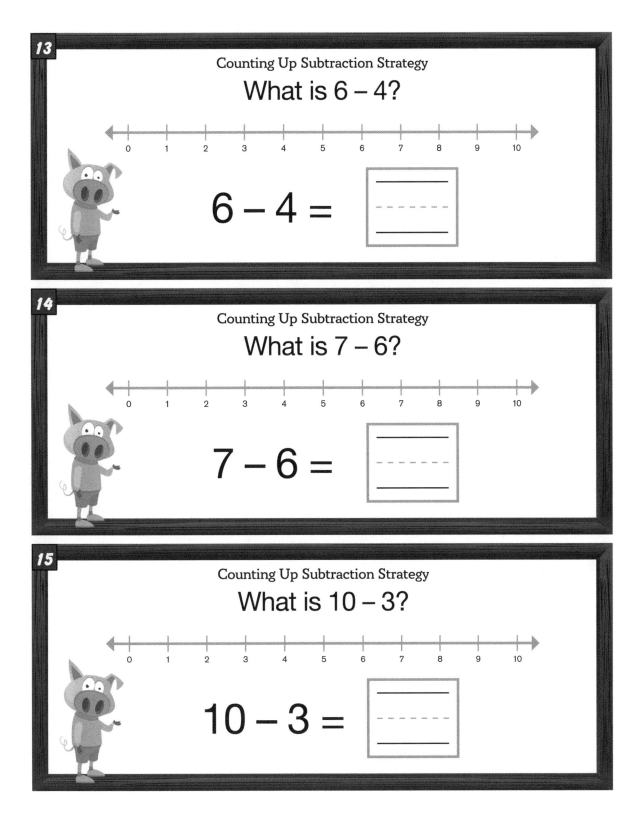

13

Counting Up Subtraction Strategy

What is 6 – 4?

0 1 2 3 4 5 6 7 8 9 10

6 – 4 =

14

Counting Up Subtraction Strategy

What is 7 – 6?

0 1 2 3 4 5 6 7 8 9 10

7 – 6 =

15

Counting Up Subtraction Strategy

What is 10 – 3?

0 1 2 3 4 5 6 7 8 9 10

10 – 3 =

16

Counting Up Subtraction Strategy

What is 9 − 2?

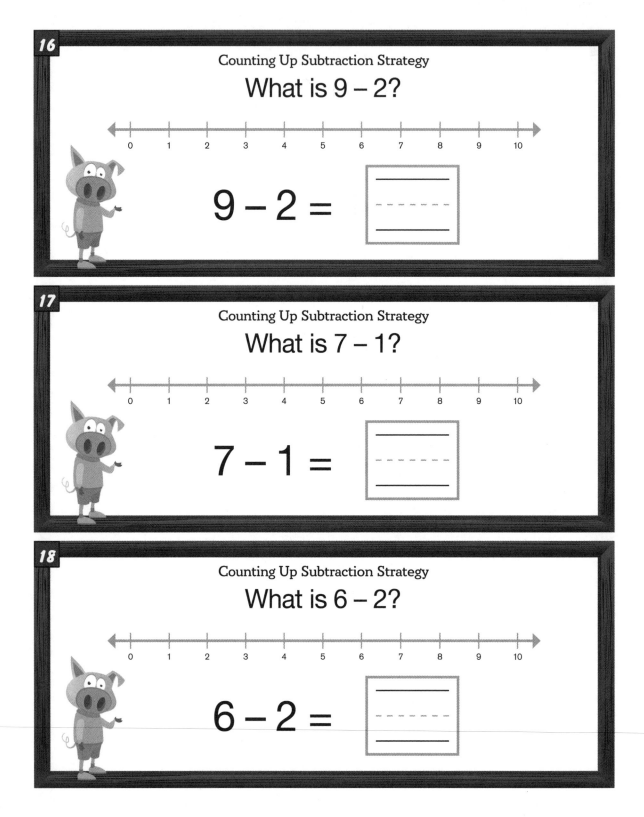

0 1 2 3 4 5 6 7 8 9 10

9 − 2 =

17

Counting Up Subtraction Strategy

What is 7 − 1?

0 1 2 3 4 5 6 7 8 9 10

7 − 1 =

18

Counting Up Subtraction Strategy

What is 6 − 2?

0 1 2 3 4 5 6 7 8 9 10

6 − 2 =

19

Counting Up Subtraction Strategy

What is 5 – 5?

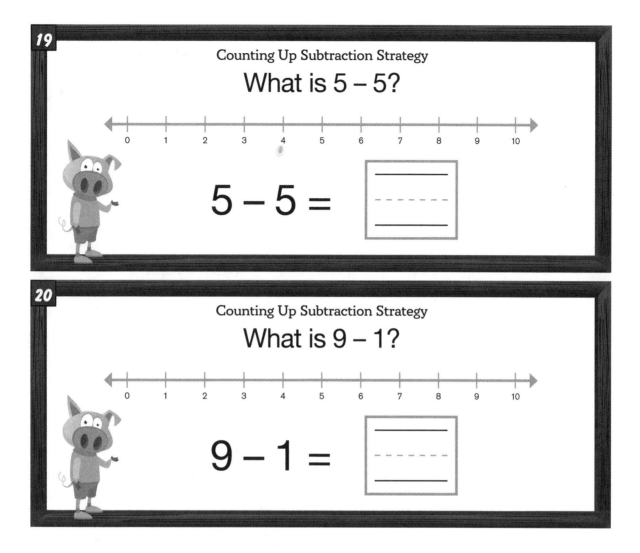

$$5 - 5 =$$

20

Counting Up Subtraction Strategy

What is 9 – 1?

$$9 - 1 =$$

ANSWER KEY:
Subtracting on a Number Line (Counting Up Strategy)

QUESTION	ANSWER	QUESTION	ANSWER
1.	4	11.	6
2.	4	12.	2
3.	3	13.	2
4.	2	14.	1
5.	2	15.	7
6.	1	16.	7
7.	5	17.	6
8.	6	18.	4
9.	1	19.	0
10.	4	20.	8

Adding by Making a 10

OBJECTIVE: Students decompose numbers leading to 10 in order to find the solutions to number sentences. Once all task cards have been solved, discuss and share solutions.

MATERIALS NEEDED: Task cards

DIRECTIONS: Copy or project the task cards. Show several examples before using the task cards. In the example below, we are adding 8 and 9. To make addition easy, make a 10 using either addend. Below, we decomposed the first addend to 7 + 1. Now we can combine the 1 with the 9 to make a 10. Addition is easy since we are adding a 10. Therefore, 7 + 10 has a sum of 17. How will the problem be different if we decompose the 9 to 2 + 7? Will we still get the same sum?

EXAMPLE

Adding by Making a 10

What is 8 + 9?

$8 + 9$

$7 + 1$

$7 + 1 + 9$

$7 + 10 = 17$

Decompose the numbers. Identify the tens, then add the rest.

1 Add by Making a 10

$$7 + 4 =$$

↓ decompose

=

2 Add by Making a 10

$$8 + 6 =$$

↓ decompose

=

3 Add by Making a 10

$$9 + 9 =$$

↓ decompose

=

Math Fluency Activities for K–2 Teachers

4

Add by Making a 10

$$6 + 9 =$$

↓ decompose

↓

$=$ [   ]

5

Add by Making a 10

$$9 + 7 =$$

↓ decompose

↓

$=$ [   ]

6

Add by Making a 10

$$8 + 4 =$$

↓ decompose

↓

$=$ [   ]

7

Add by Making a 10

$$7 + 8 =$$

↓ decompose

↓

=

8

Add by Making a 10

$$6 + 6 =$$

↓ decompose

↓

=

9

Add by Making a 10

$$5 + 8 =$$

↓ decompose

↓

=

Math Fluency Activities for K–2 Teachers

10 Add by Making a 10

$$8 + 9 =$$

↓ decompose

_____

- - - - - - - - -

_____

↓

- - - - - - - - - - - - -   =

_____

11 Add by Making a 10

$$6 + 7 =$$

↓ decompose

_____

- - - - - - - - -

_____

↓

- - - - - - - - - - - - -   =

_____

12 Add by Making a 10

$$8 + 5 =$$

↓ decompose

_____

- - - - - - - - -

_____

↓

- - - - - - - - - - - - -   =

_____

13

Add by Making a 10

$$5 + 9 =$$

↓ decompose

↓

$$=$$

14

Add by Making a 10

$$7 + 5 =$$

↓ decompose

↓

$$=$$

15

Add by Making a 10

$$9 + 3 =$$

↓ decompose

↓

$$=$$

16 Add by Making a 10

$$6 + 5 =$$

↓ decompose

_____

- - - - - - - - - - - - - -

_____

↓

- - - - - - - - - - - - - -

_____ = ☐

17 Add by Making a 10

$$3 + 8 =$$

↓ decompose

_____

- - - - - - - - - - - - - -

_____

↓

- - - - - - - - - - - - - -

= ☐

18 Add by Making a 10

$$9 + 4 =$$

↓ decompose

_____

- - - - - - - - - - - - - -

_____

↓

- - - - - - - - - - - - - -

_____ = ☐

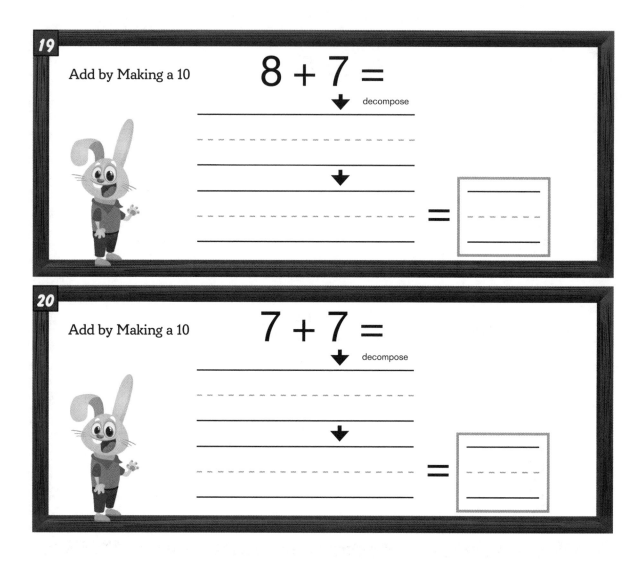

19

Add by Making a 10

$$8 + 7 =$$

↓ decompose

↓

=

20

Add by Making a 10

$$7 + 7 =$$

↓ decompose

↓

=

ANSWER KEY:
Adding By Making a 10

QUESTION	ANSWER
1.	$(7 + 3) + 1 = 11$
2.	$(8 + 2) + 4 = 14$
3.	$(9 + 1) + 8 = 18$
4.	$(6 + 4) + 5 = 15$
5.	$(9 + 1) + 6 = 16$
6.	$(8 + 2) + 2 = 12$
7.	$(7 + 3) + 5 = 15$
8.	$(6 + 4) + 2 = 12$
9.	$(5 + 5) + 3 = 13$
10.	$(8 + 2) + 7 = 17$

QUESTION	ANSWER
11.	$(6 + 4) + 3 = 13$
12.	$(8 + 2) + 3 = 13$
13.	$(5 + 5) + 4 = 14$
14.	$(7 + 3) + 2 = 12$
15.	$(9 + 1) + 2 = 12$
16.	$(6 + 4) + 1 = 11$
17.	$(3 + 7) + 1 = 11$
18.	$(9 + 1) + 3 = 13$
19.	$(8 + 2) + 5 = 15$
20.	$(7 + 3) + 4 = 14$

Using Doubles

OBJECTIVE: Students decompose numbers leading to doubles in order to find the solutions to the number sentences. Once all task cards have been solved, discuss and share solutions.

MATERIALS NEEDED: Task cards

DIRECTIONS: Copy the task cards or project the cards for the whole class. Show several examples before using the task cards. Doubles are often easy for students to remember. With this in mind, we can decompose one addend to make a double with the other addend. In the example below, we decomposed the 9 to 8 + 1. Now we have a double, 8 + 8, which has a sum of 16. Adding the double with 1, we have our total sum of 17.

EXAMPLE

Add by Using Doubles
What is 8 + 9?

$$8 + 9$$

$$8 + 1$$

$$8 + 8 + 1$$

$$16 + 1 = 17$$

Doubles are easier facts to remember. Decompose one number to make a double. Add the doubles and then the rest.

1 Add by Using Doubles

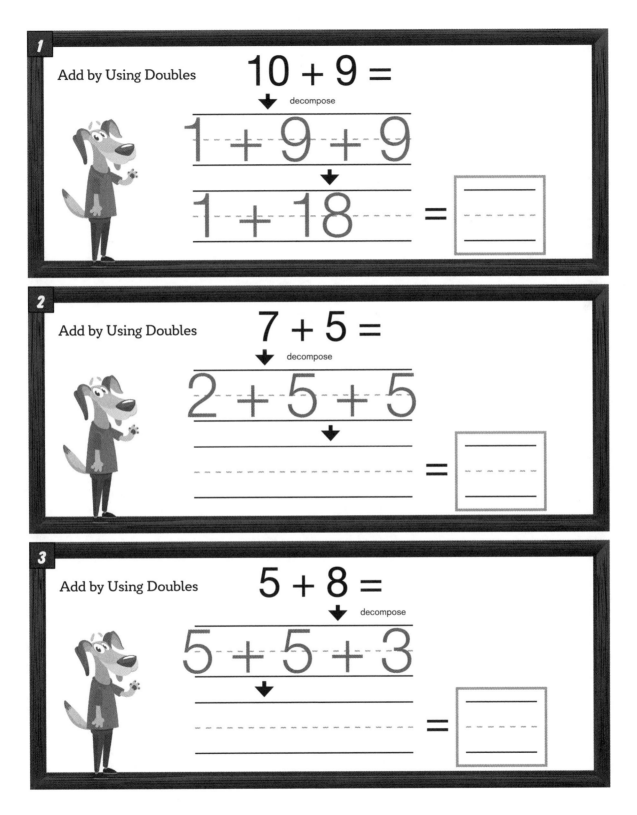

$$10 + 9 =$$

↓ decompose

$$1 + 9 + 9$$

↓

$$1 + 18 \quad = \quad \boxed{}$$

2 Add by Using Doubles

$$7 + 5 =$$

↓ decompose

$$2 + 5 + 5$$

↓

$$\underline{} \quad = \quad \boxed{}$$

3 Add by Using Doubles

$$5 + 8 =$$

↓ decompose

$$5 + 5 + 3$$

↓

$$\underline{} \quad = \quad \boxed{}$$

4

Add by Using Doubles

$$6 + 7 =$$

↓ decompose

$$6 + 6 + 1$$

↓

$$=$$ ☐

5

Add by Using Doubles

$$9 + 5 =$$

↓ decompose

$$4 + 5 + 5$$

↓

$$=$$ ☐

6

Add by Using Doubles

$$6 + 4 =$$

↓ decompose

$$2 + 4 + 4$$

↓

$$=$$ ☐

7

Add by Using Doubles

$$9 + 8 =$$

↓ decompose

_____

- - - - - - - - - - -

_____

↓

_____

- - - - - - - - - - -

_____

= [ ]

8

Add by Using Doubles

$$8 + 6 =$$

↓ decompose

_____

- - - - - - - - - - -

_____

↓

_____

- - - - - - - - - - -

_____

= [ ]

9

Add by Using Doubles

$$9 + 6 =$$

↓ decompose

_____

- - - - - - - - - - -

_____

↓

_____

- - - - - - - - - - -

_____

= [ ]

10

Add by Using Doubles

$7 + 8 =$

decompose

=

11

Add by Using Doubles

$9 + 7 =$

decompose

=

12

Add by Using Doubles

$7 + 4 =$

decompose

=

Math Fluency Activities for K–2 Teachers

13

Add by Using Doubles

$$5 + 3 =$$

↓ decompose

_____

- - - - - - - - - - - - -

↓

_____

- - - - - - - - - - - - -

_____

= [_____]

14

Add by Using Doubles

$$5 + 4 =$$

↓ decompose

_____

- - - - - - - - - - - - -

↓

_____

- - - - - - - - - - - - -

_____

= [_____]

15

Add by Using Doubles

$$5 + 6 =$$

↓ decompose

_____

- - - - - - - - - - - - -

↓

_____

- - - - - - - - - - - - -

_____

= [_____]

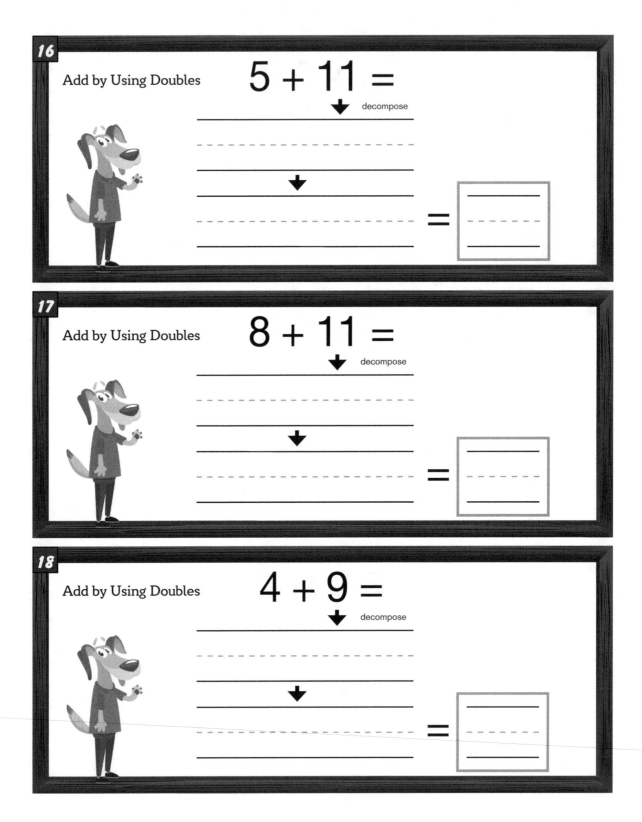

16

Add by Using Doubles

$5 + 11 =$

↓ decompose

= [ ]

17

Add by Using Doubles

$8 + 11 =$

↓ decompose

= [ ]

18

Add by Using Doubles

$4 + 9 =$

↓ decompose

= [ ]

19

Add by Using Doubles

$$4 + 3 =$$

_____

- - - - - - - - - - - - - - - -

_____

_____

- - - - - - - - - - - - - - - -

_____   =   ☐

20

Add by Using Doubles

$$5 + 11 =$$

_____

- - - - - - - - - - - - - - - -

_____

_____

- - - - - - - - - - - - - - - -

_____   =   ☐

ANSWER KEY:
Using Doubles

QUESTION	ANSWER
1.	$1 + (9 + 9) = 19$
2.	$2 + (5 + 5) = 12$
3.	$(5 + 5) + 3 = 13$
4.	$(6 + 6) + 1 = 13$
5.	$4 + (5 + 5) = 14$
6.	$2 + (4 + 4) = 10$
7.	$1 + (8 + 8) = 17$
8.	$2 + (6 + 6) = 14$
9.	$3 + (6 + 6) = 15$
10.	$(7 + 7) + 1 = 15$

QUESTION	ANSWER
11.	$2 + (7 + 7) = 16$
12.	$3 + (4 + 4) = 11$
13.	$2 + (3 + 3) = 8$
14.	$1 + (4 + 4) = 9$
15.	$(5 + 5) + 1 = 11$
16.	$(5 + 5) + 6 = 16$
17.	$(8 + 8) + 3 = 19$
18.	$(4 + 4) + 5 = 13$
19.	$1 + (3 + 3) = 7$
20.	$(5 + 5) + 6 = 16$

Related Addition Facts

OBJECTIVE: Students use number bonds to see the relationship between addition and subtraction. Using their understanding of part-part-whole, students write related number sentences. Once all task cards have been solved, discuss and share results.

MATERIALS NEEDED: Task cards

DIRECTIONS: Copy or project the task cards for the whole class. Show several examples before using the task cards. In the example below, we have a whole of 13 with parts of 4 and 9. Look for the relationship between the three numbers using addition and subtraction. Our related facts are shown below. This activity is ideal for helping students see the whole and learn how to find a missing part or find the whole when you know both parts.

EXAMPLE

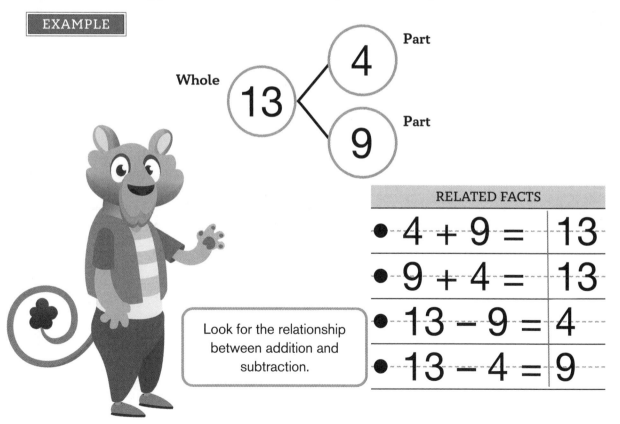

Whole 13 **Part** 4 **Part** 9

Look for the relationship between addition and subtraction.

RELATED FACTS
• 4 + 9 = 13
• 9 + 4 = 13
• 13 − 9 = 4
• 13 − 4 = 9

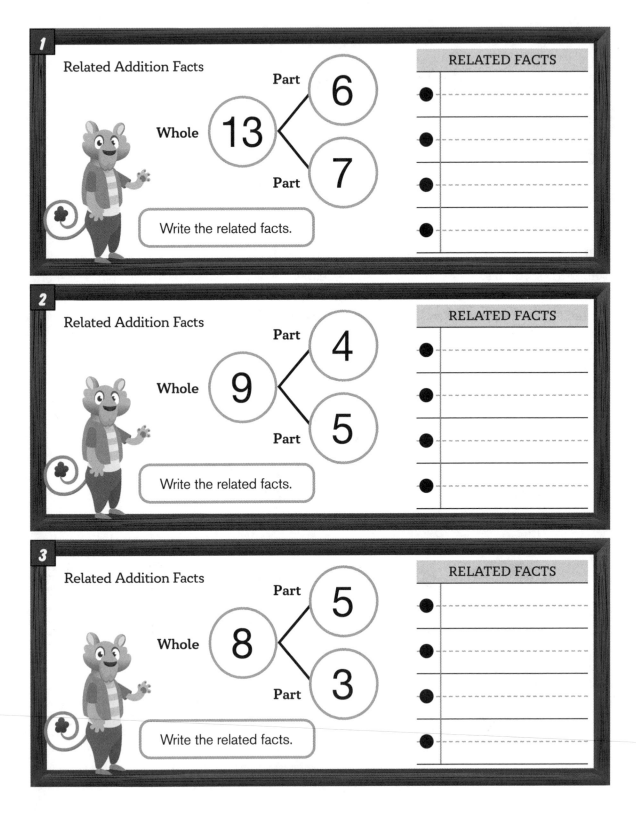

1

Related Addition Facts

Whole **13**

Part **6**

Part **7**

Write the related facts.

RELATED FACTS

2

Related Addition Facts

Whole **9**

Part **4**

Part **5**

Write the related facts.

RELATED FACTS

3

Related Addition Facts

Whole **8**

Part **5**

Part **3**

Write the related facts.

RELATED FACTS

4

Related Addition Facts

Part **7**

Whole **12**

Part **5**

RELATED FACTS

- _____
- _____
- _____
- _____

Write the related facts.

5

Related Addition Facts

Part **4**

Whole **10**

Part **6**

RELATED FACTS

- _____
- _____
- _____
- _____

Write the related facts.

6

Related Addition Facts

Part **3**

Whole **5**

Part **2**

RELATED FACTS

- _____
- _____
- _____
- _____

Write the related facts.

7

Related Addition Facts

Whole · **11**

Part · **6**

Part · **5**

Write the related facts.

RELATED FACTS

- _____
- _____
- _____
- _____

8

Related Addition Facts

Whole · **9**

Part · **7**

Part · **2**

Write the related facts.

RELATED FACTS

- _____
- _____
- _____
- _____

9

Related Addition Facts

Whole · **7**

Part · **5**

Part · **2**

Write the related facts.

RELATED FACTS

- _____
- _____
- _____
- _____

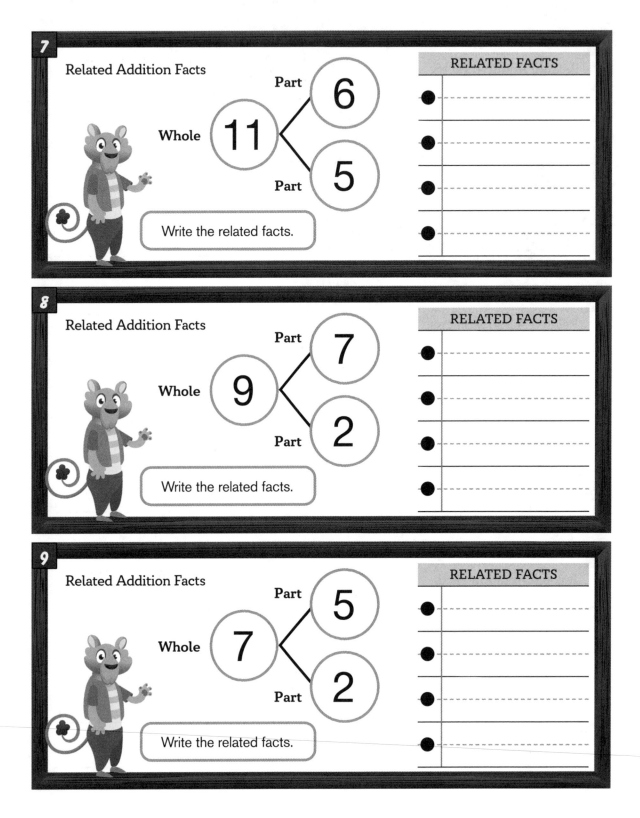

Math Fluency Activities for K–2 Teachers

10

Related Addition Facts

Part

2

Whole

8

Part

6

Write the related facts.

RELATED FACTS

- - - - - - - - -
- - - - - - - - -
- - - - - - - - -
- - - - - - - - -

11

Related Addition Facts

Part

7

Whole

12

Part

?

Write the related facts.

RELATED FACTS

- - - - - - - - -
- - - - - - - - -
- - - - - - - - -
- - - - - - - - -

12

Related Addition Facts

Part

?

Whole

10

Part

8

Write the related facts.

RELATED FACTS

- - - - - - - - -
- - - - - - - - -
- - - - - - - - -
- - - - - - - - -

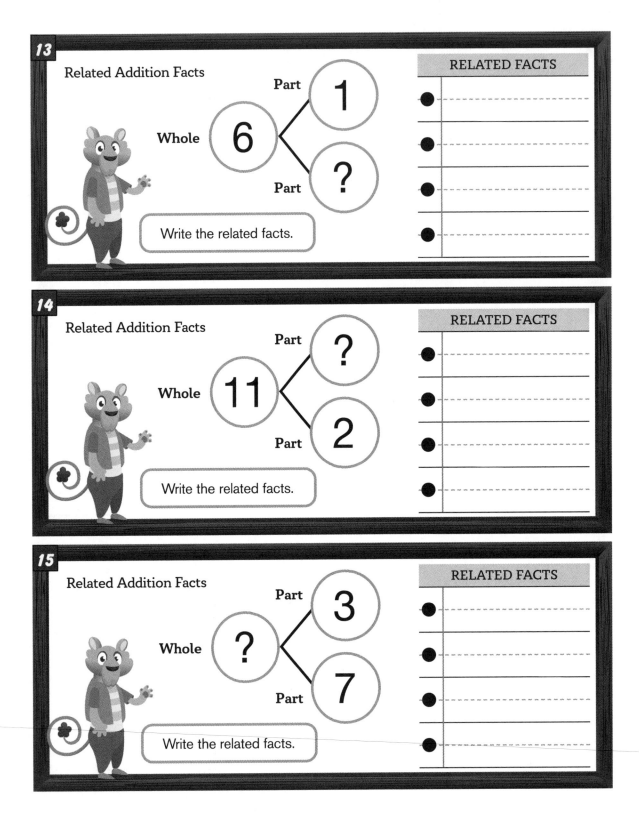

13

Related Addition Facts

Whole **6**

Part **1**

Part **?**

Write the related facts.

RELATED FACTS

14

Related Addition Facts

Whole **11**

Part **?**

Part **2**

Write the related facts.

RELATED FACTS

15

Related Addition Facts

Whole **?**

Part **3**

Part **7**

Write the related facts.

RELATED FACTS

16

Related Addition Facts

Whole **9**

Part **?**

Part **1**

Write the related facts.

RELATED FACTS

-
-
-
-

17

Related Addition Facts

Whole **3**

Part **2**

Part **?**

Write the related facts.

RELATED FACTS

-
-
-
-

18

Related Addition Facts

Whole **?**

Part **4**

Part **2**

Write the related facts.

RELATED FACTS

-
-
-
-

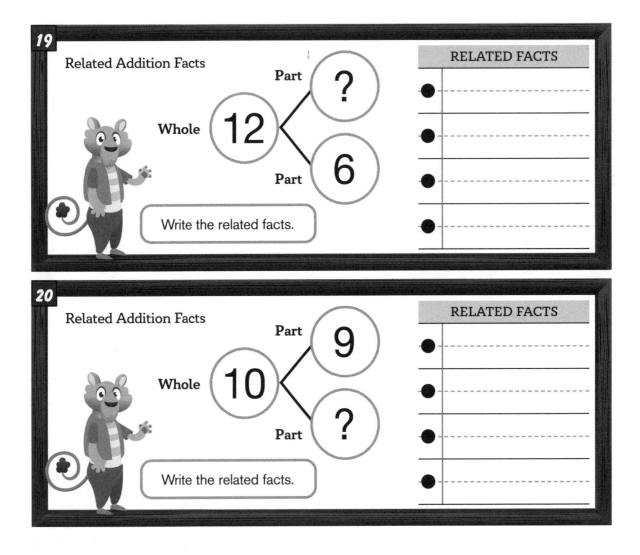

19

Related Addition Facts

Whole **12**

Part **?**

Part **6**

Write the related facts.

RELATED FACTS

20

Related Addition Facts

Whole **10**

Part **9**

Part **?**

Write the related facts.

RELATED FACTS

ANSWER KEY:
Related Addition Facts

QUESTION	ANSWERS			
1.	13 = 6 + 7	13 = 7 + 6	13 − 6 = 7	13 − 7 = 6
2.	9 = 5 + 4	9 = 4 + 5	9 − 4 = 5	9 − 5 = 4
3.	8 = 5 + 3	8 = 3 + 5	8 − 3 = 5	8 − 5 = 3
4.	12 = 7 + 5	12 = 5 + 7	12 − 5 = 7	12 − 7 = 5
5.	10 = 4 + 6	10 = 6 + 4	10 − 4 = 6	10 − 6 = 4
6.	5 = 3 + 2	5 = 2 + 3	5 − 2 = 3	5 − 3 = 2
7.	11 = 6 + 5	11 = 5 + 6	11 − 6 = 5	11 − 5 = 6
8.	9 = 7 + 2	9 = 2 + 7	9 − 7 = 2	9 − 2 = 7
9.	7 = 5 + 2	7 = 2 + 5	7 − 5 = 2	7 − 2 = 5
10.	8 = 6 + 2	8 = 2 + 6	8 − 2 = 6	8 − 6 = 2
11.	12 = 7 + 5	12 = 5 + 7	12 − 5 = 7	12 − 7 = 5
12.	10 = 8 + 2	10 = 2 + 8	10 − 8 = 2	10 − 2 = 8
13.	6 = 1 + 5	6 = 5 + 1	6 − 5 = 1	6 − 1 = 5
14.	11 = 2 + 9	11 = 9 + 2	11 − 9 = 2	11 − 2 = 9

RELATED ADDITION FACTS

QUESTION	ANSWER	ANSWER	ANSWER	ANSWER
15.	10 = 3 + 7	10 = 7 + 3	10 − 3 = 7	10 − 7 = 3
16.	9 = 1 + 8	9 = 8 + 1	9 − 8 = 1	9 − 1 = 8
17.	3 = 2 + 1	3 = 1 + 2	3 − 1 = 2	3 − 2 = 1
18.	6 = 4 + 2	6 = 2 + 4	6 − 2 = 4	6 − 4 = 2
19.	12 = 6 + 6	12 = 6 + 6	12 − 6 = 6	12 − 6 = 6
20.	10 = 9 + 1	10 = 1 + 9	10 − 1 = 9	10 − 9 = 1

Facts Strategy Check

+	0	1	2	3	4	5	6	7	8	9	10
0											
1											
2											
3											
4											
5											
6											
7											
8											
9											
10											

★ Do not time.

★ Do not have students compete against other students.

★ Have students set personal goals.

★ Look for growth.

★ Highlight facts they know.

★ Focus on facts still needing mastery.

Facts I Know!

Name: _____

+	0	1	2	3	4	5	6	7	8	9	10
0											
1											
2											
3											
4											
5											
6											
7											
8											
9											
10											

CHAPTER 3

Grade 2

GRADE	REQUIRED FLUENCY
2	**2.OA.B.2** Fluently add and subtract within 20 using mental strategies. By end of Grade 2, know from memory all sums of two one-digit numbers.
2	**2.NBT.B.5** Fluently add and subtract within 100 using strategies based on place value, properties of operations, and/or the relationship between addition and subtraction.

Activities for grade 2 students included here for the 2.OA.B.2 standard will help students be fluent when adding and subtracting within 20 based on mental math strategies. The following strategies are essential for conceptual understanding and procedural fluency: counting on, decomposing a number leading to 10, relationships between addition and subtraction, and equivalent or easier sums. These strategies are included to help students move from conceptual understanding to procedural fluency. Begin with concrete activities; once these are mastered, move students on to representational activities, which will then help them master abstract mathematics.

Instructional activities include the following:

Concrete

Activity 1. Counting On Using Connecting Cubes (*page 181*)

Activity 2. Regrouping on a Ten-Frame (*page 198*)

Activity 3. Subtracting on a Ten-Frame (*page 210*)

Representational

Abstract

The following activities are aligned to the last fluency standard, 2.NBT.B.5, for grades K–2. The other three fluency standards focus on operations and algebraic thinking. This standard takes math one step further through place value.

Fluency is developed through ongoing practice. The activities here are designed for practice to help students understand the meanings of operations and the relationships between numbers. If students are not being successful with basic facts, make sure to drop back to foundational ideas from earlier grades. Keep in mind that drilling does not help a student master basic facts. Learning strategies is central to understanding and supported by the activities here. This last set of engaging activities will focus on base ten and the strategies that can help students become fluent in addition and subtraction.

Representational

Abstract

Counting On Using Connecting Cubes

OBJECTIVE: Students will use cubes and task cards to find the solutions to the number sentences. Once all task cards have been solved, discuss and share solutions.

Tasks cards (11" x 17" to fit the number of connecting cubes lined up on a number line). If you can't copy the task cards on 11" x 17" paper, display for student use or simply draw a number line that matches the length of a connecting cube.

MATERIALS NEEDED: Connecting cubes (any kind); task cards

DIRECTIONS: Copy the task cards or display for students. This activity will add to what students already learned and hopefully mastered from grade 1, Chapter 2, Activity 1. If you find your students are struggling, intervene by stepping back to Activity 1 from grade 1. If you project the cards, use a virtual connecting cube manipulative to drag and drop the cubes to find the number sentence. In the first example below, have students place 14 connecting cubes (the first addend) on the number line. Now, add 4 more cubes (the second addend) to show a sum of 18. In the second example, we have a subtraction problem. Since the minuend is 18, start with 18 cubes. Now we are subtracting 4, the subtrahend; we need to remove 4 cubes to find the difference, or distance between the two numbers. Fourteen cubes are left, which shows our difference, or the distance between 18 and 4.

EXAMPLE

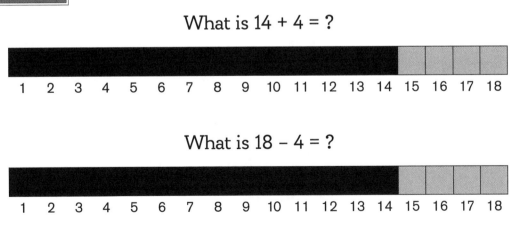

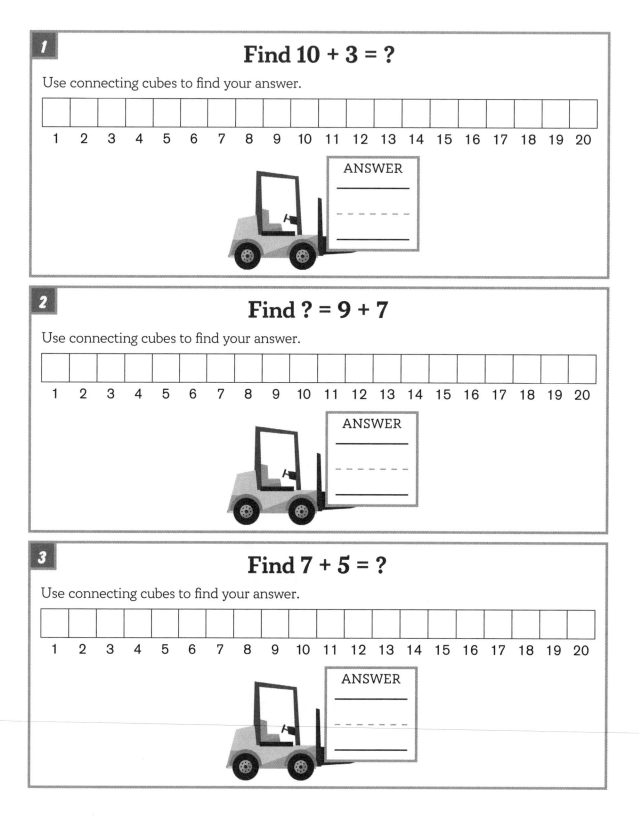

1 **Find 10 + 3 = ?**

Use connecting cubes to find your answer.

1	2	3	4	5	6	7	8	9	10	11	12	13	14	15	16	17	18	19	20

ANSWER

2 **Find ? = 9 + 7**

Use connecting cubes to find your answer.

1	2	3	4	5	6	7	8	9	10	11	12	13	14	15	16	17	18	19	20

ANSWER

3 **Find 7 + 5 = ?**

Use connecting cubes to find your answer.

1	2	3	4	5	6	7	8	9	10	11	12	13	14	15	16	17	18	19	20

ANSWER

4 Find ? = 8 + 6

Use connecting cubes to find your answer.

1	2	3	4	5	6	7	8	9	10	11	12	13	14	15	16	17	18	19	20

ANSWER

5 Find 13 + 3 = ?

Use connecting cubes to find your answer.

1	2	3	4	5	6	7	8	9	10	11	12	13	14	15	16	17	18	19	20

ANSWER

6 Find ? = 12 + 5

Use connecting cubes to find your answer.

1	2	3	4	5	6	7	8	9	10	11	12	13	14	15	16	17	18	19	20

ANSWER

7

Find 12 + 7 = ?

Use connecting cubes to find your answer.

1	2	3	4	5	6	7	8	9	10	11	12	13	14	15	16	17	18	19	20

ANSWER

8

Find ? = 11 + 6

Use connecting cubes to find your answer.

1	2	3	4	5	6	7	8	9	10	11	12	13	14	15	16	17	18	19	20

ANSWER

9

Find 9 + 11 = ?

Use connecting cubes to find your answer.

1	2	3	4	5	6	7	8	9	10	11	12	13	14	15	16	17	18	19	20

ANSWER

10   Find 13 + ? = 17

Use connecting cubes to find your answer.

1	2	3	4	5	6	7	8	9	10	11	12	13	14	15	16	17	18	19	20

ANSWER

11   Find 12 + ? = 15

Use connecting cubes to find your answer.

1	2	3	4	5	6	7	8	9	10	11	12	13	14	15	16	17	18	19	20

ANSWER

12   Find ? + 14 = 16

Use connecting cubes to find your answer.

1	2	3	4	5	6	7	8	9	10	11	12	13	14	15	16	17	18	19	20

ANSWER

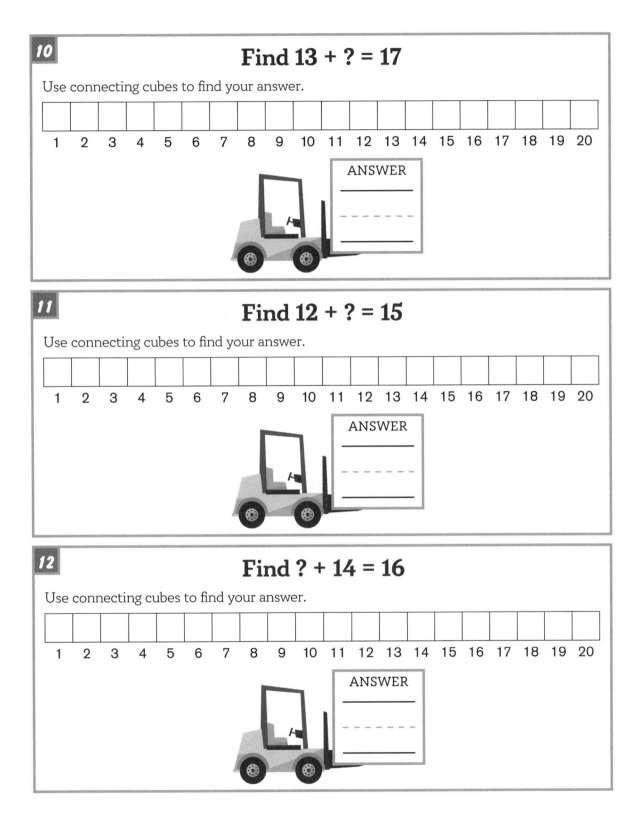

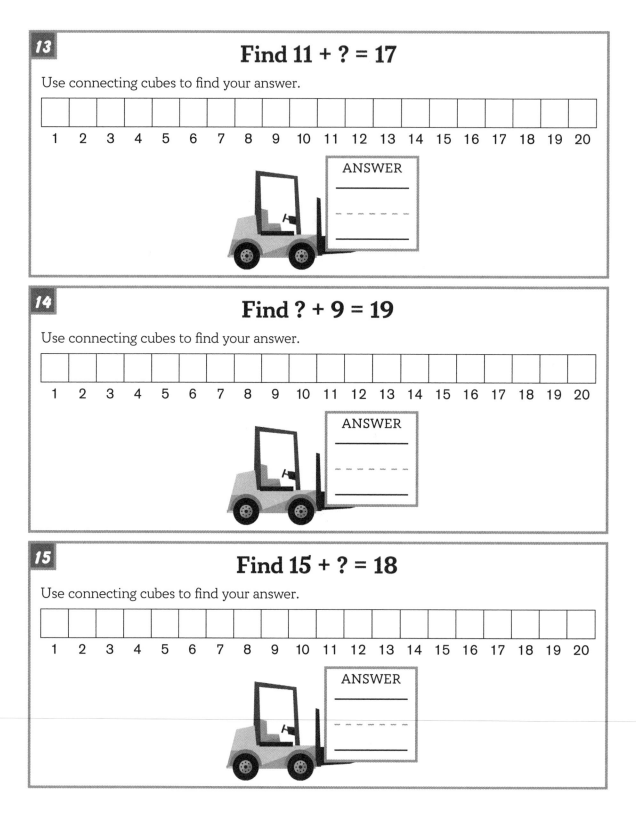

13   # Find 11 + ? = 17

Use connecting cubes to find your answer.

1	2	3	4	5	6	7	8	9	10	11	12	13	14	15	16	17	18	19	20

ANSWER

14   # Find ? + 9 = 19

Use connecting cubes to find your answer.

1	2	3	4	5	6	7	8	9	10	11	12	13	14	15	16	17	18	19	20

ANSWER

15   # Find 15 + ? = 18

Use connecting cubes to find your answer.

1	2	3	4	5	6	7	8	9	10	11	12	13	14	15	16	17	18	19	20

ANSWER

Math Fluency Activities for K–2 Teachers

16

Find ? + 6 = 20

Use connecting cubes to find your answer.

1	2	3	4	5	6	7	8	9	10	11	12	13	14	15	16	17	18	19	20

ANSWER

17

Find 9 + ? = 13

Use connecting cubes to find your answer.

1	2	3	4	5	6	7	8	9	10	11	12	13	14	15	16	17	18	19	20

ANSWER

18

Find ? + 13 = 17

Use connecting cubes to find your answer.

1	2	3	4	5	6	7	8	9	10	11	12	13	14	15	16	17	18	19	20

ANSWER

19   Find 8 + ? = 15

Use connecting cubes to find your answer.

1	2	3	4	5	6	7	8	9	10	11	12	13	14	15	16	17	18	19	20

ANSWER

20   Find ? + 13 = 20

Use connecting cubes to find your answer.

1	2	3	4	5	6	7	8	9	10	11	12	13	14	15	16	17	18	19	20

ANSWER

21   Find 16 – 4 = ?

Use connecting cubes to find your answer.

1	2	3	4	5	6	7	8	9	10	11	12	13	14	15	16	17	18	19	20

ANSWER

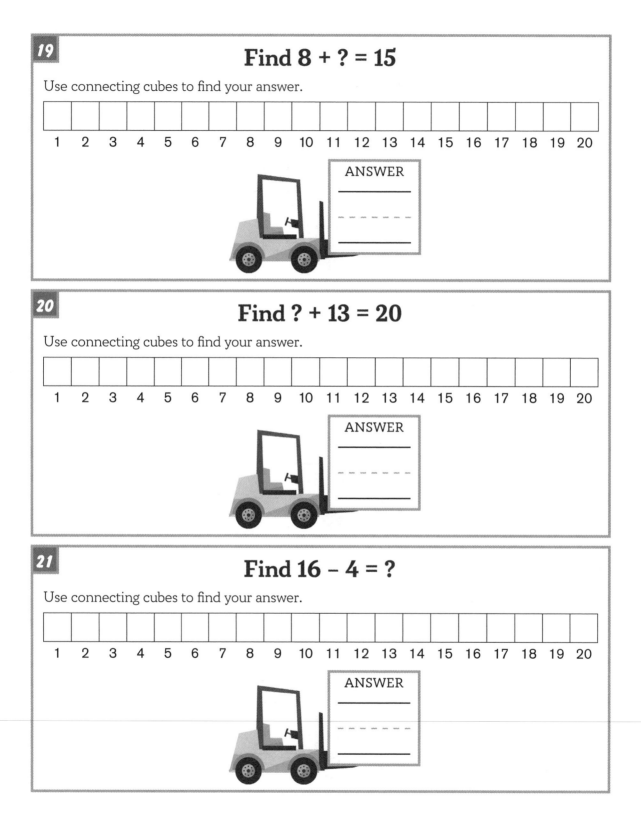

22

Find ? = 18 – 5

Use connecting cubes to find your answer.

1	2	3	4	5	6	7	8	9	10	11	12	13	14	15	16	17	18	19	20

ANSWER

23

Find 17 – 12 = ?

Use connecting cubes to find your answer.

1	2	3	4	5	6	7	8	9	10	11	12	13	14	15	16	17	18	19	20

ANSWER

24

Find ? = 20 – 6

Use connecting cubes to find your answer.

1	2	3	4	5	6	7	8	9	10	11	12	13	14	15	16	17	18	19	20

ANSWER

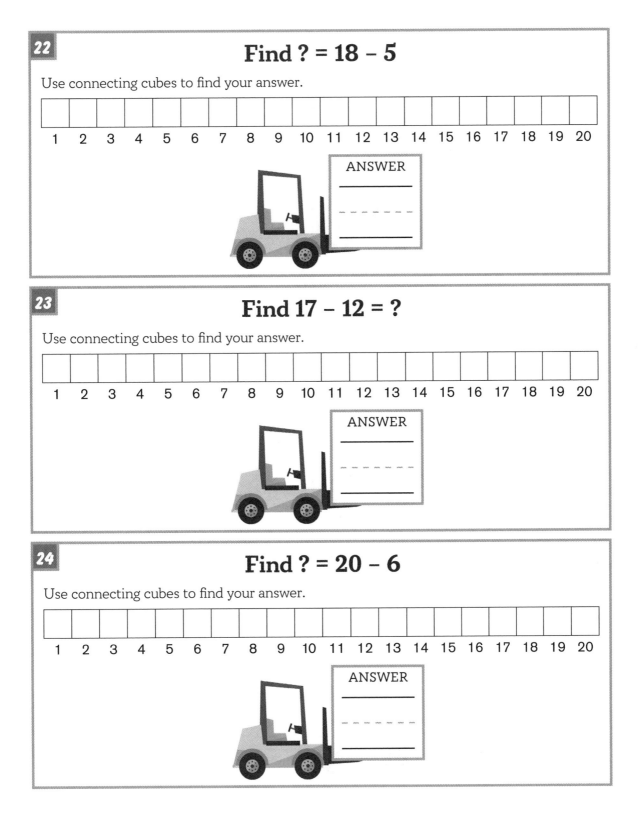

25

Find 19 − 9 = ?

Use connecting cubes to find your answer.

1	2	3	4	5	6	7	8	9	10	11	12	13	14	15	16	17	18	19	20

ANSWER

26

Find ? = 19 − 6

Use connecting cubes to find your answer.

1	2	3	4	5	6	7	8	9	10	11	12	13	14	15	16	17	18	19	20

ANSWER

27

Find 16 − 12 = ?

Use connecting cubes to find your answer.

1	2	3	4	5	6	7	8	9	10	11	12	13	14	15	16	17	18	19	20

ANSWER

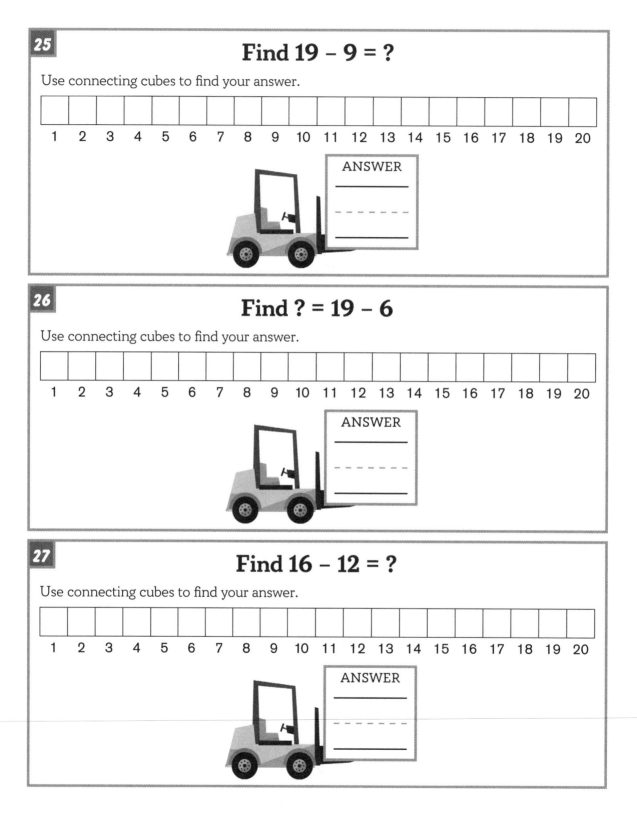

28   # Find ? = 12 – 7

Use connecting cubes to find your answer.

1	2	3	4	5	6	7	8	9	10	11	12	13	14	15	16	17	18	19	20

ANSWER

_____

- - - - - - - - - - -

_____

---

29   # Find 18 – 9 = ?

Use connecting cubes to find your answer.

1	2	3	4	5	6	7	8	9	10	11	12	13	14	15	16	17	18	19	20

ANSWER

_____

- - - - - - - - - - -

_____

---

30   # Find ? = 20 – 15

Use connecting cubes to find your answer.

1	2	3	4	5	6	7	8	9	10	11	12	13	14	15	16	17	18	19	20

ANSWER

_____

- - - - - - - - - - -

_____

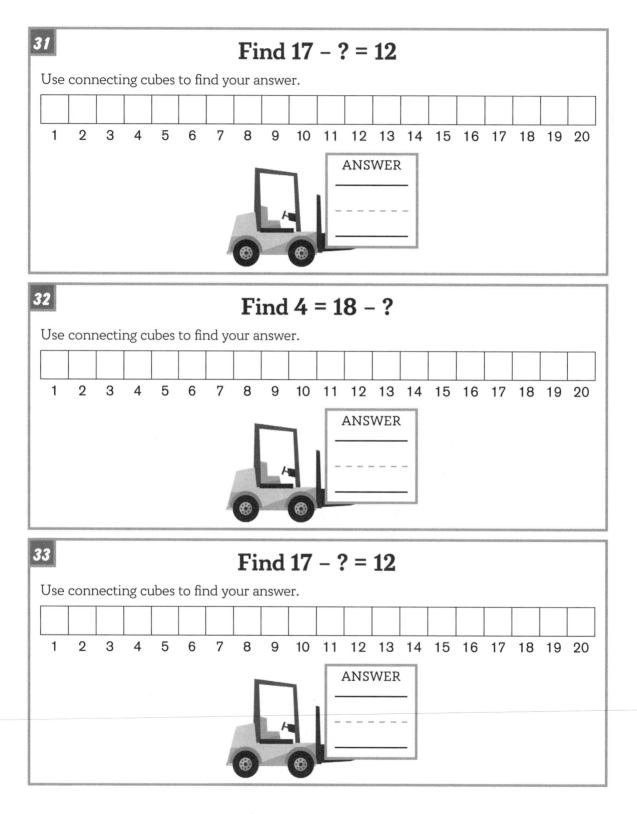

31

Find 17 − ? = 12

Use connecting cubes to find your answer.

1	2	3	4	5	6	7	8	9	10	11	12	13	14	15	16	17	18	19	20

ANSWER

32

Find 4 = 18 − ?

Use connecting cubes to find your answer.

1	2	3	4	5	6	7	8	9	10	11	12	13	14	15	16	17	18	19	20

ANSWER

33

Find 17 − ? = 12

Use connecting cubes to find your answer.

1	2	3	4	5	6	7	8	9	10	11	12	13	14	15	16	17	18	19	20

ANSWER

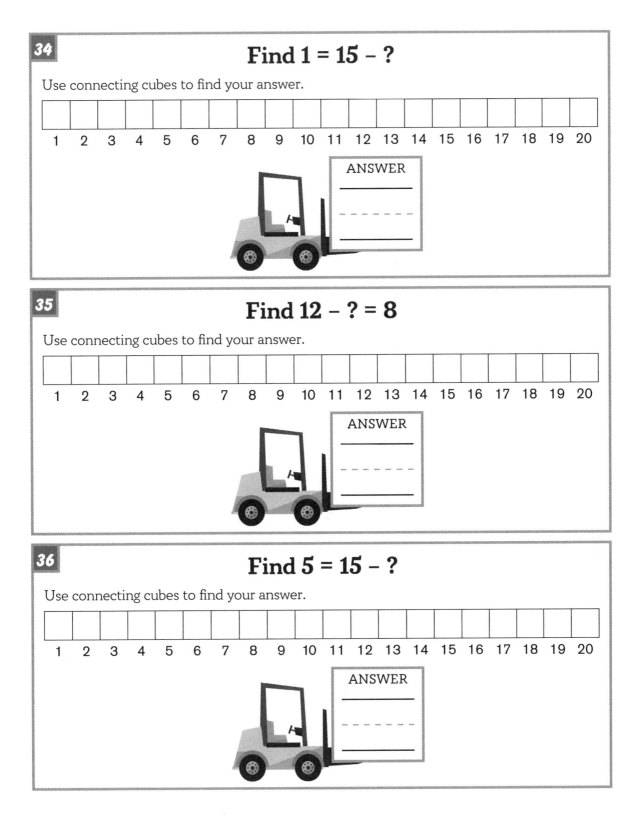

34

Find 1 = 15 – ?

Use connecting cubes to find your answer.

1	2	3	4	5	6	7	8	9	10	11	12	13	14	15	16	17	18	19	20

ANSWER

35

Find 12 – ? = 8

Use connecting cubes to find your answer.

1	2	3	4	5	6	7	8	9	10	11	12	13	14	15	16	17	18	19	20

ANSWER

36

Find 5 = 15 – ?

Use connecting cubes to find your answer.

1	2	3	4	5	6	7	8	9	10	11	12	13	14	15	16	17	18	19	20

ANSWER

37

Find 15 – ? = 3

Use connecting cubes to find your answer.

1	2	3	4	5	6	7	8	9	10	11	12	13	14	15	16	17	18	19	20

ANSWER
_____

38

Find 10 = 18 – ?

Use connecting cubes to find your answer.

1	2	3	4	5	6	7	8	9	10	11	12	13	14	15	16	17	18	19	20

ANSWER
_____

39

Find 20 – ? = 4

Use connecting cubes to find your answer.

1	2	3	4	5	6	7	8	9	10	11	12	13	14	15	16	17	18	19	20

ANSWER
_____

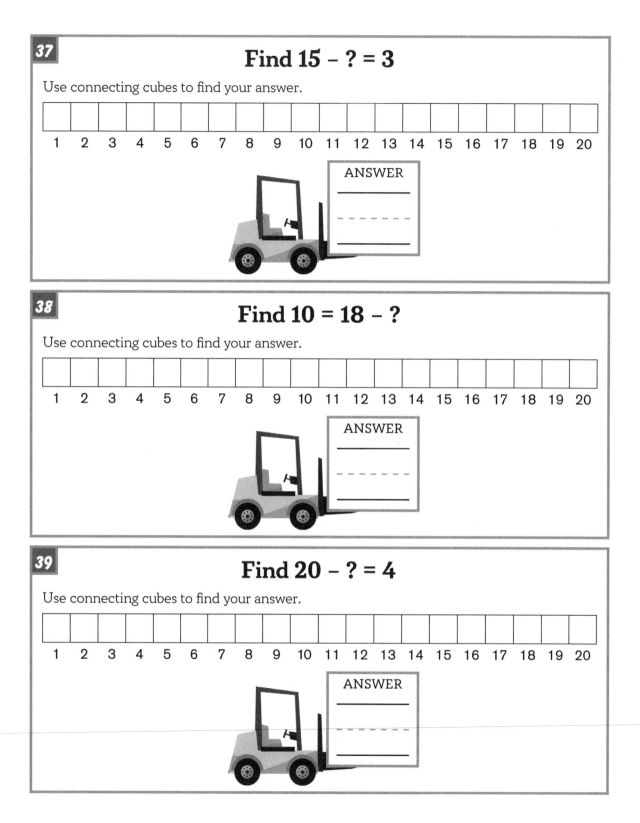

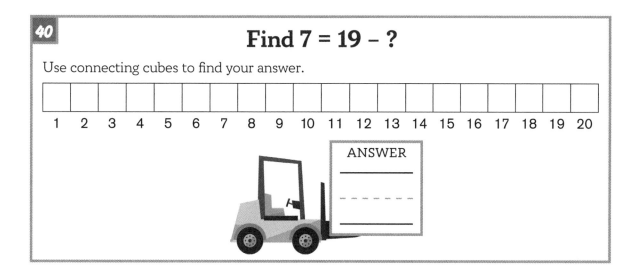

40 Find 7 = 19 – ?

Use connecting cubes to find your answer.

1	2	3	4	5	6	7	8	9	10	11	12	13	14	15	16	17	18	19	20

ANSWER
_____

- - - - - -

_____

ANSWER KEY:
Counting On Using Connecting Cubes

QUESTION	ANSWER	QUESTION	ANSWER
1.	10 + 3 = 13	11.	12 + 3 = 15
2.	16 = 9 + 7	12.	2 + 14 = 16
3.	7 + 5 = 12	13.	11 + 6 = 17
4.	14 = 8 + 6	14.	10 + 9 = 19
5.	13 + 3 = 16	15.	15 + 3 = 18
6.	17 = 12 + 5	16.	14 + 6 = 20
7.	12 + 7 = 19	17.	9 + 4 = 13
8.	17 = 11 + 6	18.	4 + 13 = 17
9.	9 + 11 = 20	19.	8 + 7 = 15
10.	13 + 4 = 17	20.	7 + 13 = 20

ANSWER KEY:
Counting On Using Connecting Cubes

QUESTION	ANSWER	QUESTION	ANSWER
21.	$16 - 4 = 12$	31.	$17 - 5 = 12$
22.	$13 = 18 - 5$	32.	$4 = 18 - 14$
23.	$17 - 12 = 5$	33.	$17 - 5 = 12$
24.	$14 = 20 - 6$	34.	$1 = 15 - 14$
25.	$19 - 9 = 10$	35.	$12 - 4 = 8$
26.	$13 = 19 - 6$	36.	$5 = 15 - 10$
27.	$16 - 12 = 4$	37.	$15 - 12 = 3$
28.	$5 = 12 - 7$	38.	$10 = 18 - 8$
29.	$18 - 9 = 9$	39.	$20 - 16 = 4$
30.	$5 = 20 - 15$	40.	$7 = 19 - 12$

Regrouping on a Ten-Frame

OBJECTIVE: Students use ten-frames on the task cards to find the solutions to the number sentences. Once all task cards have been solved, share solutions. This activity can be done as a whole class, in a small group setting, such as a guided math group, or individually.

MATERIALS NEEDED: Task cards and two-color counters

DIRECTIONS: Copy the task cards or project for all students to see. Students should place the first addend in the upper ten-frame and the second addend in the lower frame before making a 10 and finding the sum. In the example below, there are 9 red counters in the upper frame and 6 yellow counters in the lower frame. By moving one of the yellow counters to the upper frame, we have made a 10. Now addition is easy. 10 from the upper frame plus 5 from the lower frame makes a total of 15. So, 10 + 5 = 15 and 9 + 6 = 15.

EXAMPLE

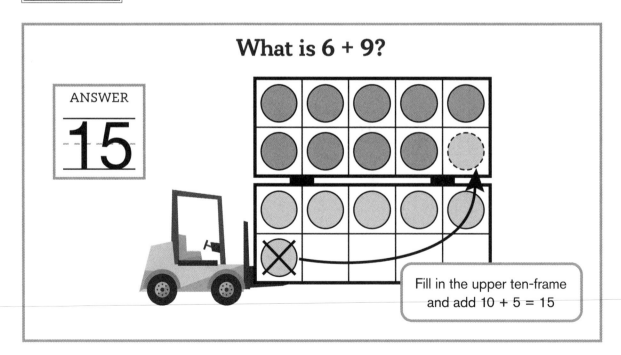

What is 6 + 9?

ANSWER

15

Fill in the upper ten-frame
and add 10 + 5 = 15

1
What is 7 + 4?

ANSWER
_____
- - - - - - - -
_____

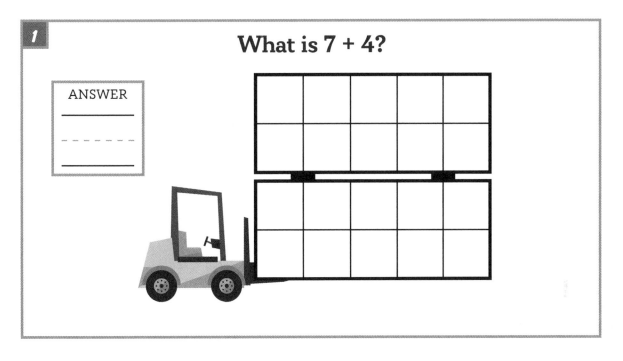

2
What is 8 + 6?

ANSWER
_____
- - - - - - - -
_____

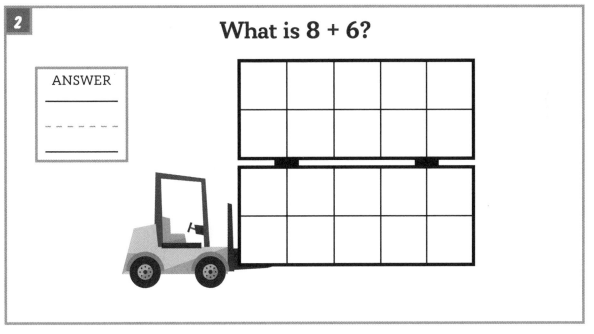

3

What is 5 + 5?

ANSWER
_____
- - - - - - -
_____

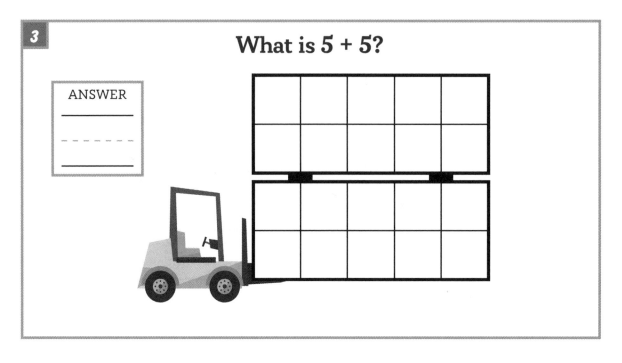

4

What is 9 + 8?

ANSWER
_____
- - - - - - -
_____

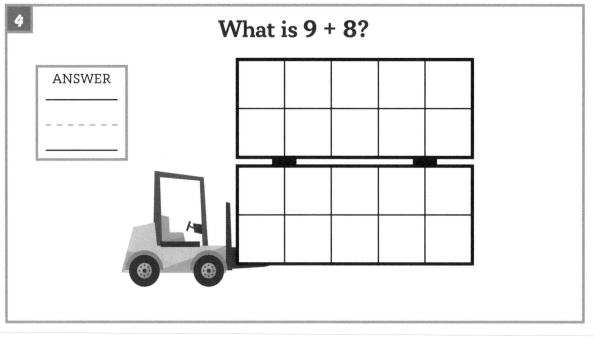

Math Fluency Activities for K–2 Teachers

5 What is 4 + 9?

ANSWER
_____
- - - - -
_____

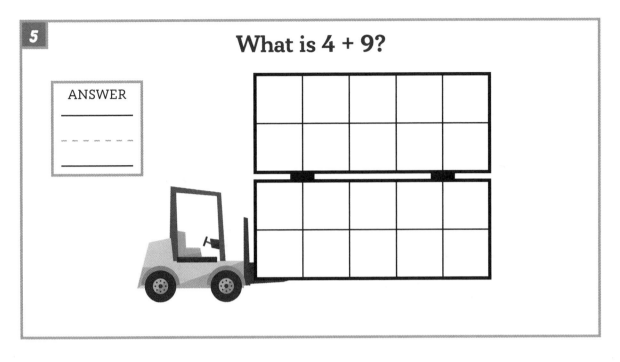

6 What is 9 + 5?

ANSWER
_____
- - - - -
_____

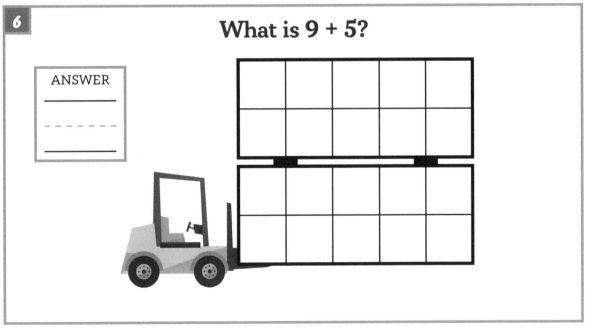

What is 8 + 7?

ANSWER

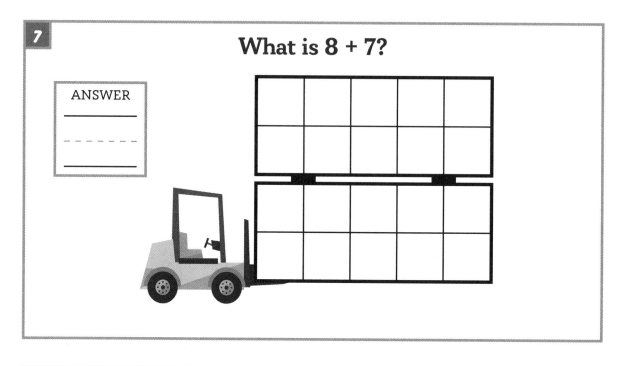

What is 6 + 6?

ANSWER

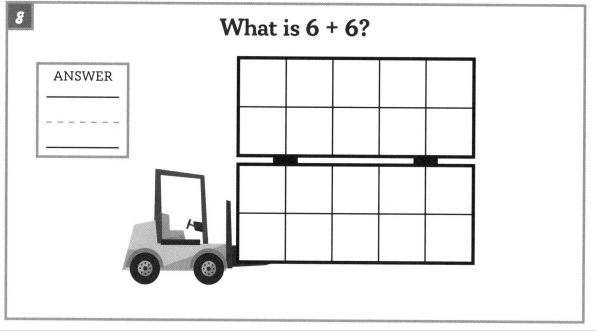

Math Fluency Activities for K–2 Teachers

What is 7 + 5?

ANSWER
_____

- - - - - - - - - -

_____

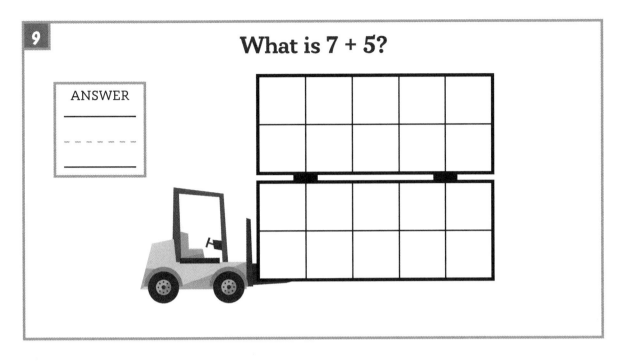

What is 6 + 5?

ANSWER
_____

- - - - - - - - - -

_____

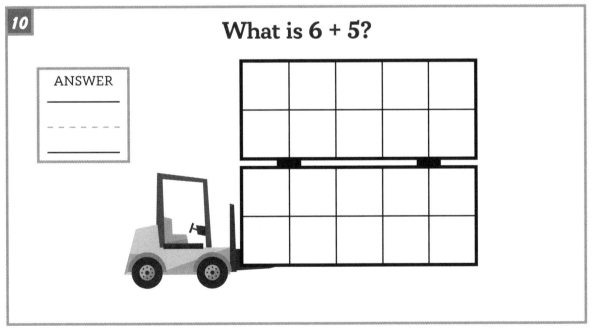

11

What is 8 + 6?

ANSWER

_____

- - - - - - - - - - -

_____

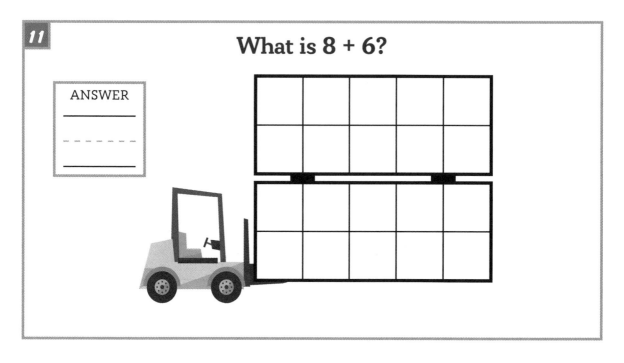

12

What is 6 + 7?

ANSWER

_____

- - - - - - - - - - -

_____

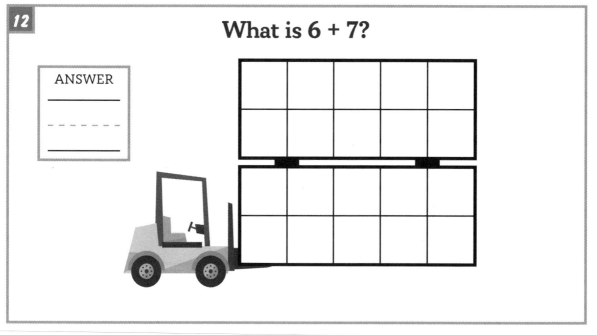

Math Fluency Activities for K–2 Teachers

13 What is 7 + 9?

ANSWER

_____

- - - - - - - - -

_____

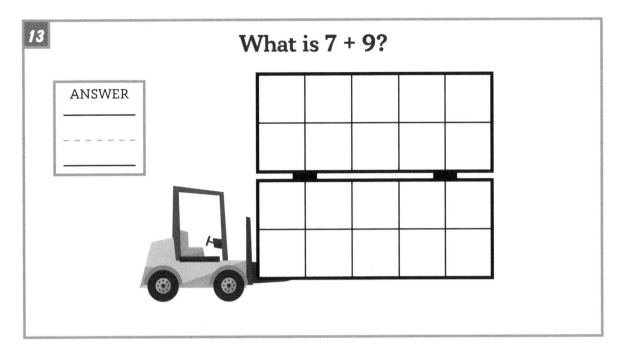

14 What is 9 + 2?

ANSWER

_____

- - - - - - - - -

_____

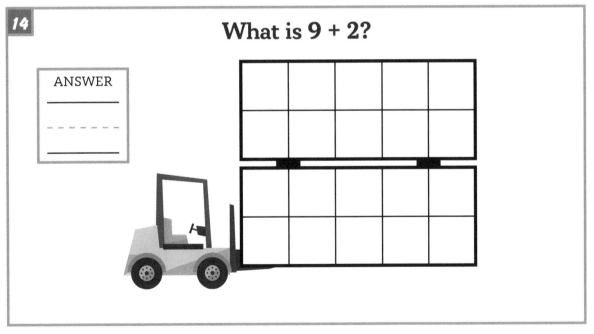

15

What is 10 + 2?

ANSWER

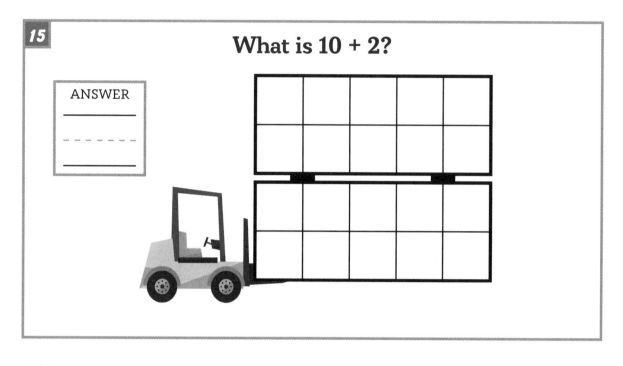

16

What is 8 + 4?

ANSWER

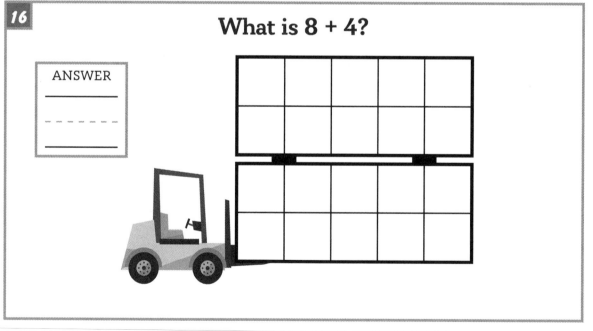

Math Fluency Activities for K–2 Teachers

17

What is 1 + 7?

ANSWER
_____
- - - - - - - - - -
_____

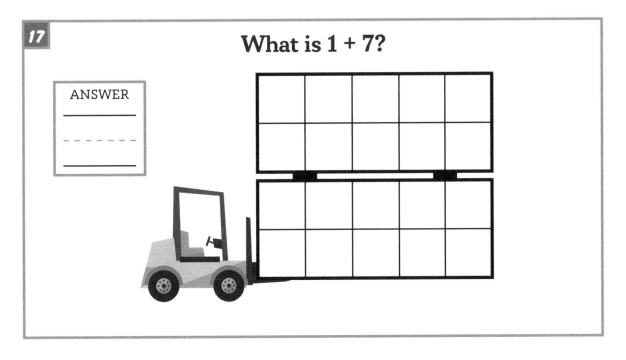

18

What is 9 + 3?

ANSWER
_____
- - - - - - - - - -
_____

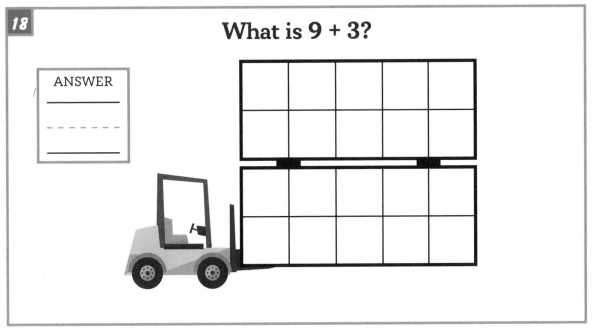

19

What is 9 + 9?

ANSWER

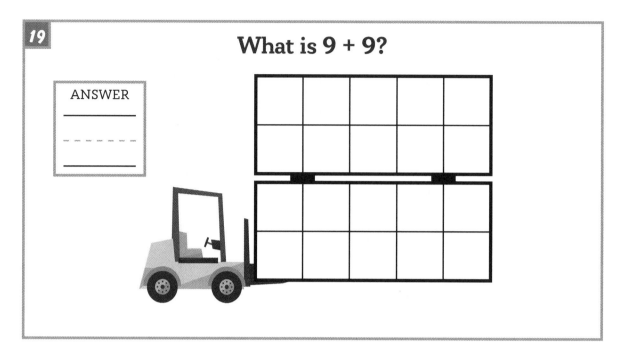

What is 8 + 5?

ANSWER

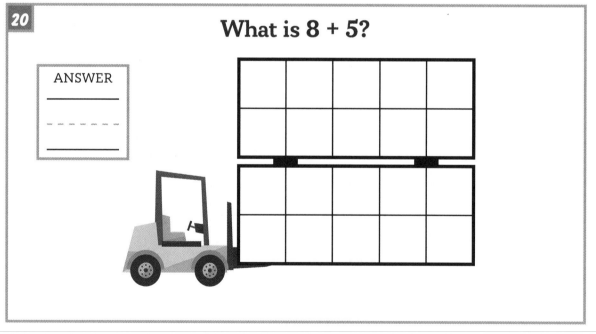

Math Fluency Activities for K–2 Teachers

ANSWER KEY:
Regrouping on a Ten-Frame

QUESTION	ANSWER		QUESTION	ANSWER
1.	11		11.	14
2.	14		12.	13
3.	10		13.	16
4.	17		14.	11
5.	13		15.	12
6.	14		16.	12
7.	15		17.	8
8.	12		18.	12
9.	12		19.	18
10.	11		20.	13

Subtracting on a Ten-Frame

OBJECTIVE: Students use ten-frames on the task cards to find the solutions to the number sentences. Once all task cards have been solved, discuss and share solutions.

MATERIALS NEEDED: Task cards and two-color counters

DIRECTIONS: Copy or display the cards for whole class instruction. Show several examples before using the task cards. If displaying, use a virtual color counter and ten-frame manipulative to drag and drop to find the solution to the problem. Students place the minuend on the ten-frames; in this example it is 15. The upper frame shows 10, and the lower frame shows 5. Decompose the subtrahend to count down to 10. Then remove the rest. In this example, if we remove 5 from the lower frame, we will be left with a 10. So, we decompose the subtrahend, 6, into 5 + 1. Our difference will be 10 minus the remaining 1 from the subtrahend, which will give us our difference of 9.

EXAMPLE

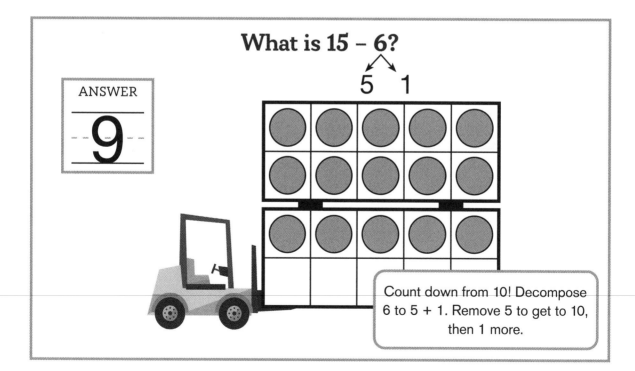

What is 15 − 6?

5   1

ANSWER

9

Count down from 10! Decompose 6 to 5 + 1. Remove 5 to get to 10, then 1 more.

1

$$11 - 4 =$$

ANSWER
_____
- - - - - - -
_____

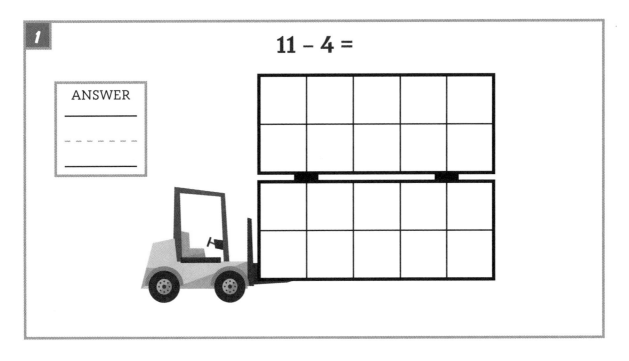

2

$$19 - 11 =$$

ANSWER
_____
- - - - - - -
_____

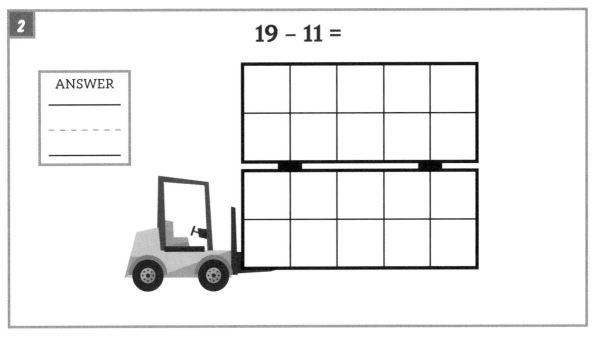

3

14 – 6 =

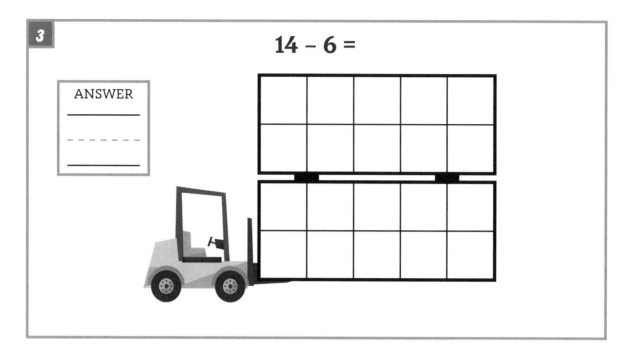

ANSWER
_____
- - - - - - - -
_____

4

17 – 8 =

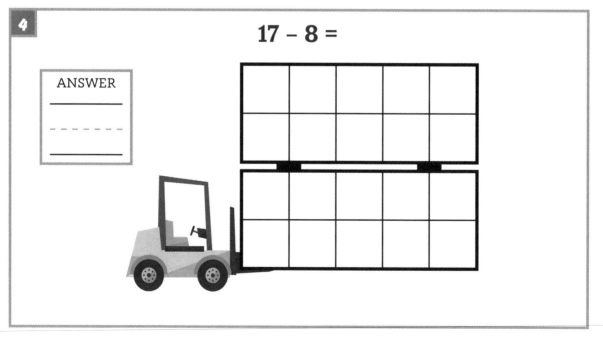

ANSWER
_____
- - - - - - - -
_____

5

$$15 - 7 =$$

ANSWER
_____
- - - - - - - - - -
_____

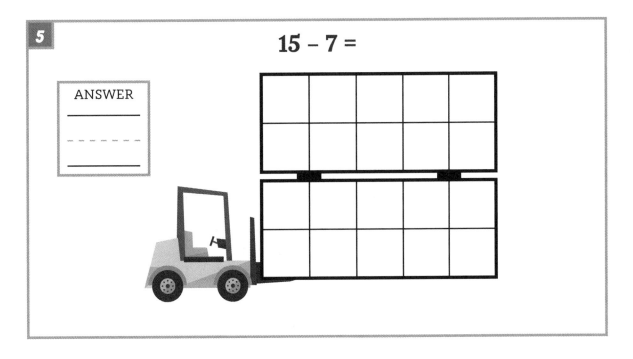

6

$$11 - 6 =$$

ANSWER
_____
- - - - - - - - - -
_____

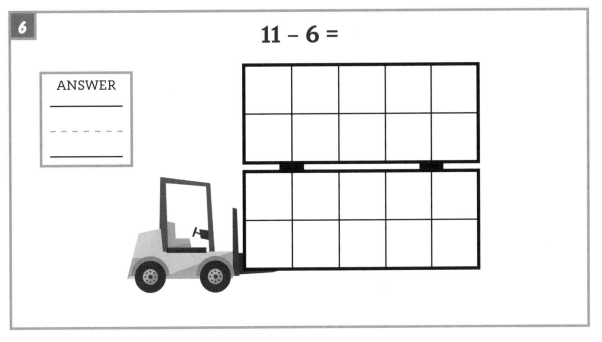

7

18 – 15 =

ANSWER
_____

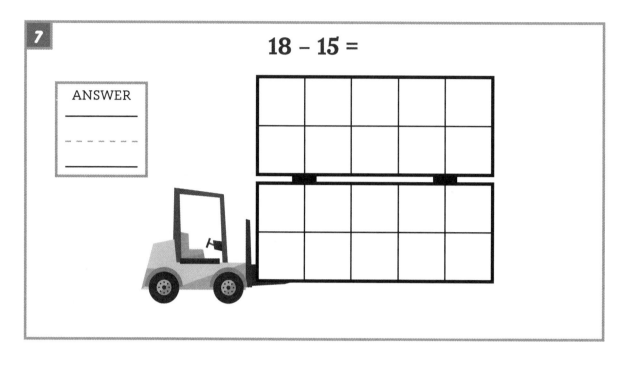

8

12 – 7 =

ANSWER
_____

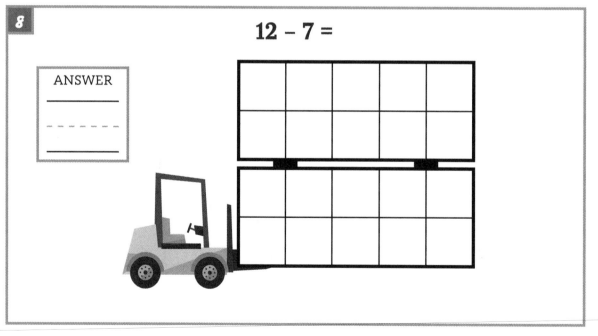

9

13 − 5 =

ANSWER
_____
- - - - - - - - -
_____

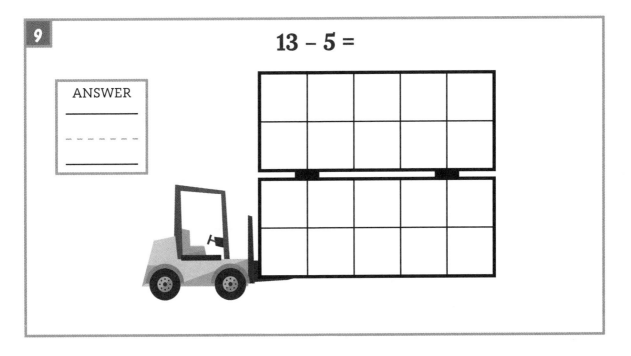

10

15 − 6 =

ANSWER
_____
- - - - - - - - -
_____

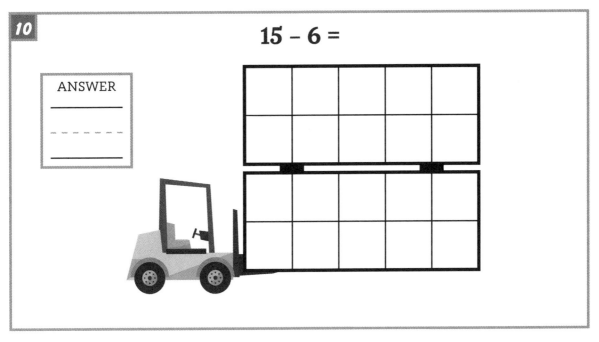

11

17 – 6 =

ANSWER
_____
- - - - - - - - - -
_____

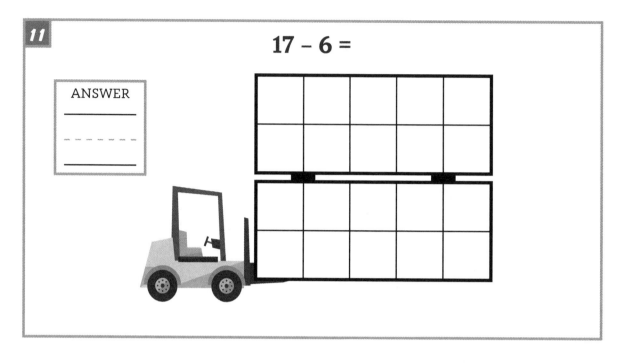

12

18 – 9 =

ANSWER
_____
- - - - - - - - - -
_____

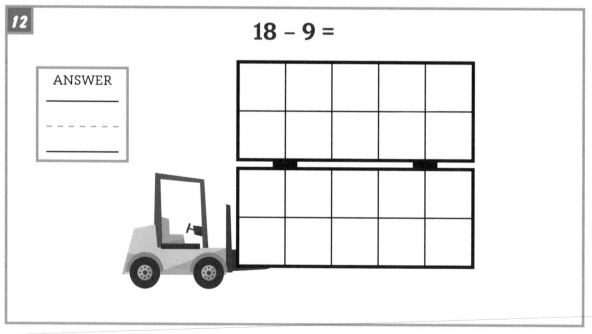

13

$$14 - 5 =$$

ANSWER
_____
- - - - - - - - - -
_____

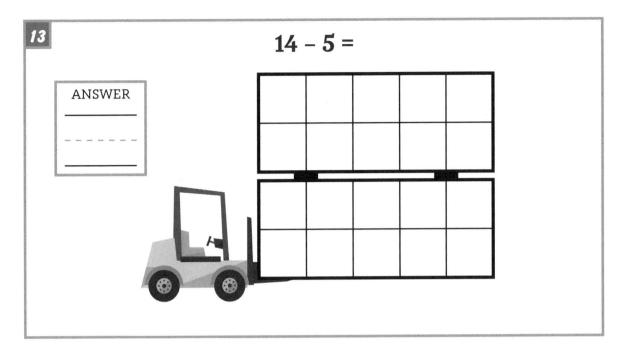

14

$$15 - 9 =$$

ANSWER
_____
- - - - - - - - - -
_____

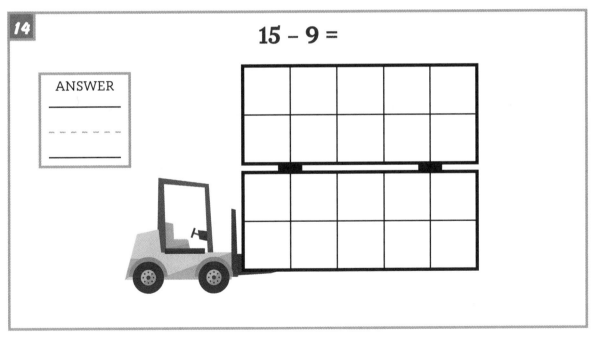

15

$$11 - 9 =$$

ANSWER

_____

- - - - - - - - - - -

_____

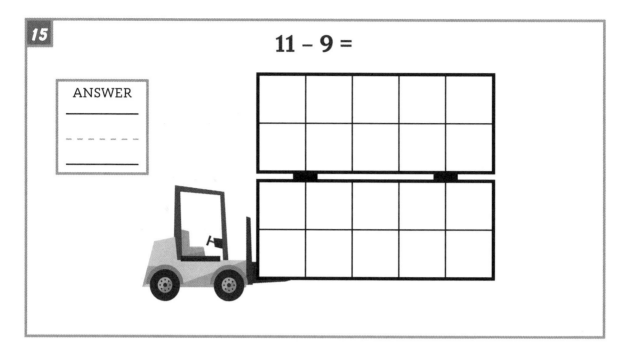

16

$$13 - 8 =$$

ANSWER

_____

- - - - - - - - - - -

_____

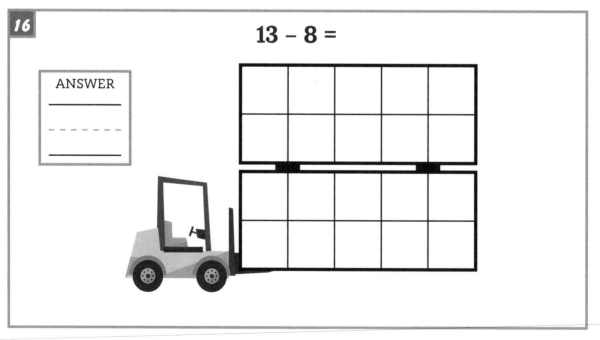

17

17 – 12 =

ANSWER

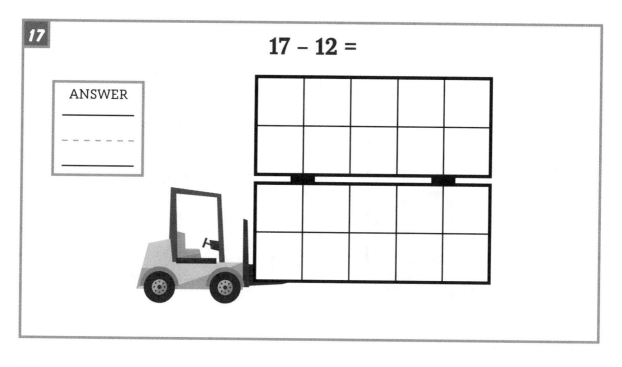

18

19 – 9 =

ANSWER

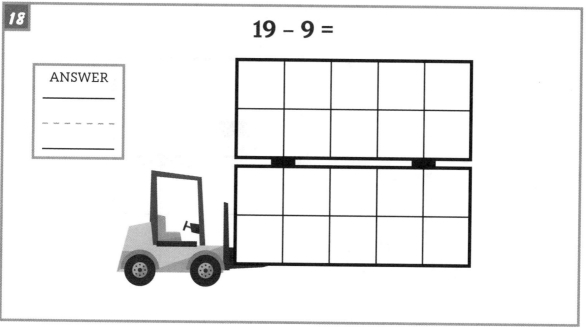

19

$$11 - 7 =$$

ANSWER
_____
- - - - - - -
_____

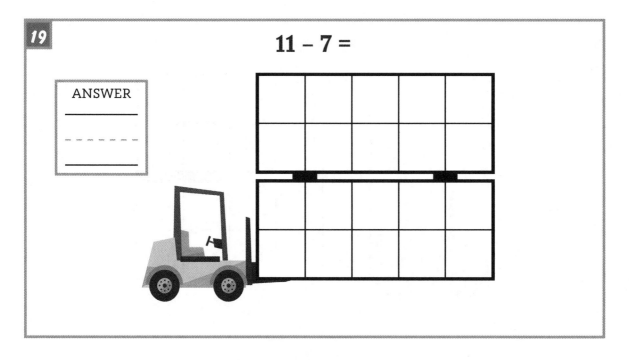

20

$$18 - 11 =$$

ANSWER
_____
- - - - - - -
_____

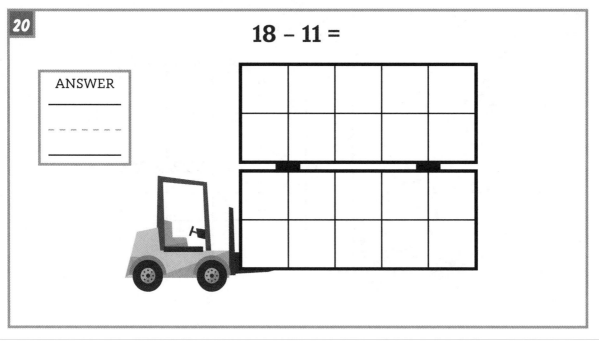

ANSWER KEY:
Subtracting on a Ten-Frame

QUESTION	ANSWER
1.	7
2.	8
3.	8
4.	9
5.	8
6.	5
7.	3
8.	5
9.	8
10.	9

QUESTION	ANSWER
11.	11
12.	9
13.	9
14.	6
15.	2
16.	5
17.	5
18.	10
19.	4
20.	7

Adding on a Number Line
(Counting On Strategy)

OBJECTIVE: Students will use a representational strategy to add numbers. Students use a number line to find the solutions to the number sentences. Once all task cards have been solved, discuss and share solutions.

MATERIALS NEEDED: Task cards

DIRECTIONS: Copy or display the task cards for student use. Begin with the first addend, and jump on the number line based on the second addend. For the example below, start at 12 (the first addend) and jump 5 units based on the second addend, which is 5. So, $12 + 5 = 17$.

EXAMPLE

Counting On Addition Strategy
What is 12 + 5?

$$12 + 5 = 17$$

Begin at 12 and count 5 more.

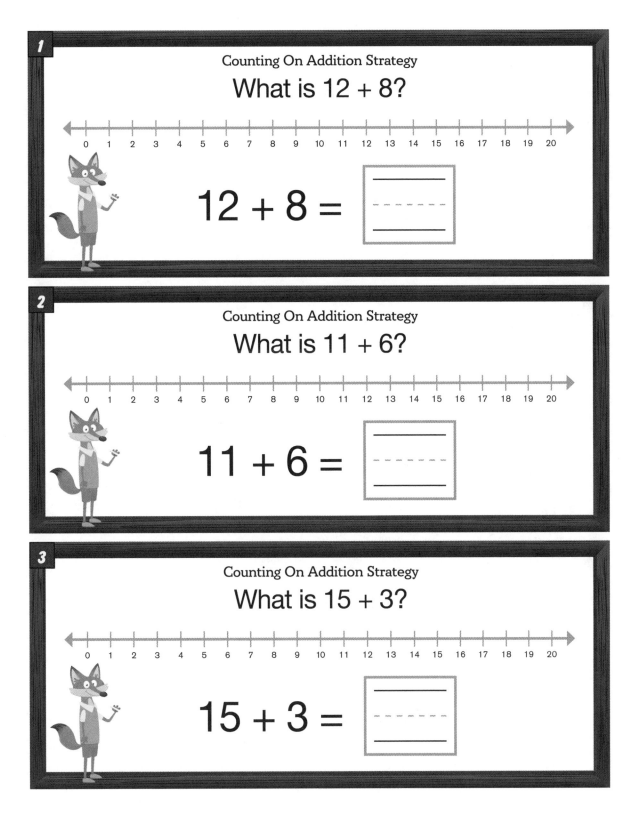

1

Counting On Addition Strategy

What is 12 + 8?

0 1 2 3 4 5 6 7 8 9 10 11 12 13 14 15 16 17 18 19 20

$$12 + 8 =$$

2

Counting On Addition Strategy

What is 11 + 6?

0 1 2 3 4 5 6 7 8 9 10 11 12 13 14 15 16 17 18 19 20

$$11 + 6 =$$

3

Counting On Addition Strategy

What is 15 + 3?

0 1 2 3 4 5 6 7 8 9 10 11 12 13 14 15 16 17 18 19 20

$$15 + 3 =$$

4

Counting On Addition Strategy

What is 18 + 1?

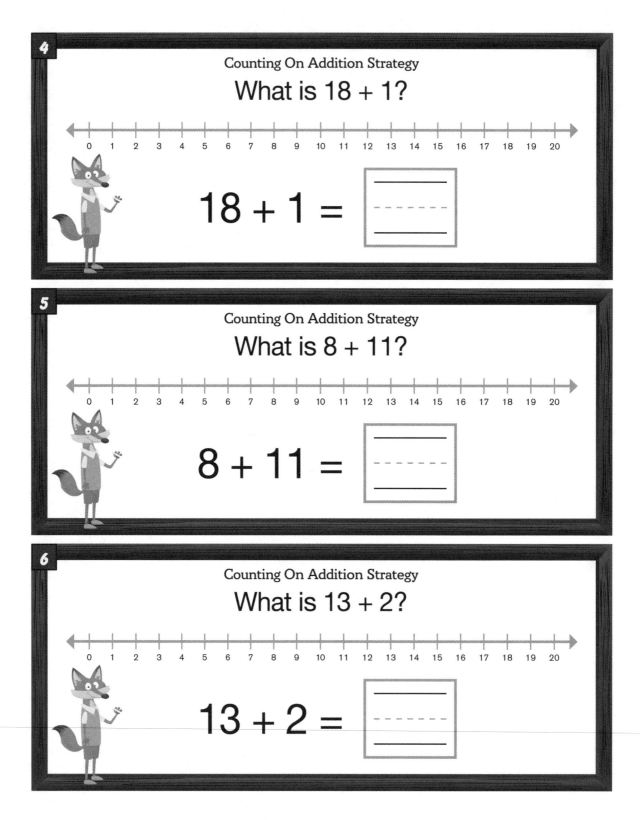

18 + 1 =

5

Counting On Addition Strategy

What is 8 + 11?

8 + 11 =

6

Counting On Addition Strategy

What is 13 + 2?

13 + 2 =

Math Fluency Activities for K–2 Teachers

7

Counting On Addition Strategy
What is 3 + 15?

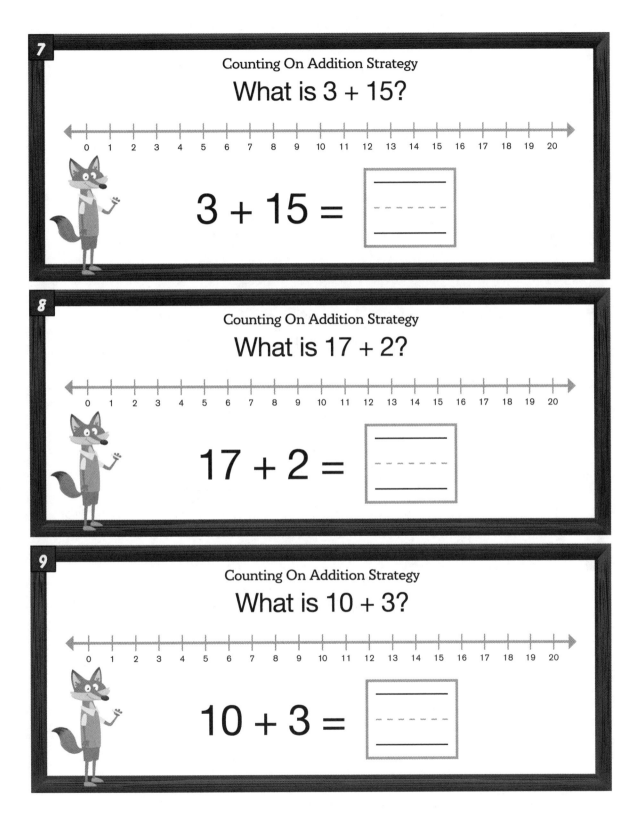

0 1 2 3 4 5 6 7 8 9 10 11 12 13 14 15 16 17 18 19 20

3 + 15 =

8

Counting On Addition Strategy
What is 17 + 2?

0 1 2 3 4 5 6 7 8 9 10 11 12 13 14 15 16 17 18 19 20

17 + 2 =

9

Counting On Addition Strategy
What is 10 + 3?

0 1 2 3 4 5 6 7 8 9 10 11 12 13 14 15 16 17 18 19 20

10 + 3 =

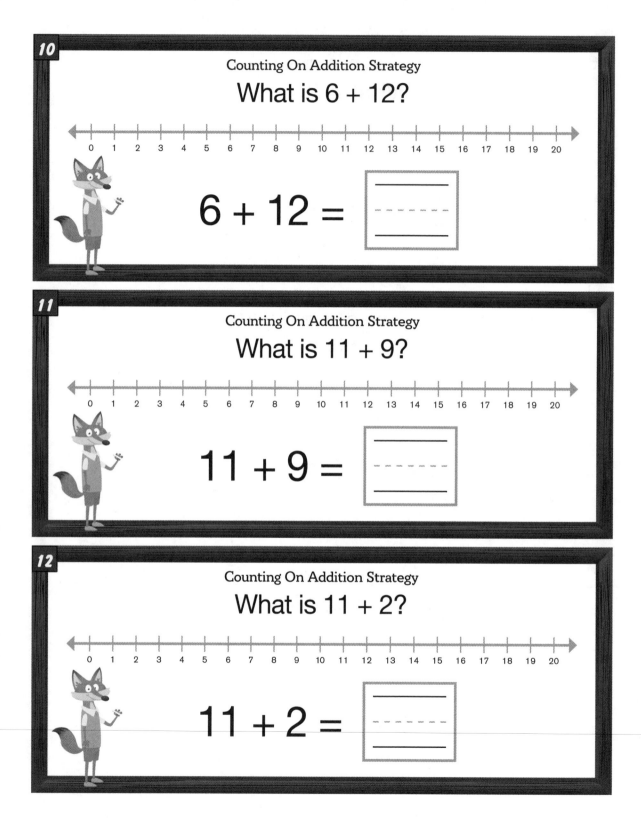

10

Counting On Addition Strategy
What is 6 + 12?

0 1 2 3 4 5 6 7 8 9 10 11 12 13 14 15 16 17 18 19 20

6 + 12 =

11

Counting On Addition Strategy
What is 11 + 9?

0 1 2 3 4 5 6 7 8 9 10 11 12 13 14 15 16 17 18 19 20

11 + 9 =

12

Counting On Addition Strategy
What is 11 + 2?

0 1 2 3 4 5 6 7 8 9 10 11 12 13 14 15 16 17 18 19 20

11 + 2 =

Math Fluency Activities for K-2 Teachers

13

Counting On Addition Strategy

What is 9 + 10?

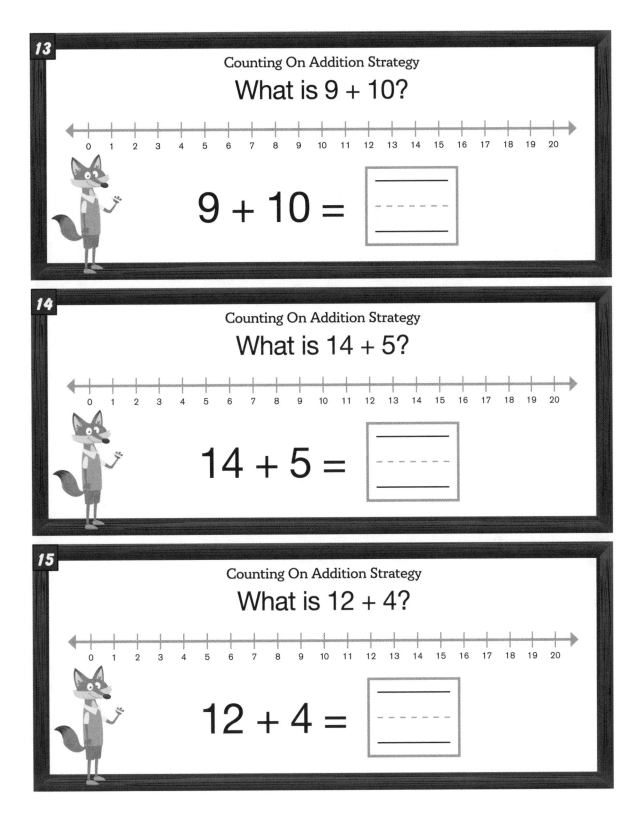

0 1 2 3 4 5 6 7 8 9 10 11 12 13 14 15 16 17 18 19 20

9 + 10 =

14

Counting On Addition Strategy

What is 14 + 5?

0 1 2 3 4 5 6 7 8 9 10 11 12 13 14 15 16 17 18 19 20

14 + 5 =

15

Counting On Addition Strategy

What is 12 + 4?

0 1 2 3 4 5 6 7 8 9 10 11 12 13 14 15 16 17 18 19 20

12 + 4 =

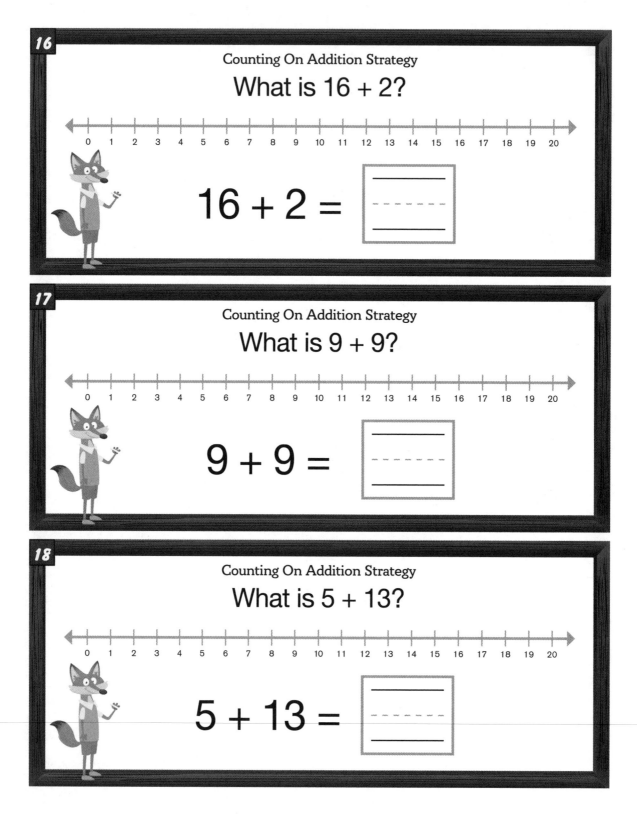

16

Counting On Addition Strategy
What is 16 + 2?

0 1 2 3 4 5 6 7 8 9 10 11 12 13 14 15 16 17 18 19 20

16 + 2 =

17

Counting On Addition Strategy
What is 9 + 9?

0 1 2 3 4 5 6 7 8 9 10 11 12 13 14 15 16 17 18 19 20

9 + 9 =

18

Counting On Addition Strategy
What is 5 + 13?

0 1 2 3 4 5 6 7 8 9 10 11 12 13 14 15 16 17 18 19 20

5 + 13 =

Math Fluency Activities for K-2 Teachers

19

Counting On Addition Strategy
What is 15 + 1?

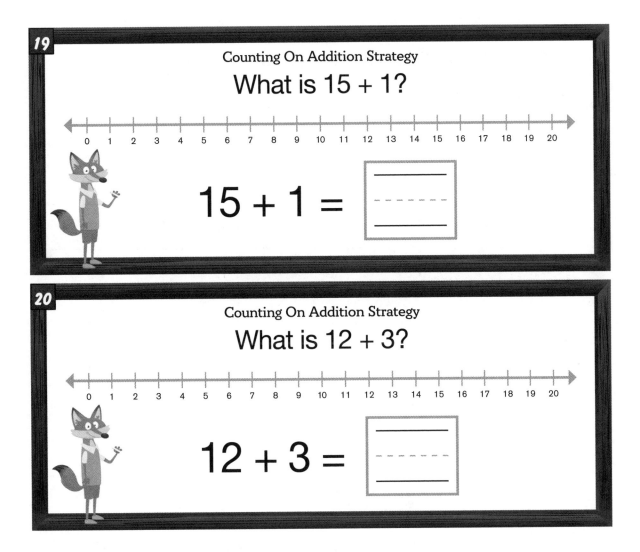

$$15 + 1 =$$

20

Counting On Addition Strategy
What is 12 + 3?

$$12 + 3 =$$

ANSWER KEY:
Adding on a Number Line (Counting On Strategy)

QUESTION	ANSWER	QUESTION	ANSWER
1.	20	11.	20
2.	17	12.	13
3.	18	13.	19
4.	19	14.	19
5.	19	15.	16
6.	15	16.	18
7.	18	17.	18
8.	19	18.	18
9.	13	19.	16
10.	18	20.	15

Subtracting on a Number Line (Counting Back Strategy)

OBJECTIVE: Students use a number line to find the solutions to the number sentences.

MATERIALS NEEDED: Task cards

DIRECTIONS: Copy or display the task cards for student use. This activity is an extension of grade 1, Activity 6. For struggling learners, revisit grade 1, Activity 6 before continuing with this grade 2 activity. Start with the larger number (minuend) on the number line and count back on the number line until you reach the second number in the sentence (the subtrahend) to find the difference. In this example, we start at 9, the minuend, and jump 5 units to reach the subtrahend of 4. We can easily see that the difference or distance between the two numbers is 5. Show several examples before using the task cards.

EXAMPLE

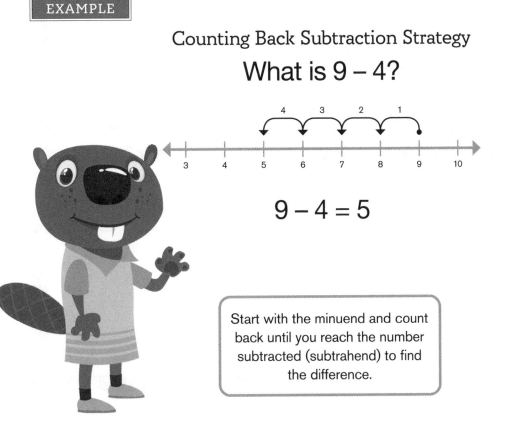

Counting Back Subtraction Strategy
What is 9 – 4?

$$9 - 4 = 5$$

Start with the minuend and count back until you reach the number subtracted (subtrahend) to find the difference.

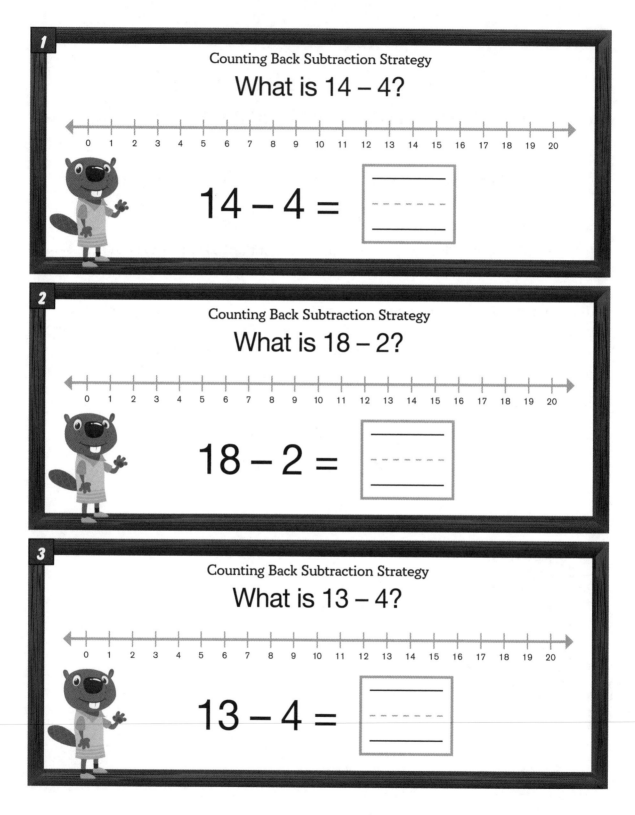

1

Counting Back Subtraction Strategy

What is 14 – 4?

0 1 2 3 4 5 6 7 8 9 10 11 12 13 14 15 16 17 18 19 20

14 – 4 =

2

Counting Back Subtraction Strategy

What is 18 – 2?

0 1 2 3 4 5 6 7 8 9 10 11 12 13 14 15 16 17 18 19 20

18 – 2 =

3

Counting Back Subtraction Strategy

What is 13 – 4?

0 1 2 3 4 5 6 7 8 9 10 11 12 13 14 15 16 17 18 19 20

13 – 4 =

Math Fluency Activities for K–2 Teachers

4

Counting Back Subtraction Strategy

What is 17 – 5?

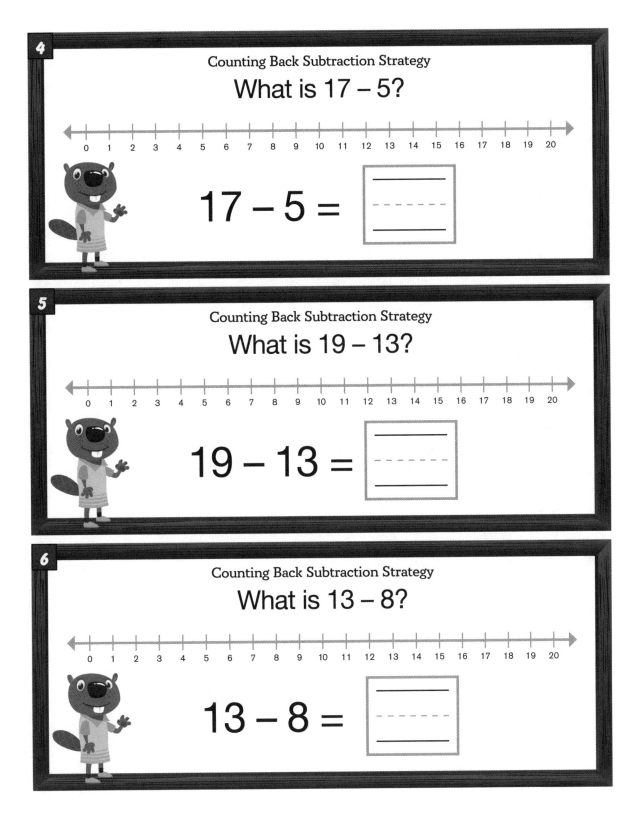

0 1 2 3 4 5 6 7 8 9 10 11 12 13 14 15 16 17 18 19 20

17 – 5 =

5

Counting Back Subtraction Strategy

What is 19 – 13?

0 1 2 3 4 5 6 7 8 9 10 11 12 13 14 15 16 17 18 19 20

19 – 13 =

6

Counting Back Subtraction Strategy

What is 13 – 8?

0 1 2 3 4 5 6 7 8 9 10 11 12 13 14 15 16 17 18 19 20

13 – 8 =

7

Counting Back Subtraction Strategy

What is 12 – 2?

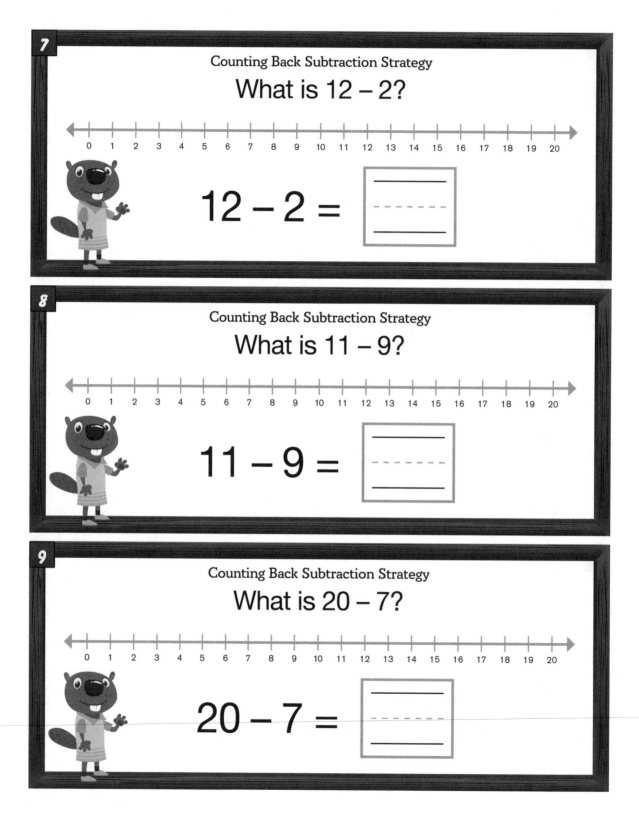

12 – 2 =

8

Counting Back Subtraction Strategy

What is 11 – 9?

11 – 9 =

9

Counting Back Subtraction Strategy

What is 20 – 7?

20 – 7 =

Math Fluency Activities for K–2 Teachers

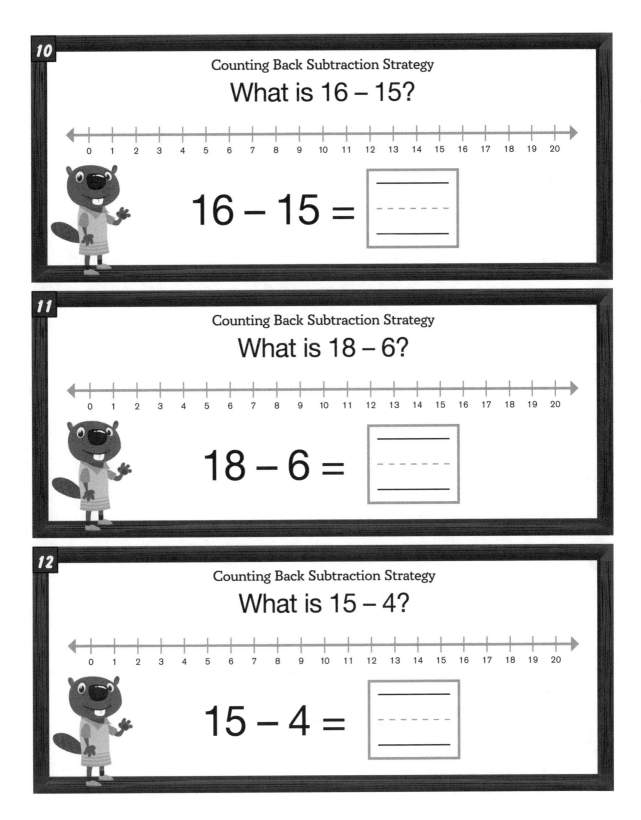

10

Counting Back Subtraction Strategy

What is 16 − 15?

0 1 2 3 4 5 6 7 8 9 10 11 12 13 14 15 16 17 18 19 20

16 − 15 =

11

Counting Back Subtraction Strategy

What is 18 − 6?

0 1 2 3 4 5 6 7 8 9 10 11 12 13 14 15 16 17 18 19 20

18 − 6 =

12

Counting Back Subtraction Strategy

What is 15 − 4?

0 1 2 3 4 5 6 7 8 9 10 11 12 13 14 15 16 17 18 19 20

15 − 4 =

Counting Back Subtraction Strategy
What is 16 – 8?

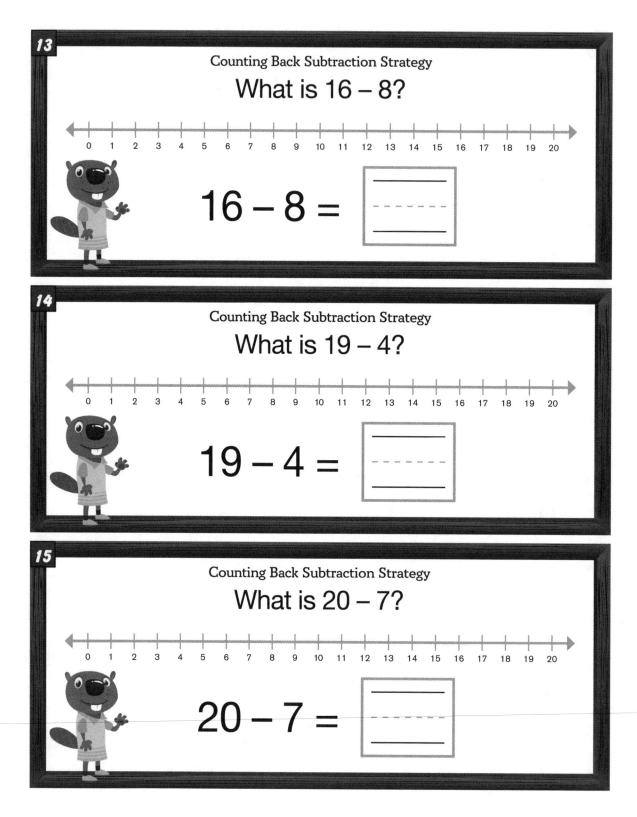

16 – 8 =

Counting Back Subtraction Strategy
What is 19 – 4?

19 – 4 =

Counting Back Subtraction Strategy
What is 20 – 7?

20 – 7 =

16

Counting Back Subtraction Strategy

What is 15 – 5?

0 1 2 3 4 5 6 7 8 9 10 11 12 13 14 15 16 17 18 19 20

15 – 5 = _____

17

Counting Back Subtraction Strategy

What is 17 – 2?

0 1 2 3 4 5 6 7 8 9 10 11 12 13 14 15 16 17 18 19 20

17 – 2 = _____

18

Counting Back Subtraction Strategy

What is 20 – 14?

0 1 2 3 4 5 6 7 8 9 10 11 12 13 14 15 16 17 18 19 20

20 – 14 = _____

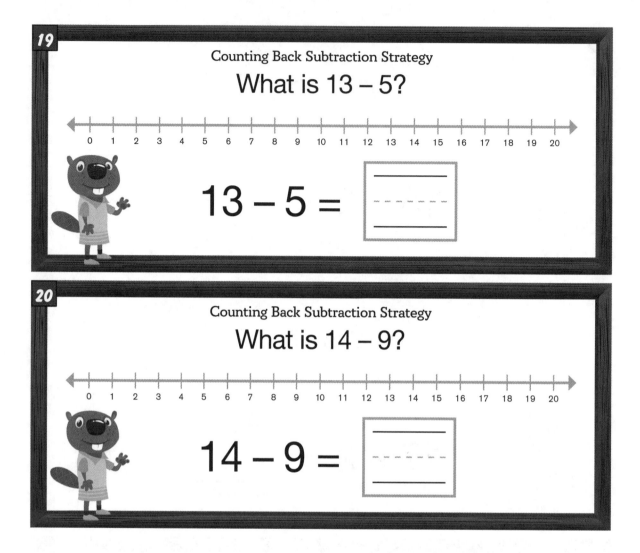

19

Counting Back Subtraction Strategy

What is 13 − 5?

0 1 2 3 4 5 6 7 8 9 10 11 12 13 14 15 16 17 18 19 20

$$13 - 5 = $$

20

Counting Back Subtraction Strategy

What is 14 − 9?

0 1 2 3 4 5 6 7 8 9 10 11 12 13 14 15 16 17 18 19 20

$$14 - 9 = $$

Math Fluency Activities for K–2 Teachers

ANSWER KEY:
Subtracting on a Number Line (Counting Back Strategy)

QUESTION	ANSWER
1.	10
2.	16
3.	9
4.	12
5.	6
6.	5
7.	10
8.	2
9.	13
10.	1

QUESTION	ANSWER
11.	12
12.	11
13.	8
14.	15
15.	13
16.	10
17.	15
18.	6
19.	8
20.	5

Subtracting on a Number Line (Counting Up Strategy)

> **OBJECTIVE:** Students use a number line to find the solutions to the number sentences.

MATERIALS NEEDED: Task cards

DIRECTIONS: Copy or project the task cards. This activity is an extension of grade 1, Activity 7. For struggling learners, step back to smaller numbers as in Activity 7 from grade 1. Show several examples before using the task cards. For example, in the problem below, start with the smaller number, 13 (the subtrahend), on the number line. From the subtrahend, count the number of jumps it takes to reach the minuend (18). In this instance, it takes 5 jumps to go from 13 to reach 18, the subtrahend. So, the difference or distance between the two numbers is 5, our solution to 18 – 13.

EXAMPLE

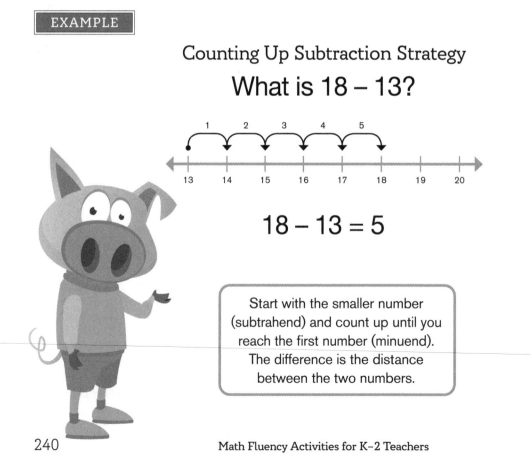

Counting Up Subtraction Strategy
What is 18 – 13?

$$18 - 13 = 5$$

> Start with the smaller number (subtrahend) and count up until you reach the first number (minuend). The difference is the distance between the two numbers.

Math Fluency Activities for K–2 Teachers

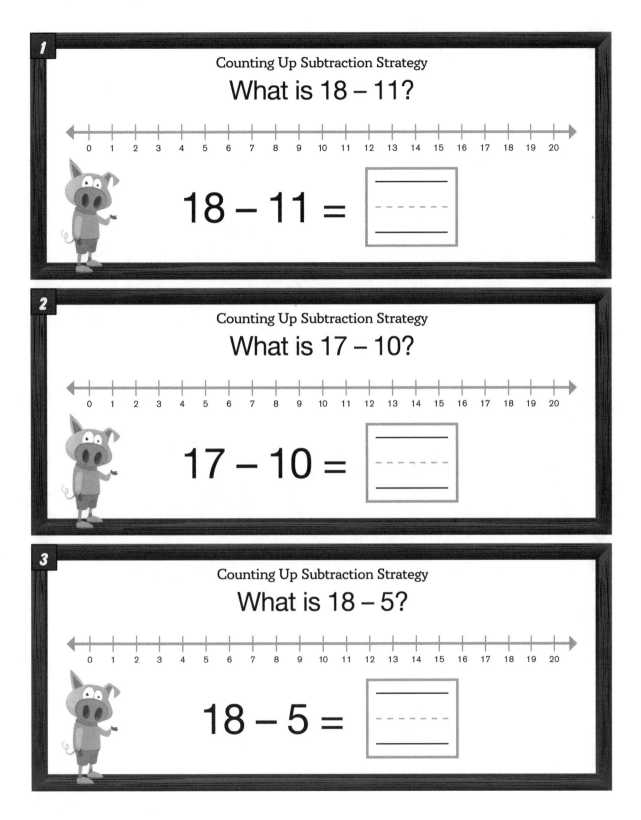

1

Counting Up Subtraction Strategy
What is 18 − 11?

0 1 2 3 4 5 6 7 8 9 10 11 12 13 14 15 16 17 18 19 20

18 − 11 =

2

Counting Up Subtraction Strategy
What is 17 − 10?

0 1 2 3 4 5 6 7 8 9 10 11 12 13 14 15 16 17 18 19 20

17 − 10 =

3

Counting Up Subtraction Strategy
What is 18 − 5?

0 1 2 3 4 5 6 7 8 9 10 11 12 13 14 15 16 17 18 19 20

18 − 5 =

4

Counting Up Subtraction Strategy
What is 15 – 13?

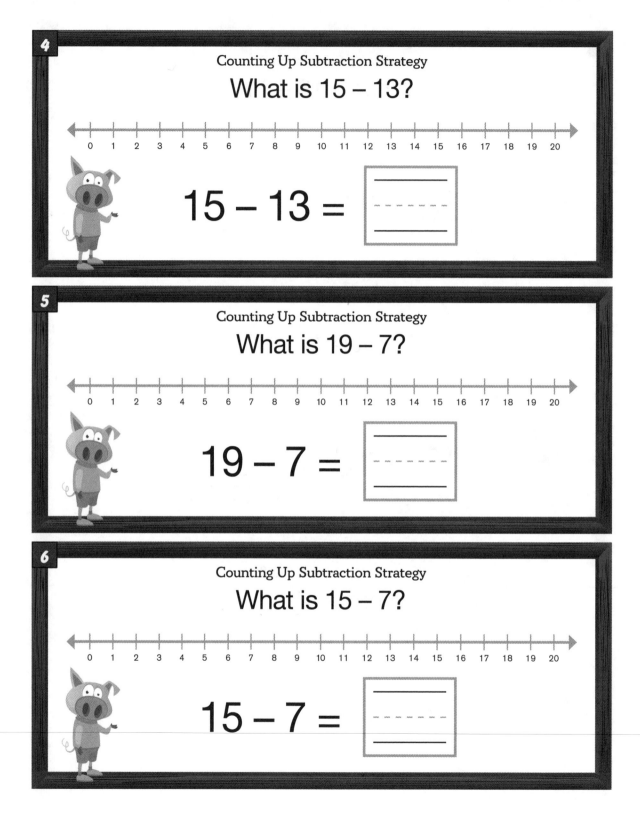

0 1 2 3 4 5 6 7 8 9 10 11 12 13 14 15 16 17 18 19 20

$$15 - 13 = \boxed{}$$

5

Counting Up Subtraction Strategy
What is 19 – 7?

0 1 2 3 4 5 6 7 8 9 10 11 12 13 14 15 16 17 18 19 20

$$19 - 7 = \boxed{}$$

6

Counting Up Subtraction Strategy
What is 15 – 7?

0 1 2 3 4 5 6 7 8 9 10 11 12 13 14 15 16 17 18 19 20

$$15 - 7 = \boxed{}$$

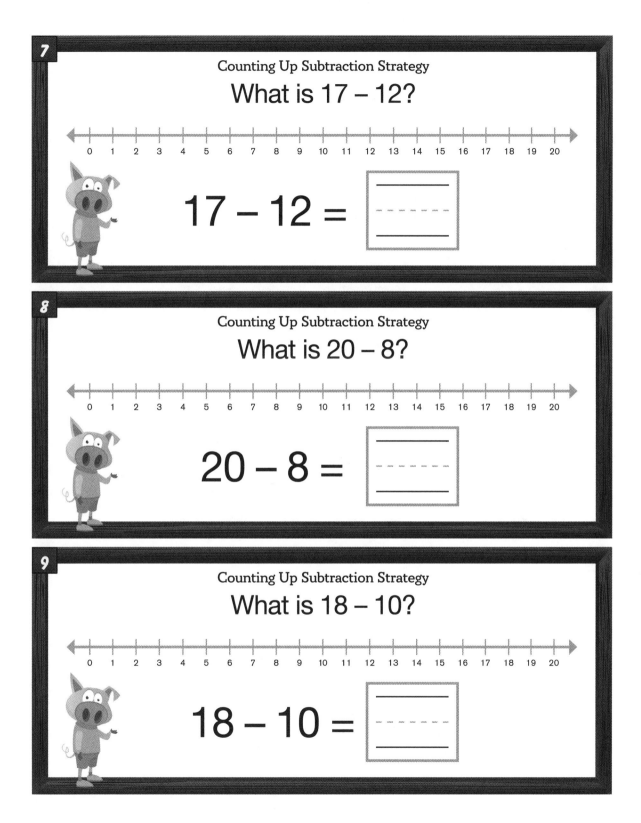

7

Counting Up Subtraction Strategy

What is 17 – 12?

0 1 2 3 4 5 6 7 8 9 10 11 12 13 14 15 16 17 18 19 20

17 – 12 =

8

Counting Up Subtraction Strategy

What is 20 – 8?

0 1 2 3 4 5 6 7 8 9 10 11 12 13 14 15 16 17 18 19 20

20 – 8 =

9

Counting Up Subtraction Strategy

What is 18 – 10?

0 1 2 3 4 5 6 7 8 9 10 11 12 13 14 15 16 17 18 19 20

18 – 10 =

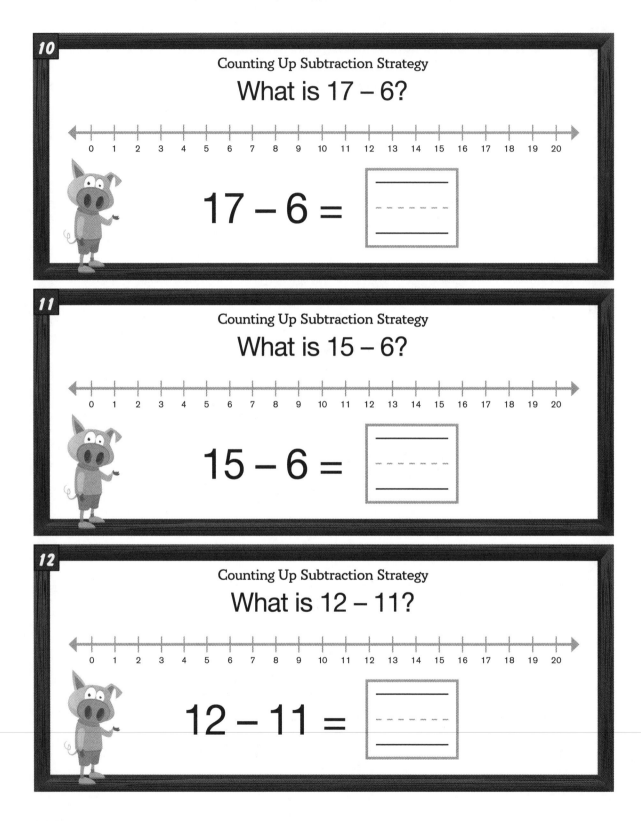

10

Counting Up Subtraction Strategy

What is 17 – 6?

0 1 2 3 4 5 6 7 8 9 10 11 12 13 14 15 16 17 18 19 20

17 – 6 =

11

Counting Up Subtraction Strategy

What is 15 – 6?

0 1 2 3 4 5 6 7 8 9 10 11 12 13 14 15 16 17 18 19 20

15 – 6 =

12

Counting Up Subtraction Strategy

What is 12 – 11?

0 1 2 3 4 5 6 7 8 9 10 11 12 13 14 15 16 17 18 19 20

12 – 11 =

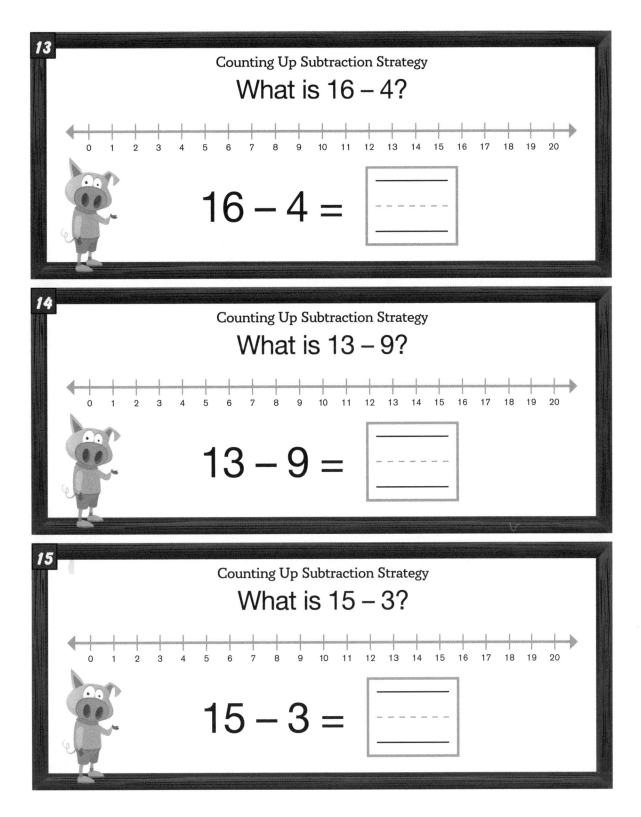

13 Counting Up Subtraction Strategy

What is 16 – 4?

0 1 2 3 4 5 6 7 8 9 10 11 12 13 14 15 16 17 18 19 20

16 – 4 =

14 Counting Up Subtraction Strategy

What is 13 – 9?

0 1 2 3 4 5 6 7 8 9 10 11 12 13 14 15 16 17 18 19 20

13 – 9 =

15 Counting Up Subtraction Strategy

What is 15 – 3?

0 1 2 3 4 5 6 7 8 9 10 11 12 13 14 15 16 17 18 19 20

15 – 3 =

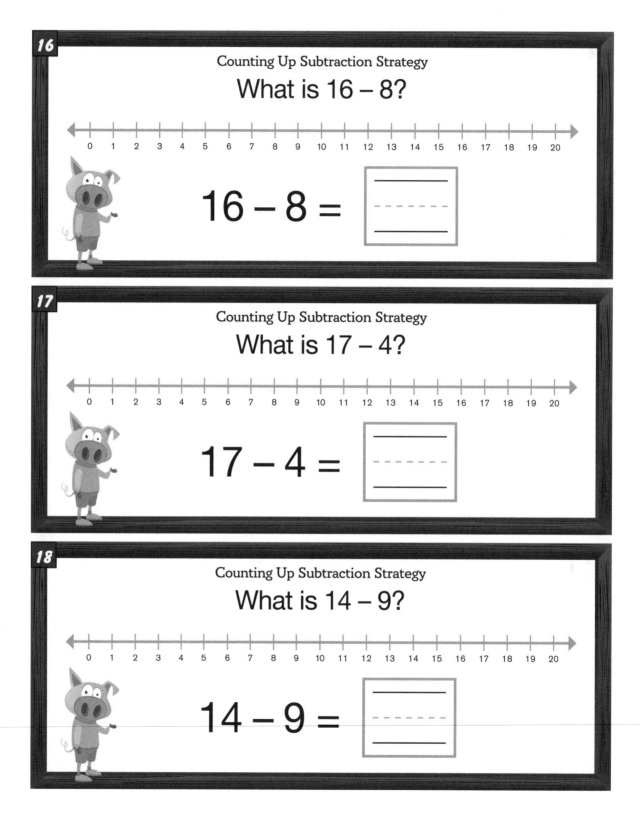

16

Counting Up Subtraction Strategy

What is 16 – 8?

0 1 2 3 4 5 6 7 8 9 10 11 12 13 14 15 16 17 18 19 20

16 – 8 =

17

Counting Up Subtraction Strategy

What is 17 – 4?

0 1 2 3 4 5 6 7 8 9 10 11 12 13 14 15 16 17 18 19 20

17 – 4 =

18

Counting Up Subtraction Strategy

What is 14 – 9?

0 1 2 3 4 5 6 7 8 9 10 11 12 13 14 15 16 17 18 19 20

14 – 9 =

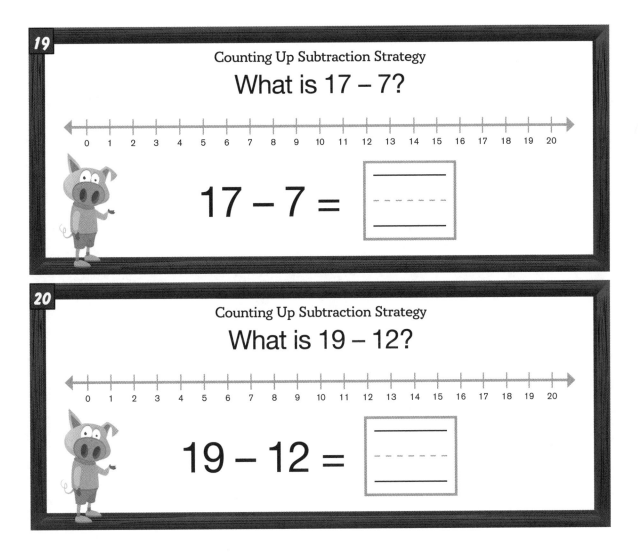

19 Counting Up Subtraction Strategy
What is 17 – 7?

0 1 2 3 4 5 6 7 8 9 10 11 12 13 14 15 16 17 18 19 20

17 – 7 = ☐

20 Counting Up Subtraction Strategy
What is 19 – 12?

0 1 2 3 4 5 6 7 8 9 10 11 12 13 14 15 16 17 18 19 20

19 – 12 = ☐

ANSWER KEY:
Subtracting on a Number Line (Counting Up Strategy)

QUESTION	ANSWER
1.	7
2.	7
3.	13
4.	2
5.	12
6.	8
7.	5
8.	12
9.	8
10.	11

QUESTION	ANSWER
11.	9
12.	1
13.	12
14.	4
15.	12
16.	8
17.	13
18.	5
19.	10
20.	7

Subtracting by Counting Down to 10

OBJECTIVE: Students decompose numbers leading to 10 in order to find the solutions to the number sentences. Again, this is an abstract strategy. Make sure students have mastered concrete and representational strategies before moving to abstract thought.

MATERIALS NEEDED: Task cards

DIRECTIONS: Copy or display the task cards. Show several examples before using the task cards. In the example below, the subtrahend was decomposed to 5 + 6 in order to make a 10 with the minuend, 15. Because 15 – 5 = 10, subtraction is so much easier. Discuss what would happen if you decomposed the minuend instead of the subtrahend. What numbers would you decompose the minuend into? How would this help with subtraction?

EXAMPLE

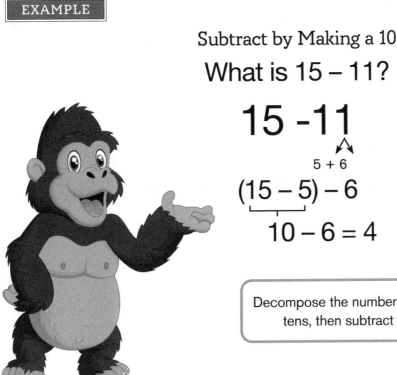

Subtract by Making a 10

What is 15 – 11?

$$15 - 11$$

$$5 + 6$$

$$(15 - 5) - 6$$

$$10 - 6 = 4$$

Decompose the numbers. Identify the tens, then subtract the rest.

1

Subtracting by Making a 10   17 – 9 =

↓ decompose

↓

=

2

Subtracting by Making a 10   11 – 8 =

↓ decompose

↓

=

3

Subtracting by Making a 10   19 – 11 =

↓ decompose

↓

=

4

Subtracting by Making a 10 $16 - 12 =$

↓ decompose

_____

- - - - - - - - - - - - - - - -

_____

↓

_____

- - - - - - - - - - - - - - - -

_____

= [_____]

5

Subtracting by Making a 10 $12 - 7 =$

↓ decompose

_____

- - - - - - - - - - - - - - - -

_____

↓

_____

- - - - - - - - - - - - - - - -

_____

= [_____]

6

Subtracting by Making a 10 $18 - 12 =$

↓ decompose

_____

- - - - - - - - - - - - - - - -

_____

↓

_____

- - - - - - - - - - - - - - - -

_____

= [_____]

7

Subtracting by Making a 10 $15 - 12 =$

↓ decompose

↓

$=$

8

Subtracting by Making a 10 $14 - 7 =$

↓ decompose

↓

$=$

9

Subtracting by Making a 10 $16 - 7 =$

↓ decompose

↓

$=$

Math Fluency Activities for K–2 Teachers

10

Subtracting by Making a 10

$$13 - 9 =$$

↓ decompose

_____

- - - - - - - - - - - -

_____

↓

_____

- - - - - - - - - - - -

_____

= [_____]

11

Subtracting by Making a 10

$$18 - 15 =$$

↓ decompose

_____

- - - - - - - - - - - -

_____

↓

_____

- - - - - - - - - - - -

_____

= [_____]

12

Subtracting by Making a 10

$$14 - 6 =$$

↓ decompose

_____

- - - - - - - - - - - -

_____

↓

_____

- - - - - - - - - - - -

_____

= [_____]

13

Subtracting by Making a 10   # 19 − 14 =

↓ decompose

_____

- - - - - - - - - -

_____

↓

- - - - - - - - - -

_____   =   [_____]

14

Subtracting by Making a 10   # 17 − 8 =

↓ decompose

_____

- - - - - - - - - -

_____

↓

- - - - - - - - - -

_____   =   [_____]

15

Subtracting by Making a 10   # 13 − 8 =

↓ decompose

_____

- - - - - - - - - -

_____

↓

- - - - - - - - - -

_____   =   [_____]

Math Fluency Activities for K–2 Teachers

16

Subtracting by Making a 10

$$11 - 4 =$$

↓ decompose

_____

- - - - - - - - - - - - - - - -

_____

↓

- - - - - - - - - - - - - - - -

_____

= [   ]

17

Subtracting by Making a 10

$$13 - 5 =$$

↓ decompose

_____

- - - - - - - - - - - - - - - -

_____

↓

- - - - - - - - - - - - - - - -

_____

= [   ]

18

Subtracting by Making a 10

$$11 - 7 =$$

↓ decompose

_____

- - - - - - - - - - - - - - - -

_____

↓

- - - - - - - - - - - - - - - -

_____

= [   ]

19

Subtracting by Making a 10

17 − 12 =

↓ decompose

_____

- - - - - - - - - - - - - - - - - -

_____

↓

- - - - - - - - - - - - - - - - - -

_____

= | _____ |
    | - - - - - |
    | _____ |

20

Subtracting by Making a 10

18 − 13 =

↓ decompose

_____

- - - - - - - - - - - - - - - - - -

_____

↓

- - - - - - - - - - - - - - - - - -

_____

= | _____ |
    | - - - - - |
    | _____ |

ANSWER KEY:
Subtracting by Counting Down to 10

QUESTION	ANSWER
1.	8
2.	3
3.	8
4.	4
5.	5
6.	6
7.	3
8.	7
9.	9
10.	4

QUESTION	ANSWER
11.	3
12.	8
13.	5
14.	9
15.	5
16.	7
17.	8
18.	4
19.	5
20.	5

Using Doubles

> **OBJECTIVE:** Students decompose numbers leading to doubles in order to find the solutions to number sentences. Make sure concrete and representational strategies are mastered before moving to an abstract strategy.

MATERIALS NEEDED: Task cards

DIRECTIONS: Copy or project the task cards. This activity will be an extension of grade 1, Activity 9 (Using Doubles). If an intervention is needed prior to this activity, step back to this activity in grade 1. Show several examples before using the task cards. For example, in the problem below, 11 (the second addend) was decomposed to $8 + 3$. Now we can make a double by adding the 8 to the first addend, 8, to make 16. Now addition is easy. We know double 8s have a sum of 16, so 16 + the leftover 3 is 19.

EXAMPLE

Add by Using Doubles

What is $8 + 11$?

$$8 + 11$$

$$8 + 3$$

$$8 + 8 + 3$$

$$16 + 3 = 19$$

> Doubles are easier facts to remember. Decompose one number to make a double. Add the doubles and then the rest.

1

Add by Using Doubles

$$11 + 9 =$$

↓ decompose

$$2 + 9 + 9$$

↓

$$2 + 18 \quad = \quad \boxed{}$$

2

Add by Using Doubles

$$13 + 5 =$$

↓ decompose

$$8 + 5 + 5$$

↓

$$\underline{} \quad = \quad \boxed{}$$

3

Add by Using Doubles

$$5 + 12 =$$

↓ decompose

$$5 + 5 + 7$$

↓

$$\underline{} \quad = \quad \boxed{}$$

4

Add by Using Doubles

$$6 + 13 =$$

↓ decompose

$$6 + 6 + 7$$

↓

_____

- - - - - - - - - - -

_____

= [ ]

5

Add by Using Doubles

$$12 + 7 =$$

↓ decompose

$$5 + 7 + 7$$

↓

_____

- - - - - - - - - - -

_____

= [ ]

6

Add by Using Doubles

$$16 + 4 =$$

↓ decompose

$$12 + 4 + 4$$

↓

_____

- - - - - - - - - - -

_____

= [ ]

Math Fluency Activities for K–2 Teachers

7

Add by Using Doubles

$$11 + 8 =$$

↓ decompose

_____

- - - - - - - - - - - -

_____

↓

_____

- - - - - - - - - - - -

_____

= [_____]

8

Add by Using Doubles

$$12 + 6 =$$

↓ decompose

_____

- - - - - - - - - - - -

_____

↓

_____

- - - - - - - - - - - -

_____

= [_____]

9

Add by Using Doubles

$$14 + 6 =$$

↓ decompose

_____

- - - - - - - - - - - -

_____

↓

_____

- - - - - - - - - - - -

_____

= [_____]

10

Add by Using Doubles

$$7 + 14 =$$

decompose

$$=$$

11

Add by Using Doubles

$$9 + 5 =$$

decompose

$$=$$

12

Add by Using Doubles

$$12 + 4 =$$

decompose

$$=$$

Math Fluency Activities for K–2 Teachers

13

Add by Using Doubles

$$11 + 7 =$$

↓ decompose

↓

=

14

Add by Using Doubles

$$11 + 7 =$$

↓ decompose

↓

=

15

Add by Using Doubles

$$5 + 14 =$$

↓ decompose

↓

=

16

Add by Using Doubles

$$5 + 15 =$$

↓ decompose

↓

=

17

Add by Using Doubles

$$6 + 12 =$$

↓ decompose

↓

=

18

Add by Using Doubles

$$8 + 12 =$$

↓ decompose

↓

=

Math Fluency Activities for K–2 Teachers

19

Add by Using Doubles

$$4 + 11 =$$

_____

- - - - - - - - - - - - - -

_____

_____

- - - - - - - - - - - - - - = $\boxed{}$

_____

20

Add by Using Doubles

$$8 + 9 =$$

_____

- - - - - - - - - - - - - -

_____

- - - - - - - - - - - - - - = $\boxed{}$

_____

ANSWER KEY:
Using Doubles

QUESTION	ANSWER		QUESTION	ANSWER
1.	20		11.	14
2.	18		12.	16
3.	17		13.	18
4.	19		14.	18
5.	19		15.	19
6.	20		16.	20
7.	19		17.	18
8.	18		18.	20
9.	20		19.	15
10.	21		20.	17

Related Addition Facts

OBJECTIVE: Students use number bonds to see the relationship between addition and subtraction. Using their understanding of part-part-whole, students write related number sentences. Once all task cards have been solved, discuss and share results.

MATERIALS NEEDED: Task cards

DIRECTIONS: Copy or project the task cards for the whole class. This activity is an extension from grade 1. If you need an intervention prior to this activity, please see Activity 10 in grade 1. Show several examples before using the task cards. In the example below, we have a whole of 13 with parts of 4 and 9. Look for the relationship between the three numbers using addition and subtraction. Our related facts are shown below. This activity is ideal for helping students see the whole and learn how to find a missing part or find the whole when you know both parts.

EXAMPLE

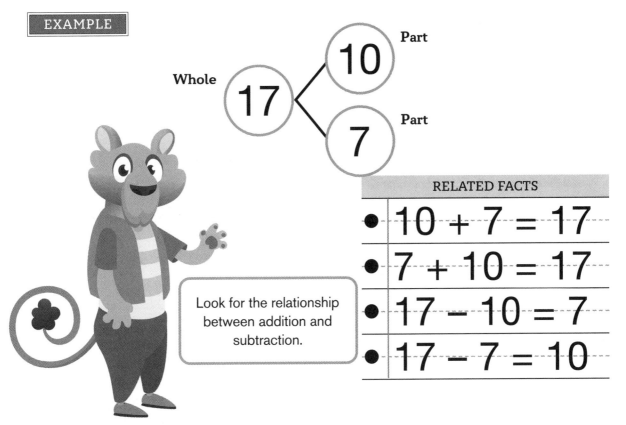

Whole

Part

10

17

Part

7

Look for the relationship between addition and subtraction.

RELATED FACTS

- $10 + 7 = 17$
- $7 + 10 = 17$
- $17 - 10 = 7$
- $17 - 7 = 10$

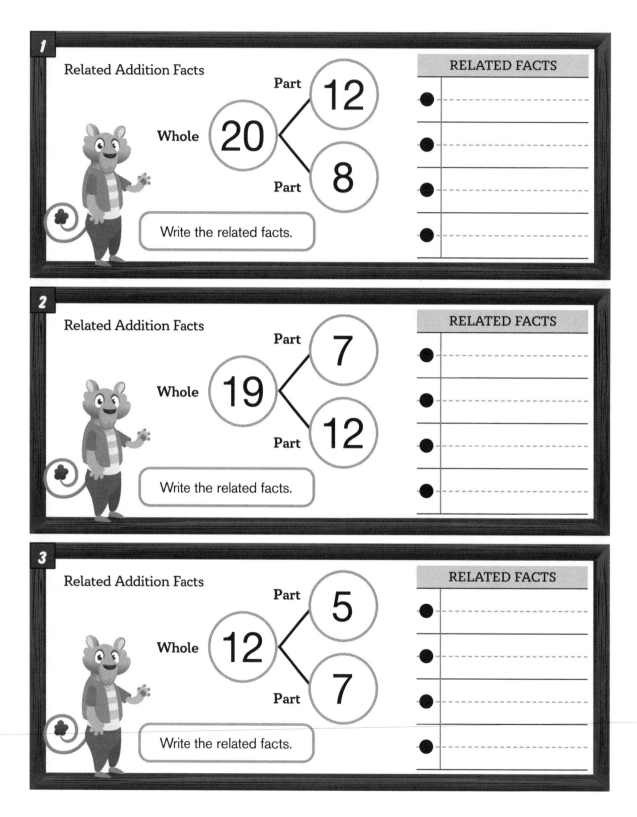

1 Related Addition Facts

Whole **20**

Part **12**

Part **8**

Write the related facts.

RELATED FACTS

- _____
- _____
- _____
- _____

2 Related Addition Facts

Whole **19**

Part **7**

Part **12**

Write the related facts.

RELATED FACTS

- _____
- _____
- _____
- _____

3 Related Addition Facts

Whole **12**

Part **5**

Part **7**

Write the related facts.

RELATED FACTS

- _____
- _____
- _____
- _____

Math Fluency Activities for K–2 Teachers

4

Related Addition Facts

Whole **12**

Part **11**

Part **1**

Write the related facts.

RELATED FACTS

5

Related Addition Facts

Whole **15**

Part **4**

Part **11**

Write the related facts.

RELATED FACTS

6

Related Addition Facts

Whole **16**

Part **11**

Part **5**

Write the related facts.

RELATED FACTS

7

Related Addition Facts

Part **6**

Whole **18**

Part **12**

Write the related facts.

8

Related Addition Facts

17

15

2

Write the related facts.

9

Related Addition Facts

Part **6**

Whole **19**

Part **13**

Write the related facts.

Math Fluency Activities for K–2 Teachers

10 Related Addition Facts

Part: **14**
Whole: **20**
Part: **6**

Write the related facts.

- _____
- _____
- _____
- _____

---

11 Related Addition Facts

Part: **4**
Whole: **12**
Part: **?**

Write the related facts.

- _____
- _____
- _____
- _____

---

12 Related Addition Facts

Part: **?**
Whole: **18**
Part: **5**

Write the related facts.

- _____
- _____
- _____
- _____

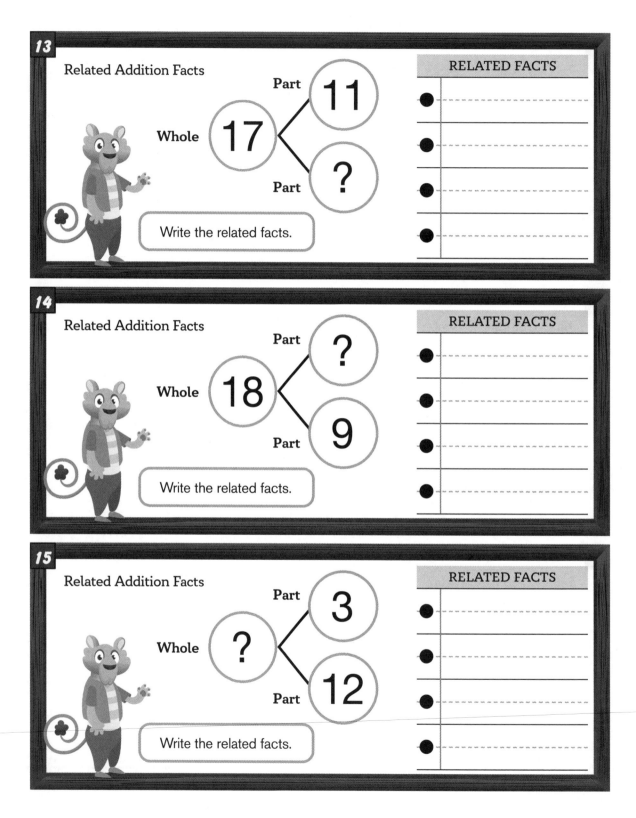

13

Related Addition Facts

Whole **17**

Part **11**

Part **?**

Write the related facts.

RELATED FACTS

14

Related Addition Facts

Whole **18**

Part **?**

Part **9**

Write the related facts.

RELATED FACTS

15

Related Addition Facts

Whole **?**

Part **3**

Part **12**

Write the related facts.

RELATED FACTS

16

Related Addition Facts

Part: ?
Whole: 19
Part: 17

Write the related facts.

RELATED FACTS

17

Related Addition Facts

Part: 2
Whole: 13
Part: ?

Write the related facts.

RELATED FACTS

18

Related Addition Facts

Part: 14
Whole: ?
Part: 2

Write the related facts.

RELATED FACTS

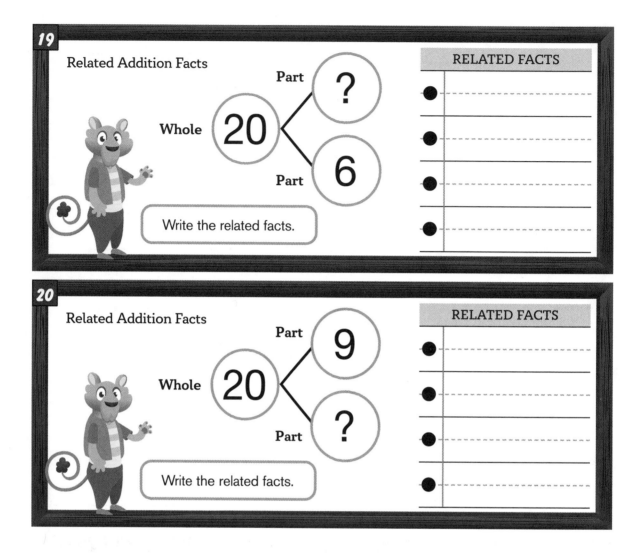

19

Related Addition Facts

Part

?

Whole **20**

Part **6**

Write the related facts.

RELATED FACTS

20

Related Addition Facts

Part **9**

Whole **20**

Part **?**

Write the related facts.

RELATED FACTS

ANSWER KEY:
Related Addition Facts

QUESTION	RELATED FACTS			
1.	$20 = 12 + 8$	$20 = 8 + 12$	$20 - 8 = 12$	$20 - 12 = 8$
2.	$19 = 12 + 7$	$19 = 7 + 12$	$19 - 7 = 12$	$19 - 12 = 7$
3.	$12 = 7 + 5$	$12 = 5 + 7$	$12 - 5 = 7$	$12 - 7 = 5$
4.	$12 = 11 + 1$	$12 = 1 + 11$	$12 - 1 = 11$	$12 - 11 = 1$
5.	$15 = 4 + 11$	$15 = 11 + 4$	$15 - 4 = 11$	$15 - 11 = 4$
6.	$16 = 5 + 11$	$16 = 11 + 5$	$16 - 11 = 5$	$16 - 5 = 11$
7.	$18 = 6 + 12$	$18 = 12 + 6$	$18 - 6 = 12$	$18 - 12 = 6$
8.	$17 = 15 + 2$	$17 = 2 + 15$	$17 - 2 = 15$	$17 - 15 = 2$
9.	$19 = 13 + 6$	$19 = 6 + 13$	$19 - 6 = 13$	$19 - 13 = 6$
10.	$20 = 14 + 6$	$20 = 6 + 14$	$20 - 6 = 14$	$20 - 14 = 6$
11.	$12 = 8 + 4$	$12 = 4 + 8$	$12 - 4 = 8$	$12 - 8 = 4$
12.	$18 = 13 + 5$	$18 = 5 + 13$	$18 - 5 = 13$	$18 - 13 = 5$
13.	$17 = 11 + 6$	$17 = 6 + 11$	$17 - 6 = 11$	$17 - 11 = 6$
14.	$18 = 9 + 9$	$18 = 9 + 9$	$18 - 9 = 9$	$18 - 9 = 9$
15.	$15 = 3 + 12$	$15 = 12 + 3$	$15 - 12 = 3$	$15 - 3 = 12$
16.	$19 = 17 + 2$	$19 = 2 + 17$	$19 - 2 = 17$	$19 - 17 = 2$
17.	$13 = 2 + 11$	$13 = 11 + 2$	$13 - 11 = 2$	$13 - 2 = 11$
18.	$16 = 14 + 2$	$16 = 2 + 14$	$16 - 2 = 14$	$16 - 14 = 2$
19.	$20 = 14 + 6$	$20 = 6 + 14$	$20 - 6 = 14$	$20 - 14 = 6$
20.	$20 = 9 + 11$	$20 = 11 + 9$	$20 - 11 = 9$	$20 - 9 = 11$

Representing Addition with Place Value Strips

OBJECTIVE: Use place value strips to help you add.

MATERIALS NEEDED: Task cards

DIRECTIONS: Copy and cut out the task cards. Students can work alone or in groups to solve the place value problem. I prefer to use mini place value strips so each student or group of students has their own set.

Construct the number using your place value strips. Set them next to the card so that you can fill in the correct numbers in both standard and expanded form. In the example below, this would be 80 + 6 (86) and 10 + 3 (13). Add from expanded form, showing and explaining your work. Write your steps and solution on the blank place value strips. Be prepared to discuss and share your results. Use the example provided to show students how to use place value strips to find the answer to the subtraction problem.

EXAMPLE

Representing Addition with Place Value Strips

86 + 13

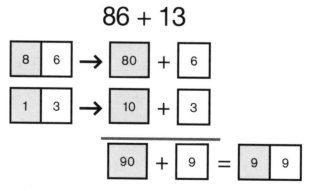

Use your place value cards to show both 86 and 13 in standard form.

Line up both numbers in a vertical format in expanded form. Add the numbers in the ones place (6 + 3 = 9) and place the sum below in the ones place. Next, add the numbers in the tens column and place the sum below in the tens place (80 +10 = 90 or 9 tens). 86 + 13 = 99. You can see this by putting the strips back in standard form.

1

Representing Addition with Place Value Strips

72 + 21

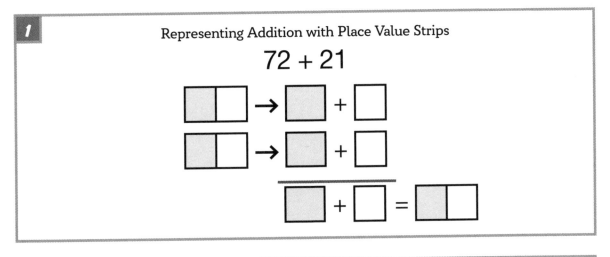

2

Representing Addition with Place Value Strips

63 + 25

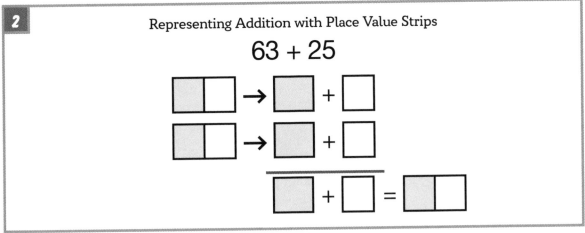

3

Representing Addition with Place Value Strips

43 + 26

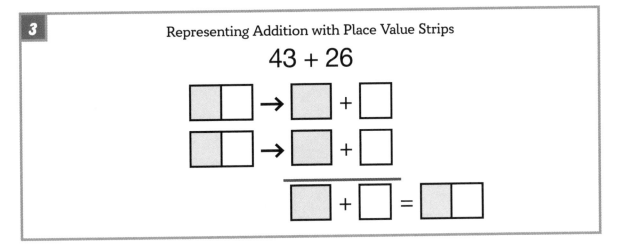

4

Representing Addition with Place Value Strips
62 + 16

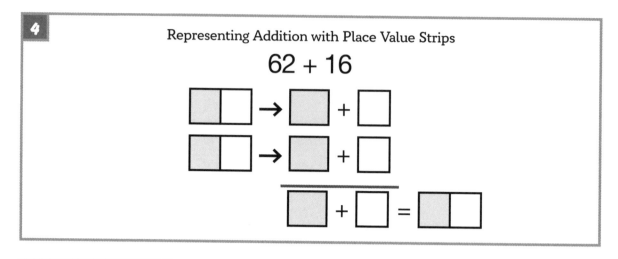

5

Representing Addition with Place Value Strips
52 + 34

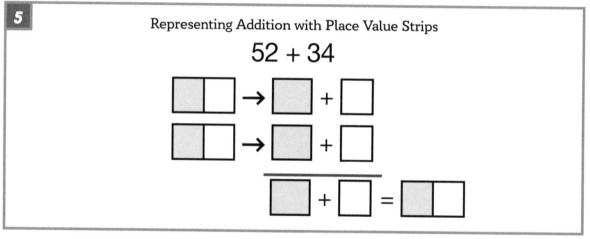

6

Representing Addition with Place Value Strips
81 + 16

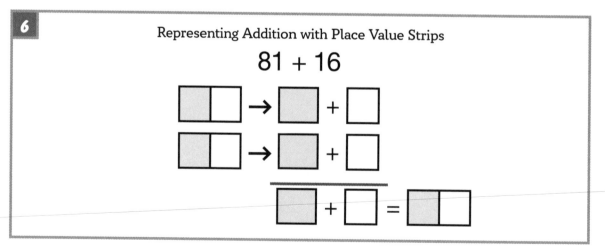

Math Fluency Activities for K–2 Teachers

7

Representing Addition with Place Value Strips

33 + 31

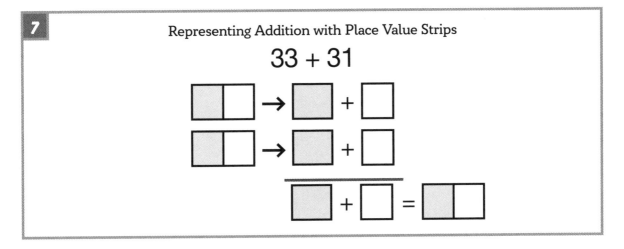

8

Representing Addition with Place Value Strips

17 + 52

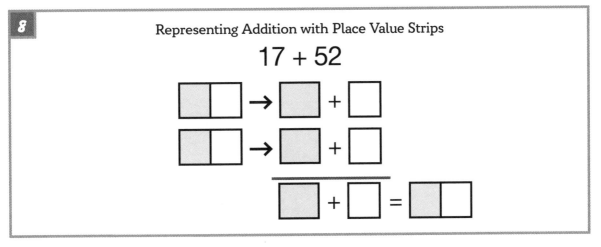

9

Representing Addition with Place Value Strips

67 + 21

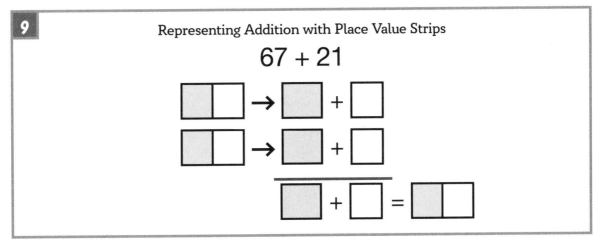

Representing Addition with Place Value Strips

26 + 12

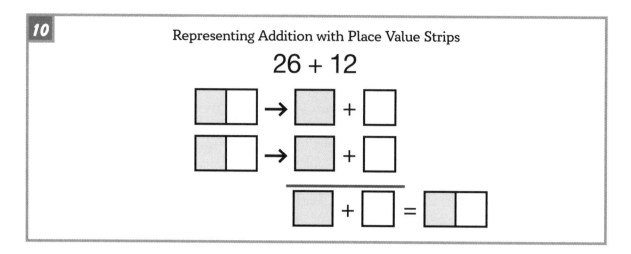

Representing Addition with Place Value Strips

58 + 30

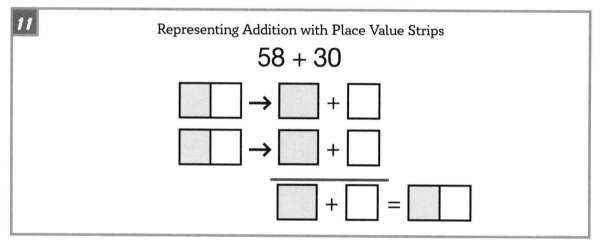

Representing Addition with Place Value Strips

77 + 21

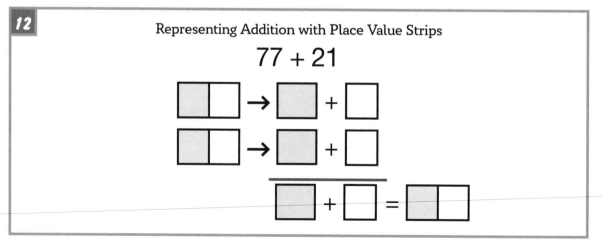

Math Fluency Activities for K–2 Teachers

13

Representing Addition with Place Value Strips

55 + 34

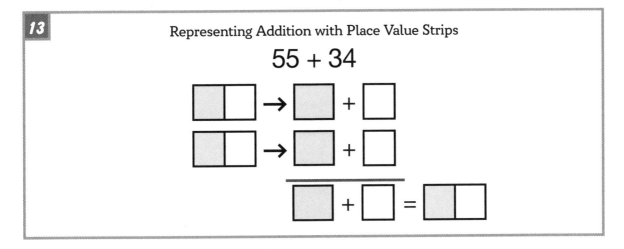

14

Representing Addition with Place Value Strips

92 + 7

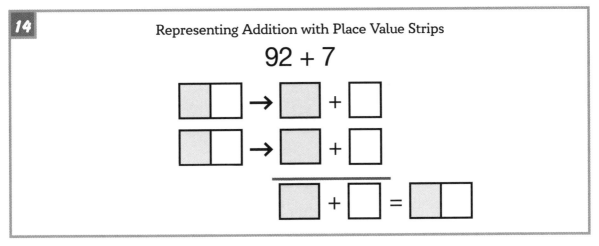

15

Representing Addition with Place Value Strips

63 + 26

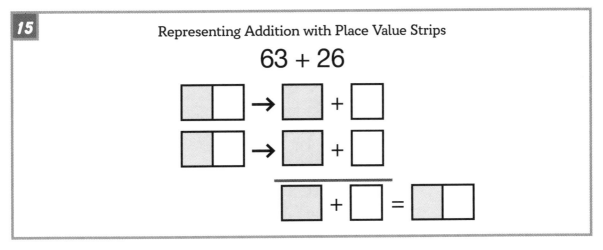

16

Representing Addition with Place Value Strips

32 + 25

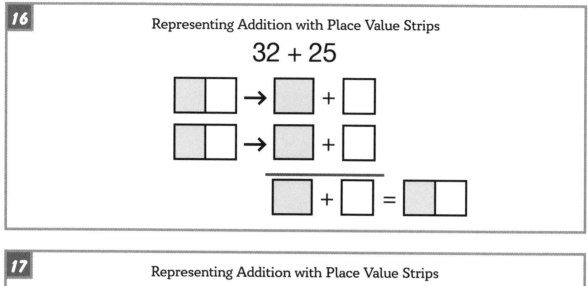

17

Representing Addition with Place Value Strips

24 + 21

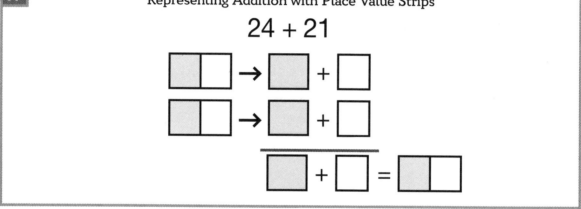

18

Representing Addition with Place Value Strips

16 + 13

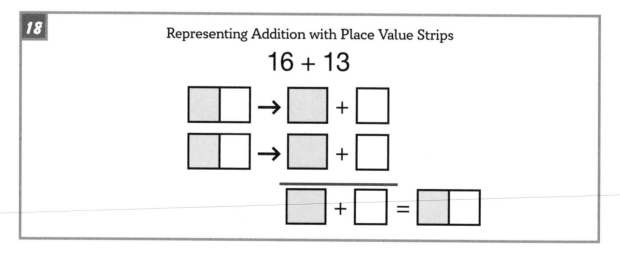

Representing Addition with Place Value Strips

66 + 23

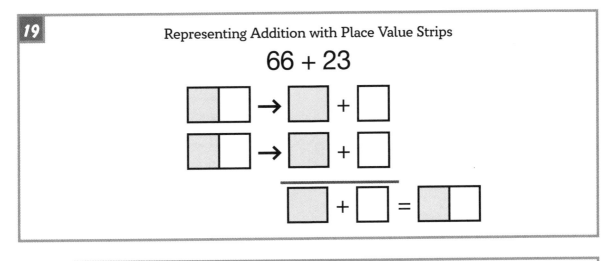

Representing Addition with Place Value Strips

71 + 28

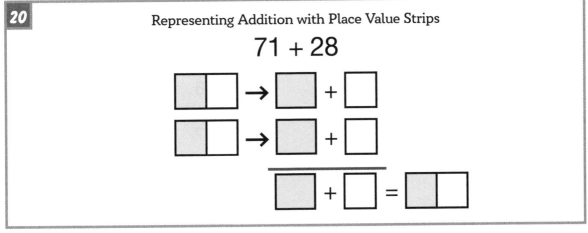

ANSWER KEY:
Representing Addition with Place Value Strips

QUESTION	ANSWER	QUESTION	ANSWER
1.	93	11.	88
2.	88	12.	98
3.	69	13.	89
4.	78	14.	99
5.	86	15.	89
6.	97	16.	57
7.	64	17.	45
8.	69	18.	29
9.	88	19.	89
10.	38	20.	99

Math Fluency Activities for K–2 Teachers

Representing Addition with Regrouping

MATERIALS NEEDED: Task cards

DIRECTIONS: Copy and cut out the task cards. Students can work alone or in groups to solve the place value problem. I prefer to use mini place value strips so each student or group of students has their own set.

Construct the numbers in both standard and expanded form using place value strips. Placing the strips near the task cards is a great visual method of learning to add numbers. Use the strips to show both standard and expanded form. Completely fill in the blank place value cards both in standard and expanded form, mirroring your place value strips. Add from expanded form, showing and explaining your work. Write your steps and solution on the blank place value strips. Be prepared to discuss and share your results. Use the example provided to show students how to use place value strips to find the answer to the addition problem.

EXAMPLE

Representing Addition with Regrouping

89 + 43

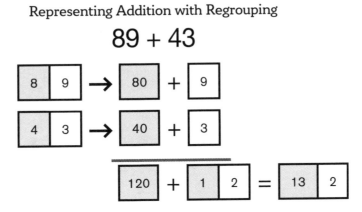

Use your place value cards to show both 89 and 43 in standard form.

Line up both numbers in a vertical format in expanded form. Add the numbers in the ones place (9 + 3 = 12 or 1 ten and 2 ones) and place the sum below in the ones place. Next, add the numbers in the tens column and place the sum below in the tens place. In the tens place we have 80 + 40 = 120, or 1 hundred and 2 tens. To find the sum, I add 100 + 20 + 10 + 2 = 132. Or, use your strips to put the numbers in standard form.

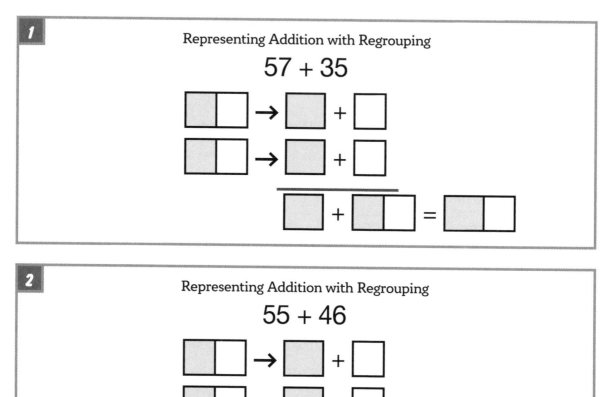

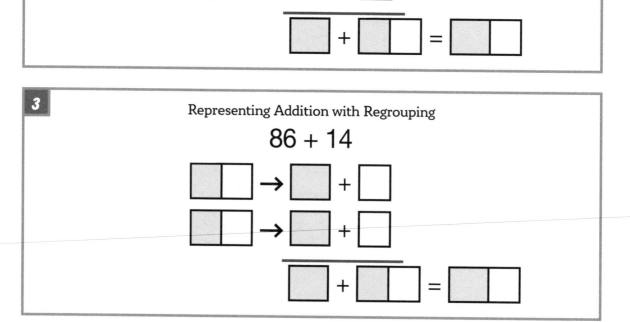

Math Fluency Activities for K–2 Teachers

4 Representing Addition with Regrouping

63 + 28

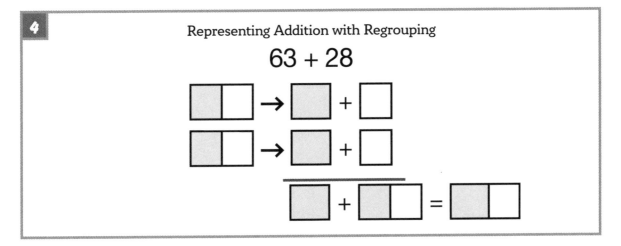

5 Representing Addition with Regrouping

29 + 34

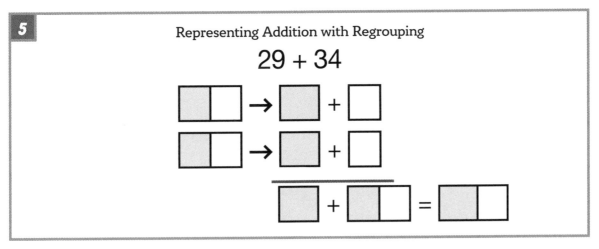

6 Representing Addition with Regrouping

44 + 28

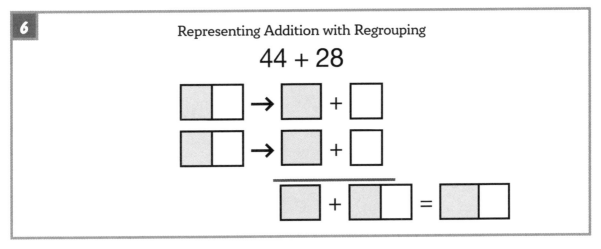

7

Representing Addition with Regrouping

17 + 19

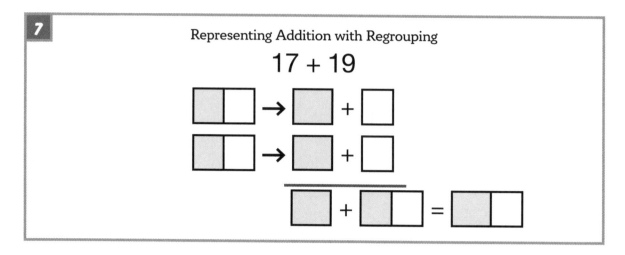

8

Representing Addition with Regrouping

75 + 26

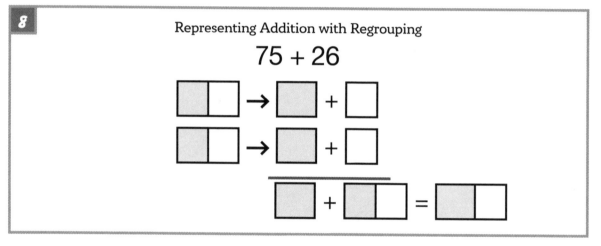

9

Representing Addition with Regrouping

87 + 24

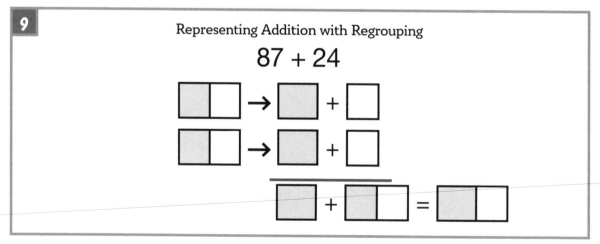

Math Fluency Activities for K–2 Teachers

Representing Addition with Regrouping

35 + 28

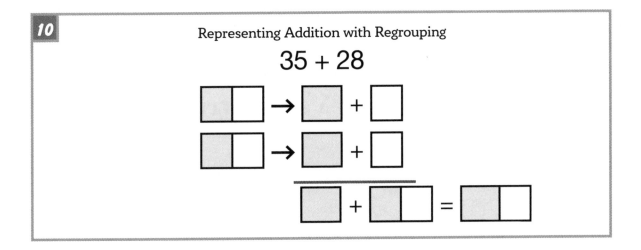

ANSWER KEY:
Representing Addition With Regrouping

QUESTION	ANSWER
1.	92
2.	101
3.	100
4.	91
5.	63

QUESTION	ANSWER
6.	72
7.	36
8.	101
9.	111
10.	63

Representing Subtraction with Place Value Strips

OBJECTIVE: Use place value strips to help you subtract.

MATERIALS NEEDED: Task cards

DIRECTIONS: Copy and cut out the task cards. Students can work alone or in groups to solve the place value problem. I prefer to use mini place value strips so each student or group of students has their own set.

Use your place value strips to construct the numbers being subtracted. In the example, you would make 58 and 45 in standard form. Set these cards next to the task cards to show how they help you write the numbers in expanded form. Use the place value strips to show how they help you completely fill in the solution on the blank task cards. Subtract from expanded form, showing and explaining your work. Write the solution on the blank place value strips provided. Be prepared to discuss and share your results. Use the example provided to show students how to use place value strips to find the answer to the subtraction problem.

EXAMPLE

Representing Subtraction with Place Value Strips

58 – 45

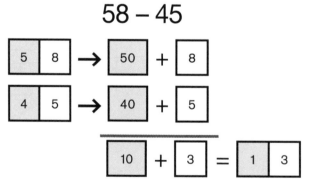

Use your place value cards to show both 58 and 45 in standard form.

Line up both numbers in a vertical format in expanded form. Subtract the numbers in the ones place (8 – 5 = 3) and place the difference below in the ones place. Next, subtract the numbers in the tens column and place the difference below in the tens place (50 – 40 = 10). Finally put the strips back in standard form to find the difference of 13.

1

Representing Subtraction with Place Value Strips

78 − 25

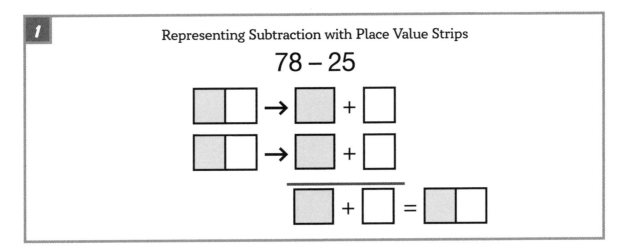

2

Representing Subtraction with Place Value Strips

57 − 36

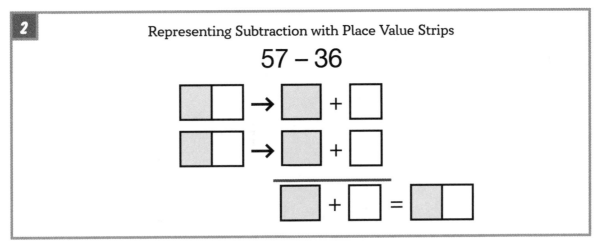

3

Representing Subtraction with Place Value Strips

89 − 13

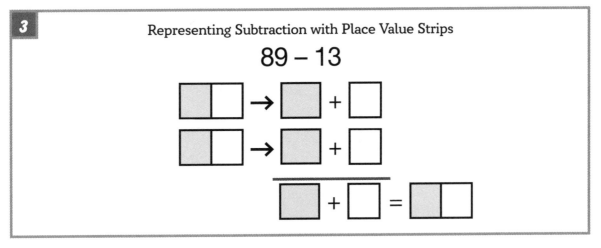

4

Representing Subtraction with Place Value Strips

67 – 26

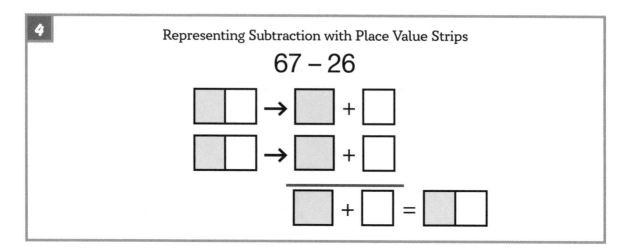

5

Representing Subtraction with Place Value Strips

43 – 22

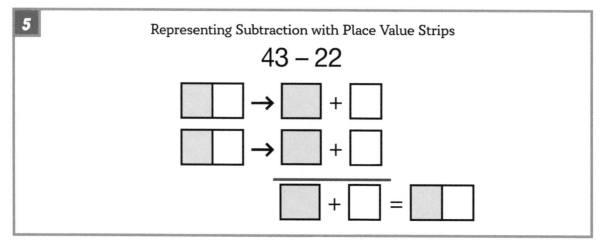

6

Representing Subtraction with Place Value Strips

63 – 21

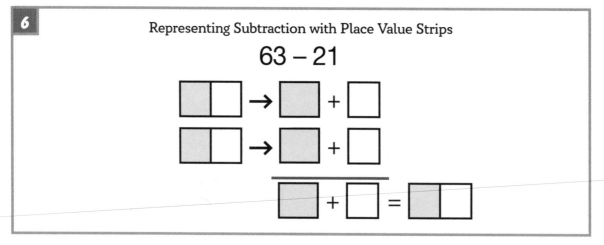

7

Representing Subtraction with Place Value Strips

49 – 32

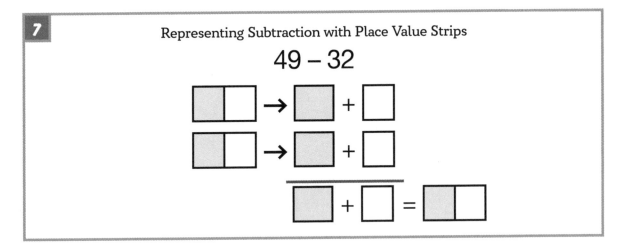

8

Representing Subtraction with Place Value Strips

78 – 54

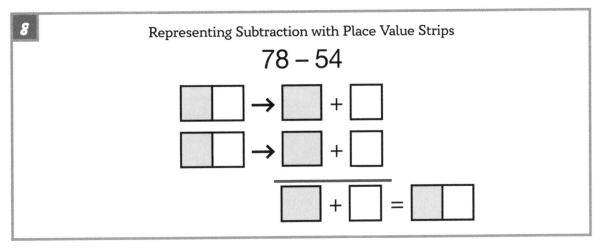

9

Representing Subtraction with Place Value Strips

88 – 56

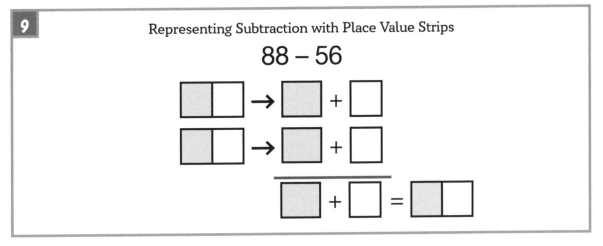

Representing Subtraction with Place Value Strips

27 – 15

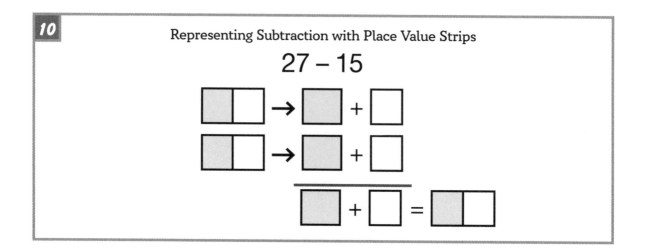

ANSWER KEY:
Representing Subtraction with Place Value Strips

QUESTION	ANSWER
1.	53
2.	21
3.	76
4.	41
5.	21

QUESTION	ANSWER
6.	42
7.	17
8.	24
9.	32
10.	12

Representing Subtraction with Regrouping

> OBJECTIVE: Use place value strips to help you subtract.

MATERIALS NEEDED: Task cards

DIRECTIONS: Copy and cut out the task cards. Students can work alone or in groups to solve the place value problem. I prefer to use mini place value strips so each student or group of students have their own set. Construct the numbers on the strips in standard form, and set these strips near the task card to help you write the number in standard and expanded form. This will help your students visualize subtraction. Completely fill in the solution on the task card using your place value strips as a guide. Write the numbers first in standard form, then expanded form. Displaying numbers in expanded form will help you visualize the subtraction and help find the difference between the two numbers. Subtract from expanded form, showing and explaining your work. Write your steps and solution on the blank place value strips. Be prepared to discuss and share your results. Use the example provided to show students how to use place value strips to find the answer to the subtraction problem.

EXAMPLE

Representing Subtraction with Regrouping

51 – 26

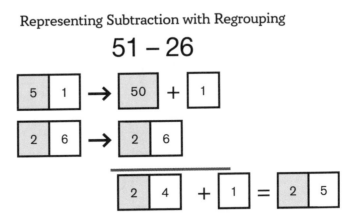

Use your place value cards to show both 51 and 26 in standard form.

Line up both numbers in a vertical format in expanded form. We will not have enough ones to subtract 6 ones in 26 from 1 one in 51. In order to subtract, we move the 6 ones to the tens column and simply place the 1 below without subtracting. Now we look at the tens place and we see we have 5 tens, or 50, and we will subtract 2 tens and 6 ones, or 26. 50 – 20 = 30 and we have to remove 6 more. 30 – 6 = 24. Once we place the 2 tens and 4 ones with the remaining 1, we can add in expanded form. 20 + 4 + 1 = 25, our difference.

1

Representing Subtraction with Regrouping

54 – 38

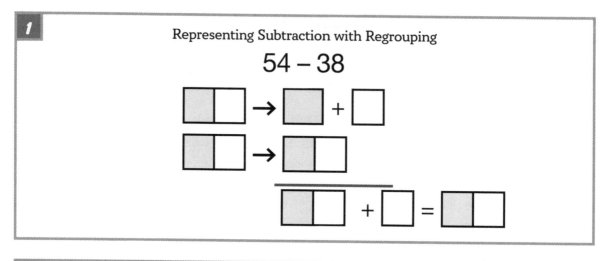

2

Representing Subtraction with Regrouping

62 – 16

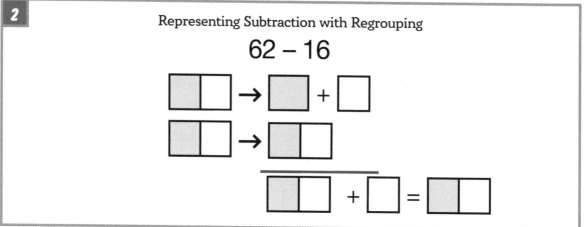

3

Representing Subtraction with Regrouping

22 – 16

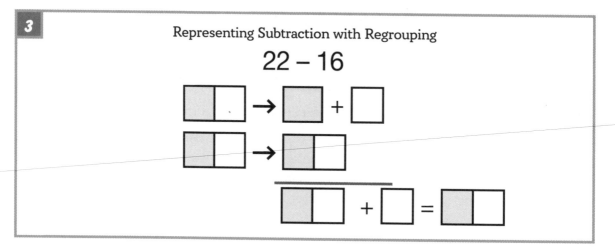

Representing Subtraction with Regrouping

91 − 34

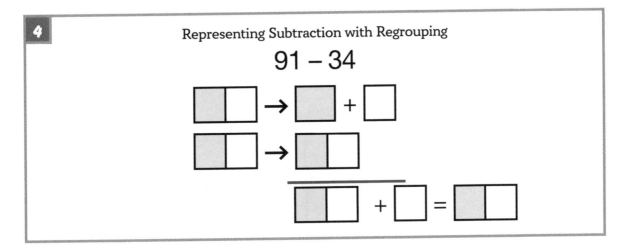

Representing Subtraction with Regrouping

156 − 38

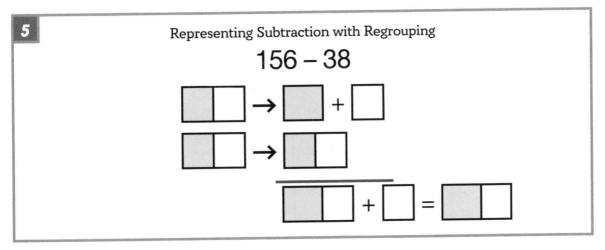

Representing Subtraction with Regrouping

74 − 48

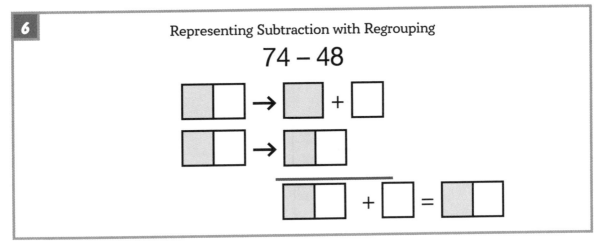

7 Representing Subtraction with Regrouping

64 − 27

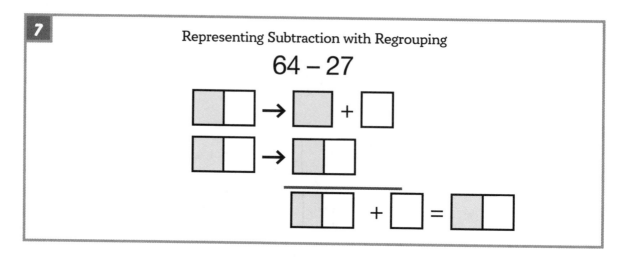

8 Representing Subtraction with Regrouping

145 − 18

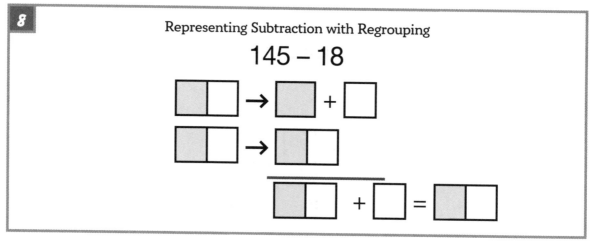

9 Representing Subtraction with Regrouping

88 − 59

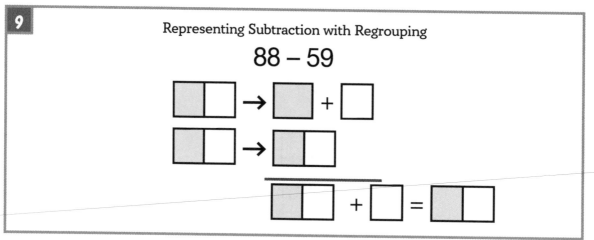

Math Fluency Activities for K–2 Teachers

Representing Subtraction with Regrouping

46 – 29

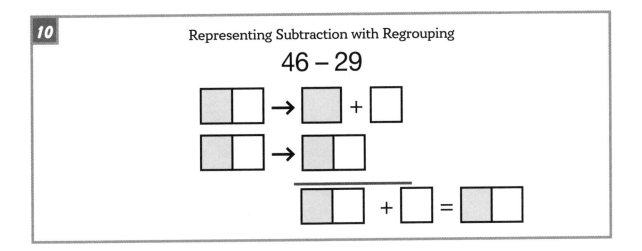

ANSWER KEY:
Representing Subtraction with Regrouping

QUESTION	ANSWER
1.	16
2.	46
3.	6
4.	57
5.	118

QUESTION	ANSWER
6.	26
7.	37
8.	127
9.	29
10.	17

Show Me the Number

OBJECTIVE: Following a solid understanding of place value, students will represent whole numbers using place value strips and then find the final value of a number based on specific numerical operations performed on the number.

MATERIALS NEEDED: Task cards

DIRECTIONS: Copy and cut out the task cards. Use your place value strips to show the number at the start of the train. As the train moves down the track, numbers are added (In) or subtracted (Out).

EXAMPLE

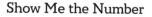

Show Me the Number

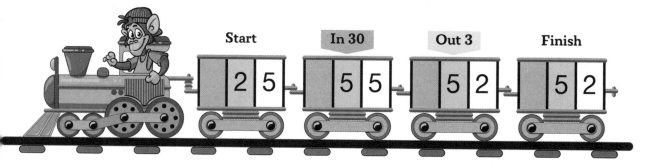

Use your place value strips to show the changes.

Record your number after each change on the place value strip provided, in standard form. Record your final number, in standard form, on the last train. Be ready to discuss and share your results. In the example above, we start with the number 25 in standard form. We add 30 (using our place value strips) to 25 to get 55, and then subtract 3 for a final value of 52. We can show this using our place value strips as we solve each step of the problem.

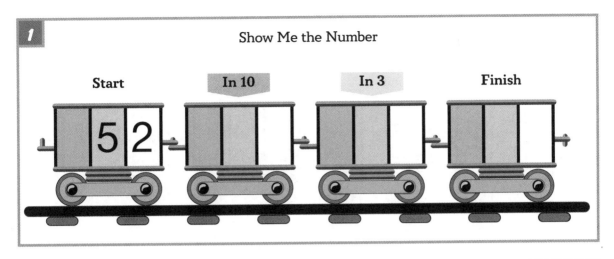

1 Show Me the Number

Start   In 10   In 3   Finish

5 2

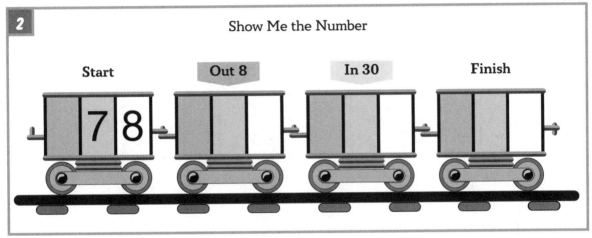

2 Show Me the Number

Start   Out 8   In 30   Finish

7 8

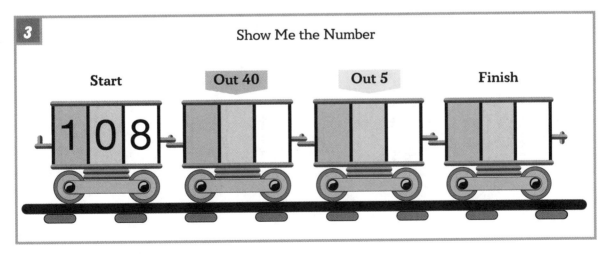

3 Show Me the Number

Start   Out 40   Out 5   Finish

1 0 8

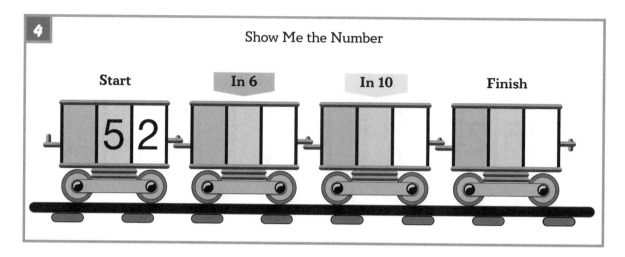

4. Show Me the Number

Start — 5 2 | In 6 | In 10 | Finish

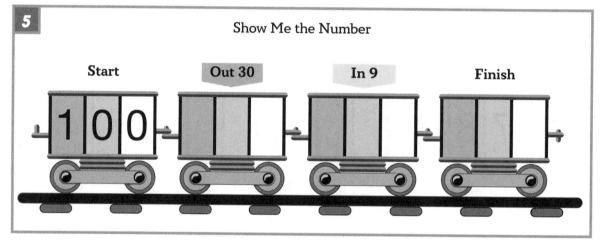

5. Show Me the Number

Start — 1 0 0 | Out 30 | In 9 | Finish

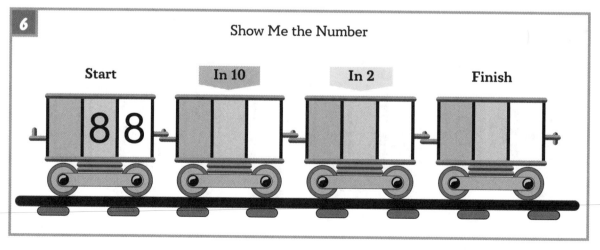

6. Show Me the Number

Start — 8 8 | In 10 | In 2 | Finish

Math Fluency Activities for K–2 Teachers

7

Show Me the Number

Start   Out 7   In 20   Finish

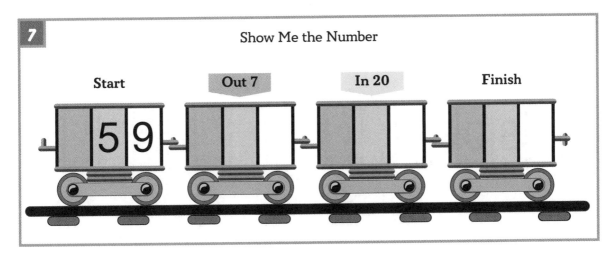

8

Show Me the Number

Start   In 40   In 7   Finish

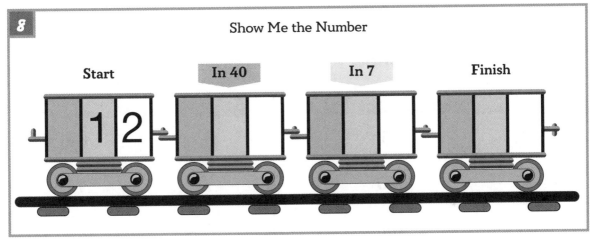

9

Show Me the Number

Start   Out 30   In 5   Finish

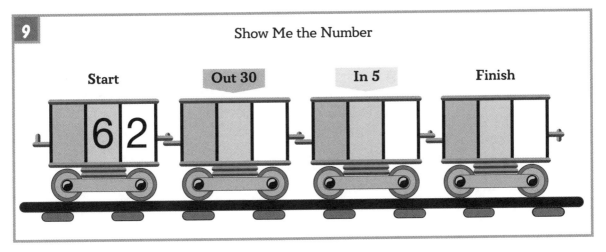

Show Me the Number

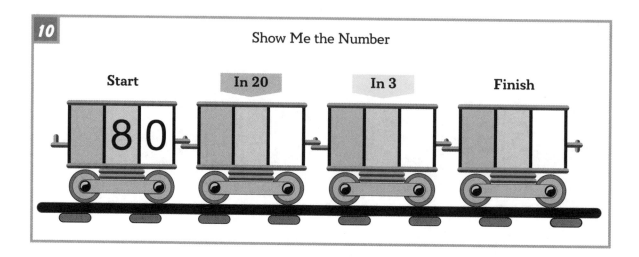

Start   In 20   In 3   Finish

ANSWER KEY:
Show Me the Number

QUESTION	ANSWER
1.	65
2.	100
3.	63
4.	68
5.	79

QUESTION	ANSWER
6.	100
7.	72
8.	59
9.	37
10.	103

Mystery Numbers

> OBJECTIVE: Use place value strips to help you find the missing number.

MATERIALS NEEDED: Task cards

DIRECTIONS: Copy and cut out the task cards. Students can work alone or in groups to solve the place value problem. I prefer to use mini place value strips so each student or group of students can have their own set. Write the solution on the blank place value strips. Be prepared to discuss and share your results.

EXAMPLE

Mystery Numbers

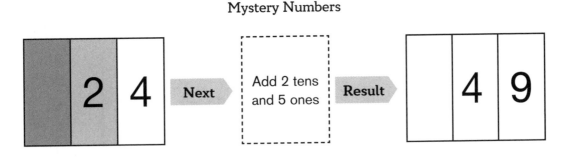

Use place value strips to help you find the mystery number. In the example shown, we start with the number 24. In expanded form, this requires selecting the strip that shows 2 tens, or 20. Place on top of the ones strip the 4 ones. Now we have the number 24. To find the mystery number, you must add an additional 2 tens, or 20, and 5 ones. When you add 2 more tens and 5 ones to the original number of 24, you have a result of 49, the mystery number.

1

Mystery Numbers

6 5 → Next → Add 2 tens and then add 4 ones → Result

2

Mystery Numbers

2 3 → Next → Double it and add 2 tens and 1 one → Result

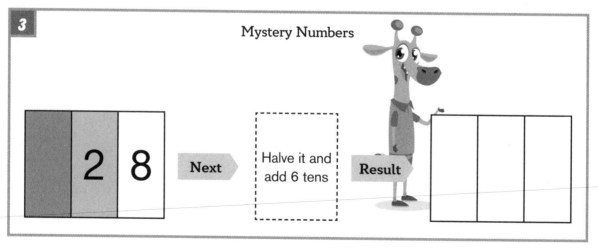

3

Mystery Numbers

2 8 → Next → Halve it and add 6 tens → Result

4   Mystery Numbers

| 5 | 2 | **Next** | Add 4 tens and 8 ones | **Result** | | | |

5   Mystery Numbers

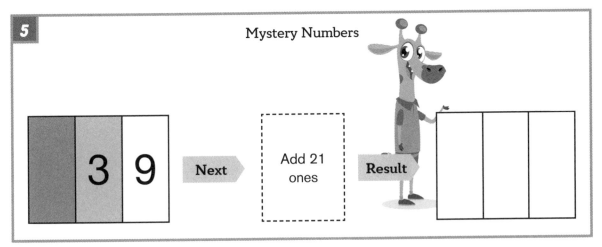

| 3 | 9 | **Next** | Add 21 ones | **Result** | | | |

6   Mystery Numbers

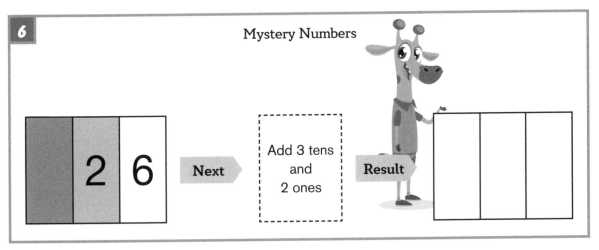

| 2 | 6 | **Next** | Add 3 tens and 2 ones | **Result** | | | |

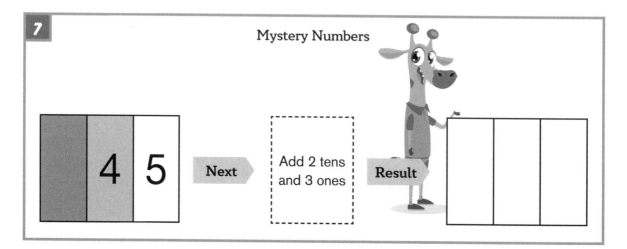

7 Mystery Numbers

4 5 → Next → Add 2 tens and 3 ones → Result

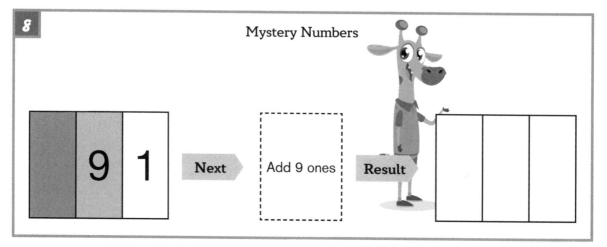

8 Mystery Numbers

9 1 → Next → Add 9 ones → Result

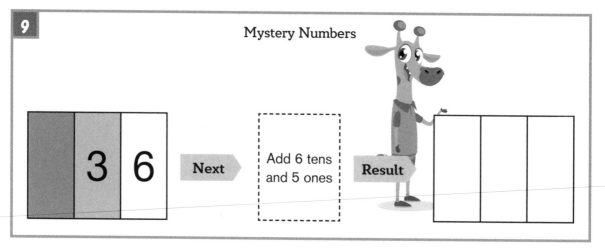

9 Mystery Numbers

3 6 → Next → Add 6 tens and 5 ones → Result

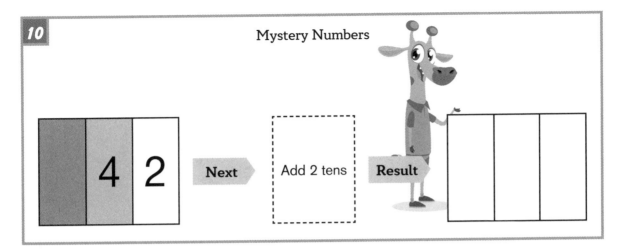

10

Mystery Numbers

| 4 | 2 |

Next

Add 2 tens

Result

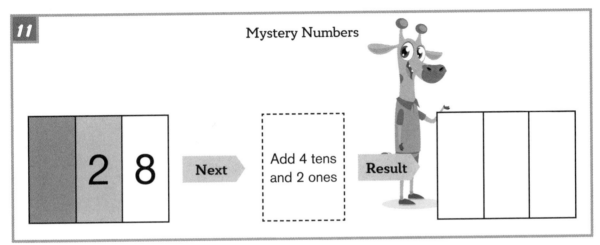

11

Mystery Numbers

| 2 | 8 |

Next

Add 4 tens
and 2 ones

Result

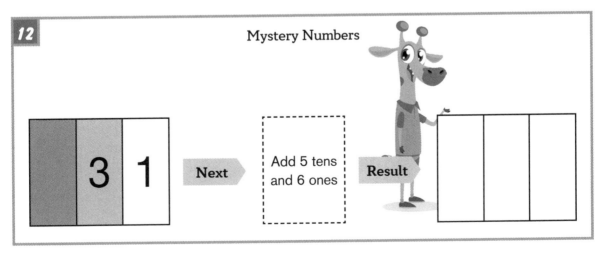

12

Mystery Numbers

| 3 | 1 |

Next

Add 5 tens
and 6 ones

Result

13 Mystery Numbers

4 4 → Next → Add 1 ten and 1 one → Result →

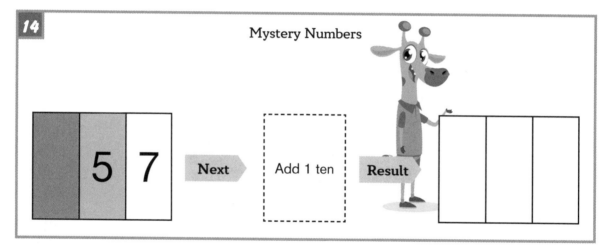

14 Mystery Numbers

5 7 → Next → Add 1 ten → Result →

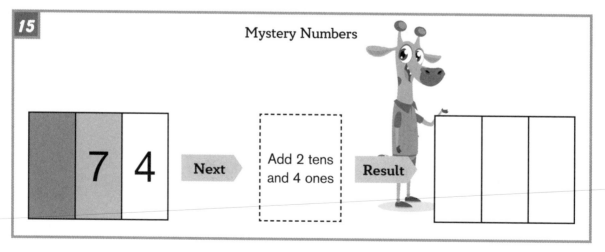

15 Mystery Numbers

7 4 → Next → Add 2 tens and 4 ones → Result →

16 Mystery Numbers

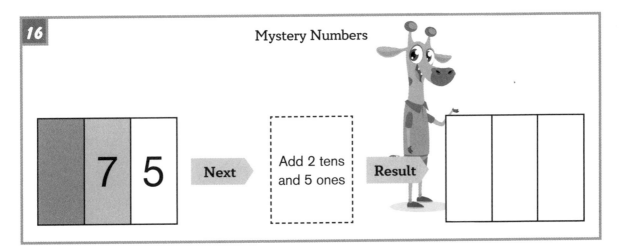

| 7 | 5 |

Next

Add 2 tens and 5 ones

Result

---

17 Mystery Numbers

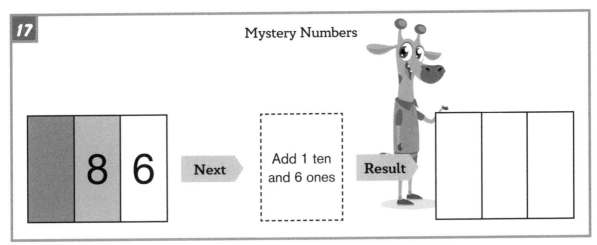

| 8 | 6 |

Next

Add 1 ten and 6 ones

Result

---

18 Mystery Numbers

| 1 | 0 | 0 |

Next

Add 1 ten and 4 ones

Result

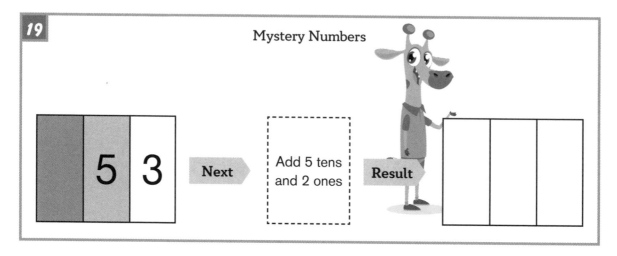

19   Mystery Numbers

| 5 | 3 |

Next

Add 5 tens and 2 ones

Result

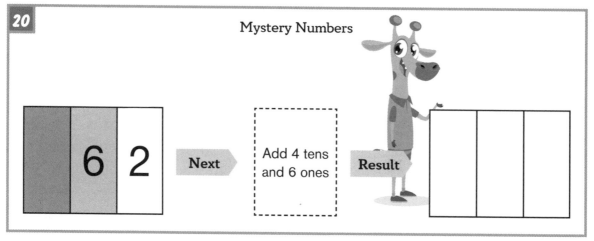

20   Mystery Numbers

| 6 | 2 |

Next

Add 4 tens and 6 ones

Result

ANSWER KEY:
Mystery Numbers

QUESTION		ANSWER	
1.		8	9
2.		6	7
3.		7	4
4.	1	0	0
5.		6	0
6.		5	8
7.		6	8
8.	1	0	0
9.	1	0	1
10.		6	2

QUESTION		ANSWER	
11.		7	0
12.		8	7
13.		5	5
14.		6	7
15.		9	8
16.	1	0	0
17.	1	0	2
18.	1	1	4
19.	1	0	5
20.	1	0	8

Adding and Subtracting on an Open Number Line

MATERIALS NEEDED: Task cards

DIRECTIONS: Copy and cut out the task cards. Place students in groups to find a solution to the task cards. Have students discuss and share results after all task cards have been solved. Use the examples below as models. Add and subtract by using place value and jumps on an open number line.

Adding on an Open Number Line

$$64 + 22$$

Expanded form of the second addend:
22 = 20 + 2

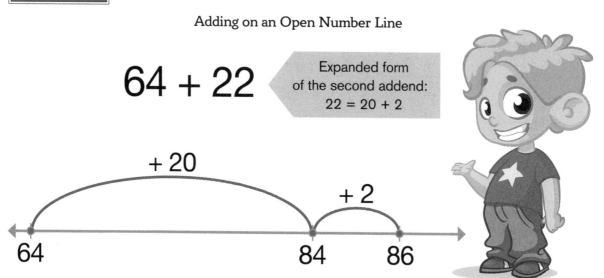

Start by writing the second addend in expanded form (22 = 20 + 2). On an open number line, jump 20 units for the tens place (64 + 20 = 84) and 2 units for the ones place (84 + 2 = 86). Therefore, (64 + 22 = 86).

Subtracting on an Open Number Line

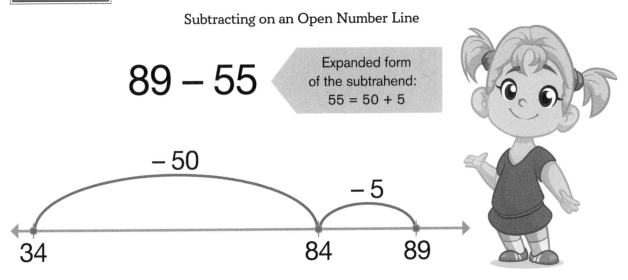

$$89 - 55$$

Expanded form
of the subtrahend:
$55 = 50 + 5$

$- 50$

$- 5$

34   84   89

Start by writing the subtrahend in expanded form ($55 = 50 + 5$). On an open number line, jump down 5 units for the ones place ($89 - 5 = 84$) and then jump 50 units down for the tens. ($84 - 50 = 34$). The distance or difference between 89 and 55 is 34.

1 Add the numbers below using an open number line and expanded place value.

65 + 23

Expanded form:

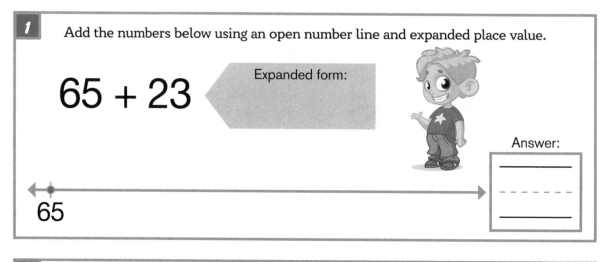

Answer:

65

---

2 Add the numbers below using an open number line and expanded place value.

29 + 45

Expanded form:

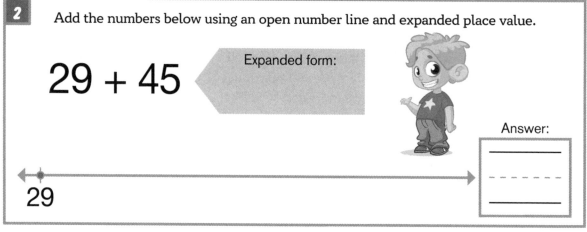

Answer:

29

---

3 Add the numbers below using an open number line and expanded place value.

74 + 26

Expanded form:

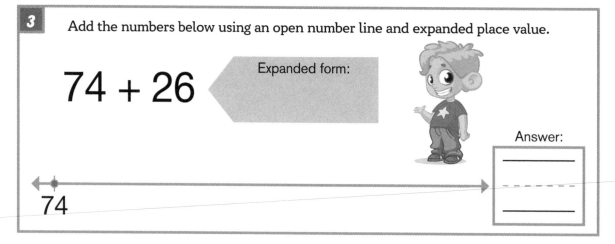

Answer:

74

316   Math Fluency Activities for K–2 Teachers

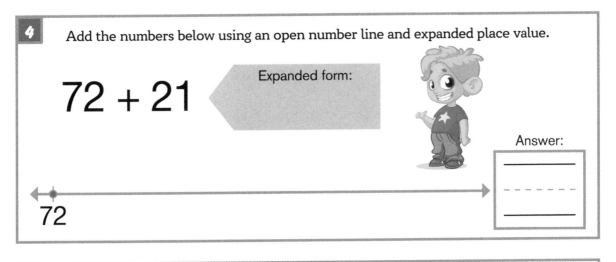

4 Add the numbers below using an open number line and expanded place value.

72 + 21

Expanded form:

Answer:

72

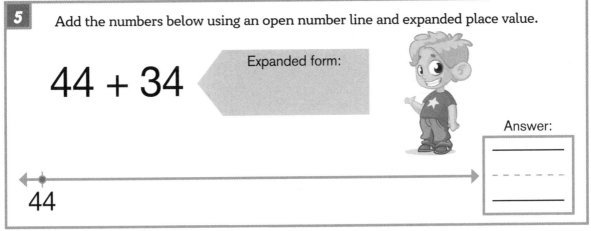

5 Add the numbers below using an open number line and expanded place value.

44 + 34

Expanded form:

Answer:

44

6 Add the numbers below using an open number line and expanded place value.

60 + 29

Expanded form:

Answer:

60

7 Add the numbers below using an open number line and expanded place value.

18 + 14

Expanded form:

Answer:
_____
- - - - - -
_____

18

8 Add the numbers below using an open number line and expanded place value.

39 + 23

Expanded form:

Answer:
_____
- - - - - -
_____

39

9 Add the numbers below using an open number line and expanded place value.

62 + 18

Expanded form:

Answer:
_____
- - - - - -
_____

62

10 Add the numbers below using an open number line and expanded place value.

25 + 28

Expanded form:

Answer:

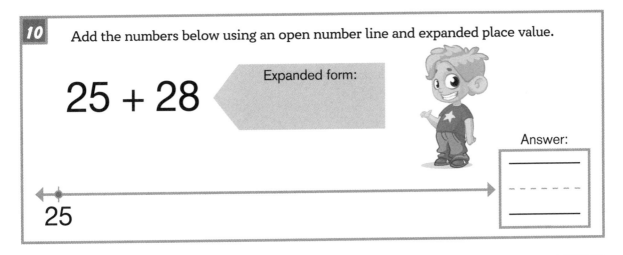

25

11 Subtract the numbers below using an open number line and expanded place value.

58 – 24

Expanded form:

Answer:

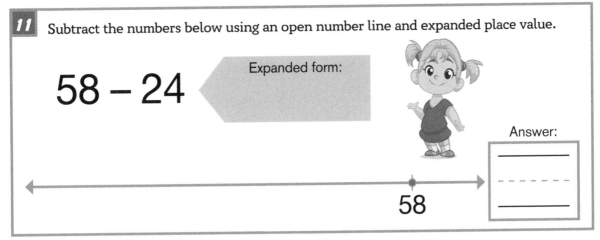

58

12 Subtract the numbers below using an open number line and expanded place value.

52 – 36

Expanded form:

Answer:

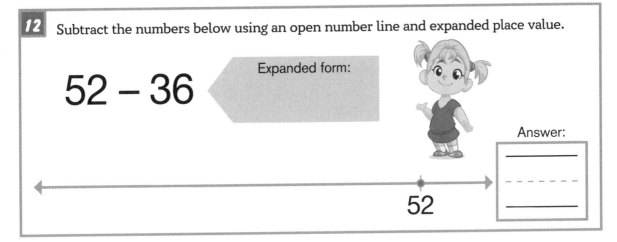

52

13 Subtract the numbers below using an open number line and expanded place value.

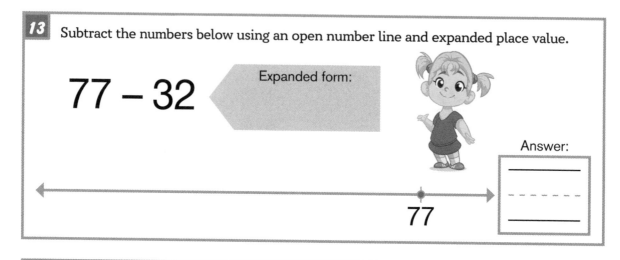

77 – 32

Expanded form:

Answer:

77

14 Subtract the numbers below using an open number line and expanded place value.

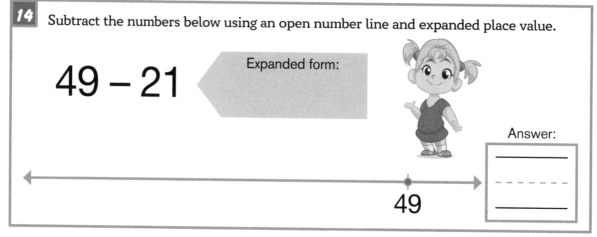

49 – 21

Expanded form:

Answer:

49

15 Subtract the numbers below using an open number line and expanded place value.

29 – 16

Expanded form:

Answer:

29

16 Subtract the numbers below using an open number line and expanded place value.

81 – 58

Expanded form:

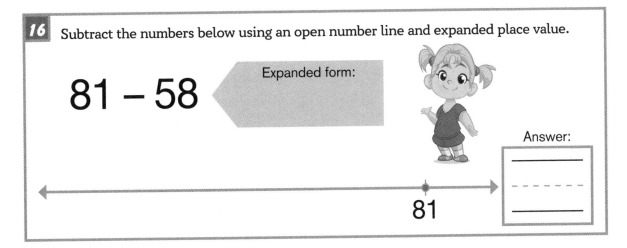

81

Answer:
_____
- - - - - - -
_____

17 Subtract the numbers below using an open number line and expanded place value.

79 – 48

Expanded form:

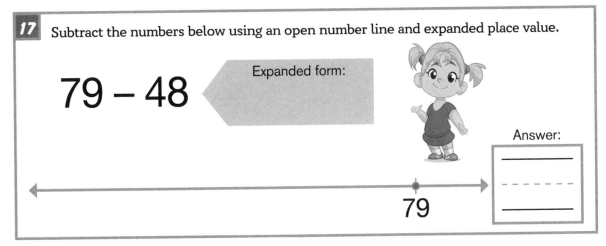

79

Answer:
_____
- - - - - - -
_____

18 Subtract the numbers below using an open number line and expanded place value.

100 – 63

Expanded form:

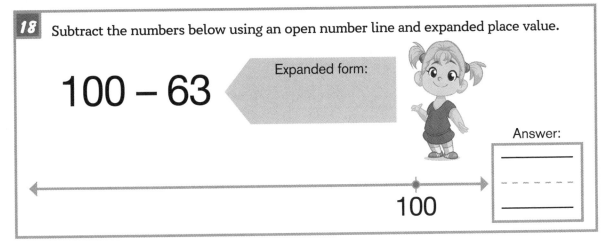

100

Answer:
_____
- - - - - - -
_____

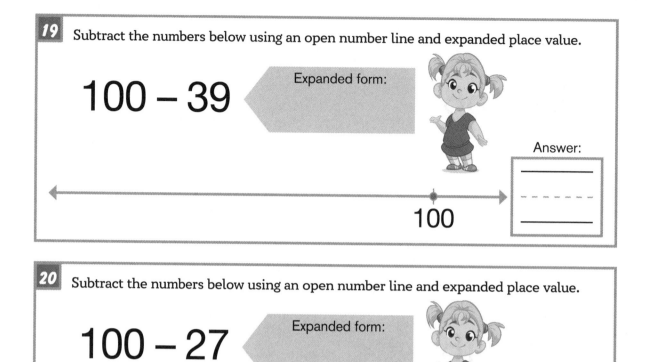

19 Subtract the numbers below using an open number line and expanded place value.

100 – 39

Expanded form:

Answer:

100

---

20 Subtract the numbers below using an open number line and expanded place value.

100 – 27

Expanded form:

Answer:

100

ANSWER KEY:
Adding and Subtracting on an Open Number Line

QUESTION	ANSWER		QUESTION	ANSWER
1.	88		11.	34
2.	74		12.	16
3.	100		13.	45
4.	93		14.	28
5.	78		15.	13
6.	89		16.	23
7.	32		17.	31
8.	62		18.	37
9.	80		19.	61
10.	53		20.	73

Adding and Subtracting Based on Place Value

OBJECTIVE: Find the sum of the numbers by using place value as you write and solve the numbers in expanded form.

MATERIALS NEEDED: Task cards

INSTRUCTIONS: Copy and cut out the task cards. Students can work alone or in a group to find the sum or difference. Write the numbers in expanded form before finding the solution. If needed, use place value strips to help you solve the problem.

EXAMPLE

Adding Based on Place Value

Add: 32 + 12

$$
\begin{array}{r}
30 + 2 \\
+\ 10 + 2 \\
\hline
40 + 4
\end{array}
$$

40 + 4 = 44 in standard form.
Therefore, 32 + 12 = 44

Decompose the number to expanded form. Add value based on place value.

Subtracting Based on Place Value

Subtract 56 − 34

$$50 + 6$$
$$- \ 30 + 4$$
$$\overline{20 + 2}$$

20 + 2 = 22 in standard form.
Therefore, 56 − 34 = 22

Decompose the number to expanded form. Subtract value based on place value.

1 Add the numbers below based on place value (use expanded form).

Add: 46 + 46

Answer:

2 Add the numbers below based on place value (use expanded form).

Add: 57 + 24

Answer:

3 Add the numbers below based on place value (use expanded form).

Add: 55 + 23

Answer:

4

Add the numbers below based on place value (use expanded form).

Add: 38 + 32

Answer:

5

Add the numbers below based on place value (use expanded form).

Add: 78 + 14

Answer:

6

Add the numbers below based on place value (use expanded form).

Add: 38 + 34

Answer:

7 Add the numbers below based on place value (use expanded form).

Add: 91 + 23

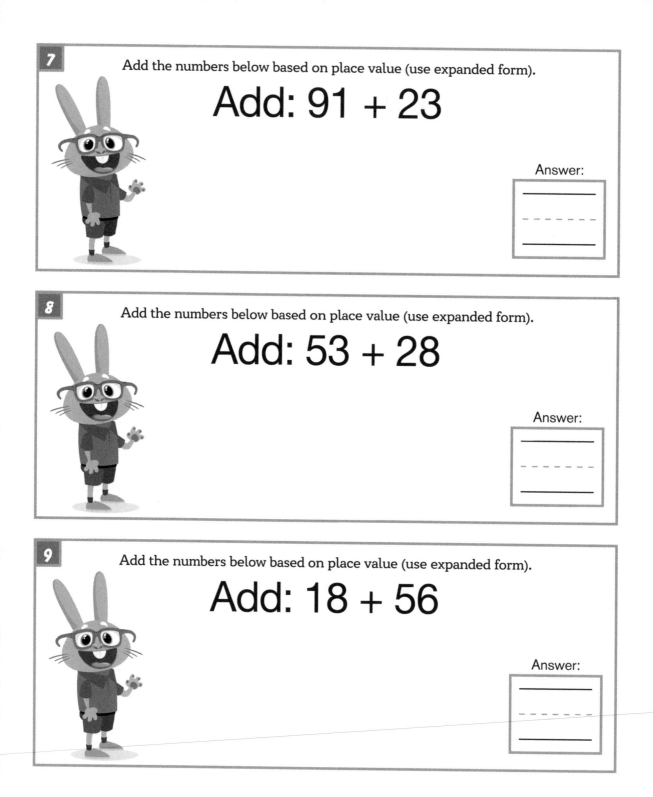

Answer:

8 Add the numbers below based on place value (use expanded form).

Add: 53 + 28

Answer:

9 Add the numbers below based on place value (use expanded form).

Add: 18 + 56

Answer:

Math Fluency Activities for K–2 Teachers

10 Add the numbers below based on place value (use expanded form).

Add: 31 + 23

Answer:

---

11 Subtract the numbers below based on place value (use expanded form).

Subtract: 89 – 63

Answer:

---

12 Subtract the numbers below based on place value (use expanded form).

Subtract: 96 – 43

Answer:

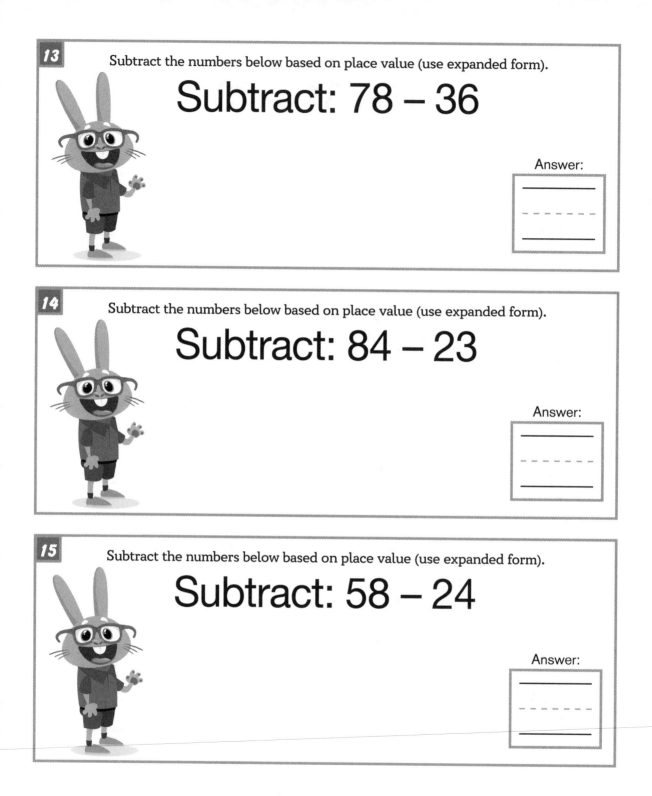

13 Subtract the numbers below based on place value (use expanded form).

Subtract: 78 – 36

Answer:
_____

14 Subtract the numbers below based on place value (use expanded form).

Subtract: 84 – 23

Answer:
_____

15 Subtract the numbers below based on place value (use expanded form).

Subtract: 58 – 24

Answer:
_____

16 Subtract the numbers below based on place value (use expanded form).

Subtract: 66 – 35

Answer:

_____

- - - - - - - - - - - - -

_____

17 Subtract the numbers below based on place value (use expanded form).

Subtract: 49 – 21

Answer:

_____

- - - - - - - - - - - - -

_____

18 Subtract the numbers below based on place value (use expanded form).

Subtract: 56 – 35

Answer:

_____

- - - - - - - - - - - - -

_____

19 Subtract the numbers below based on place value (use expanded form).

Subtract: 55 – 34

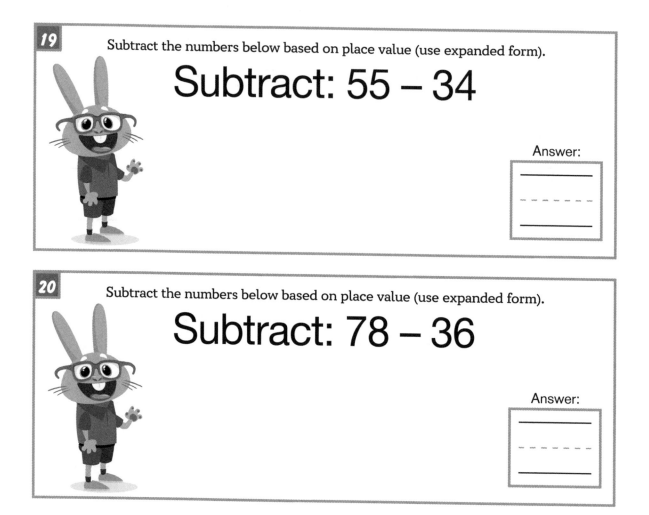

Answer:

_____

- - - - - - -

_____

20 Subtract the numbers below based on place value (use expanded form).

Subtract: 78 – 36

Answer:

_____

- - - - - - -

_____

ANSWER KEY:
Adding and Subtracting Based On Place Value

QUESTION	ANSWER
1.	92
2.	81
3.	78
4.	70
5.	92
6.	72
7.	114
8.	81
9.	74
10.	54

QUESTION	ANSWER
11.	26
12.	53
13.	42
14.	61
15.	34
16.	31
17.	28
18.	21
19.	21
20.	42

Facts Strategy Check: Counting On

+	0	1	2	3	4	5	6	7	8	9	10
0											
1											
2											
3											
4											
5											
6											
7											
8											
9											
10											

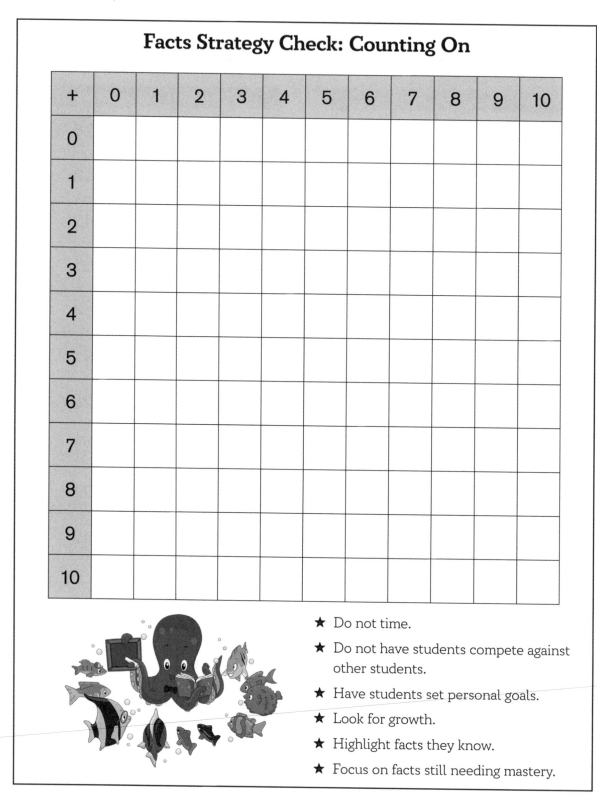

★ Do not time.

★ Do not have students compete against other students.

★ Have students set personal goals.

★ Look for growth.

★ Highlight facts they know.

★ Focus on facts still needing mastery.

Facts I Know!

Name: _____

+	0	1	2	3	4	5	6	7	8	9	10
0											
1											
2											
3											
4											
5											
6											
7											
8											
9											
10											

Acknowledgments

The activities and games in this book were in response to a need for ramping up basic skills while providing support for teachers and students as they navigate Common Core, interventions, guided math, resource classrooms, summer school, and classroom instruction. I am grateful for Olathe students and teachers that test drove and provided feedback on so many of these activities.

Many thanks to Ulysses Press, managing editor Claire Chun, design editor Jake Flaherty, and copy editor Anne Healey. I would like to thank my husband, Rich Hughes, and daughter, Dr. Laura Hughes, for supporting me throughout this process. Finally, special thanks to our son, Dr. Michael Hughes, who recently lost his battle with cancer.

About the Author

Nancy Hughes, author of the Classroom-Ready Number Talks series for kindergarten, 1st, 2nd, 3rd, 4th, 5th, 6th, 7th, and 8th grade teachers, is a former K–12 mathematics coordinator at Olathe Public Schools, the largest school district in the Kansas City region, where she also provided professional development for mathematics teachers in all grade levels. Prior to working at Olathe, Hughes taught middle school math in public and private schools. Hughes has presented math topics at conferences for the National Council of Teachers of Mathematics, Kansas City Area Teachers of Mathematics, and Kansas Area Teachers of Mathematics. She also directed the Kauffman Foundation's K–16 Professional Development program. Hughes has a BS from Kansas State University and an MS in Curriculum and Instruction from Kansas University.